101 GOOD REASONS TO BELIEVE

A COMPREHENSIVE CASE FOR CHRISTIANITY

JAMES D. SIDERAS

WestBow
P R E S S®
A DIVISION OF THOMAS NELSON
& ZONDERVAN

NIV: All Scripture quotations, unless otherwise indicated, are taken from the Holy Bible, New International Version®, NIV®. Copyright ©1973, 1978, 1984, 2011 by Biblica, Inc.™ Used by permission of Zondervan. All rights reserved worldwide. The "NIV" and "New International Version" are trademarks registered in the United States Patent and Trademark Office by Biblica, Inc. KJV: Scripture taken from the King James Version of the Bible.

This book is a work of non-fiction. Unless otherwise noted, the author and the publisher make no explicit guarantees as to the accuracy of the information contained in this book and in some cases, names of people and places have been altered to protect their privacy.

WestBow Press books may be ordered through booksellers or by contacting:

WestBow Press
A Division of Thomas Nelson & Zondervan
1663 Liberty Drive
Bloomington, IN 47403
www.westbowpress.com
1 (866) 928-1240

Because of the dynamic nature of the Internet, any web addresses or links contained in this book may have changed since publication and may no longer be valid. The views expressed in this work are solely those of the author and do not necessarily reflect the views of the publisher, and the publisher hereby disclaims any responsibility for them.

Any people depicted in stock imagery provided by Thinkstock are models, and such images are being used for illustrative purposes only. Certain stock imagery © Thinkstock.

ISBN: 978-1-9736-0997-1 (sc)
ISBN: 978-1-9736-0998-8 (hc)
ISBN: 978-1-9736-0996-4 (e)

Library of Congress Control Number: 2017918058

Print information available on the last page.

WestBow Press rev. date: 01/03/2018

RECOMMENDATIONS

James's passion for Truth that "holds fast" whether examined by academics, philosophers, scientists, business professionals, religious authorities or the "man in the street" comes through loud and clear in this brilliant collection of 101 Good Reasons to Believe. Diligently researched and grounded in historical facts, scientific evidence and Biblical truths, James tackles age old questions and the sweeping tide of current cultural beliefs with short, focused, compelling arguments. In this generation of "pick and mix" beliefs, James provides the evidence that challenges us to encounter the Unchanging God of the Bible for ourselves and each confront the question: Who do YOU say Jesus is? An indispensable resource for our time.

—Andrea Taylor-Cummings, M.Phil., D.Phil. (Oxon),
Co-Founder of SoulMates Academy

The ancient proverbs declare, *"The first to present his case seems right until another comes forward and sets the record straight"* (Prov. 18.17). With guns blazing in this masterly work, Dr. James confounds the anti-biblical viewpoint that is expounded as truth in the majority of present-day academic institutions and media sources. I'm sure that many sincere seekers and big thinkers of today, like their peers of yesteryear, will be shaken awake by the glorious Gospel that shines through these well-researched reasons to believe.

—Giles Stevens, MA (Oxon),
Evangelist and Founder of The Great Mission

101 Good Reasons to Believe is a very compelling and argumentative case for the Christian worldview. Dr. James argues brilliantly with his meticulous and analytical data from all possible sources that there can be only one option for this world to exist and that option has to be the God of the Bible. While I truly am blessed by the information and presentation of Dr. James on the existence of God I truly enjoyed the depth of the subject with which he justified the effort. Debunking the alternative worldviews is the strength of the book. I congratulate Dr. James for his excellent work and his commitment to Jesus Christ our Lord for whose glory this book stands for. This book is a well-organized and well-presented case for the Christian Faith and every one should read it.

—Praveen Kumar Pagadala,
Christian Apologist in India

ACKNOWLEDGMENTS

I am truly grateful to my wife Pascale, for without her help in managing a family of five children, this book would not have been possible. I also acknowledge Rev. Bediako Bosque-Hamilton, George Sideras, Dr. Andrea Taylor-Cummings and Gail Mills for reviewing earlier drafts of this book. Most of all, I give thanks to my Lord Jesus Christ, the author and finisher of my faith.

CONTENTS

INTRODUCTION

Since the enlightenment era, when knowledge was pursued by human reason alone, western culture has become deeply post-Christian, i.e., lost the primacy of a Christian worldview. Although most of the enlightenment thinkers who galvanized the scientific revolution were Christians, the irony is that an enlightenment mentality led to a divide between religion and science. Even today, many believe the two disciplines are incompatible.

John Worrall, Professor of Philosophy of Science at the London School of Economics argues, "Science and religion are in irreconcilable conflict ... There is no way in which you can be both properly scientifically minded and a true religious believer."[1] However, this argument is simply untrue. The historical revisionism that first generated the myth of conflict between Christianity and science—a myth that is being exposed by more and more historians—can be attributed to the writings of John William Draper (1811-1882) and Andrew Dickson White (1832-1918). For example, James Hannam, a historian with a PhD in the History of Science from Cambridge University, asserts that scientific progress during the enlightenment was often made because of the influence of Christianity.[2] Hannam also claims that Christian scholars toppled the erroneous wisdom of the ancient Greeks by laying the foundation of modern science.[3]

Throughout the scientific revolution (1500s-1700s), the close link between science and religion was taken for granted, as both were used to understand the world. In fact, because the modern scientific method is to a significant degree an outcome of theological reflection on God and nature, it is erroneous of new atheists like Richard Dawkins to claim theology has never made any contribution to science. For instance, Sir Isaac Newton (1643-1727) attempted to understand the mind of God by examining the laws of nature, and what he discovered set him apart as one of the most influential scientists in human history. Johannes Kepler (1571-1630) was also on a quest to know the wisdom of God when he discovered the laws of planetary motion, a finding that evaded so many before him. In a letter to the Baron von Herberstein in 1596, Kepler wrote, "God, like a human architect, approached the founding of the world according to order and rule and measured everything in such a manner."[4]

As surprising as it sounds, theoretical questions from medieval theology had a significant influence on what constituted scientific knowledge. Is scientific knowledge certain or provisional? What is the best scientific method for understanding nature, e.g., human reason or experience? Although Aristotle's method of deductive reasoning (logic based on one or more premises) had a stronghold over the medieval Catholic Church, Christian philosopher and scientist Sir Francis Bacon (1561-1626) sought to overthrow this method. He argued that truth could only be derived from inductive reasoning (logic based on observation of the natural world). Bacon argued, "Man, as the minister and interpreter of nature, is limited in act and understanding by his observation of the order of nature."[5]

While Christians like Galileo Galilei (1564-1642) and René Descartes (1596-1650) emphasized the power of human reason (deductive reasoning), others such as Robert Boyle (1627-1691) and Sir Isaac Newton believed human minds were limited in their power to impose logic on the natural world, and that one must rely on empirical observation (inductive reasoning) to generate knowledge. Debates such as these among Christian thinkers ultimately led to rational empiricism (a synthesis of reason and observation)—the foundation of today's dominant scientific method. In fact, many great advances in science during the Middle Ages were derived from Christians who believed that God created the universe, and that to study the natural world was to admire

His work. Thus, Christianity is not in conflict with science. On the contrary, Christianity founded science.

Considering the Church was not the enemy of science, it is somewhat surprising that the myth of conflict (peddled by Draper and White) actually took root, no thanks to philosophers like Voltaire (1694-1778). As a staunch political opponent of both church and state, Voltaire claimed the Catholic Church had a powerful control over French culture because of its close association with France's monarchy.

Voltaire reasoned that the best way to dismantle the Church's hold over people's minds was to engender doubt over its core doctrines. Towards this end, not only did Voltaire sow the seeds of the French revolution, but he also influenced many to believe Christianity was a serious impediment to science—that is to say, he engendered the belief that metaphysical (non-observable) reasoning blocked the thinking of scientists. As such, Voltaire attempted to purge Christian thinking from science by encouraging a materialistic worldview, the view in which everything that exists is merely physical—a way of thinking that is still pervasive today. A consequence of this worldview is that it excludes the existence God. In the words of Harvard Professor Richard Lewontin:

> We are forced by our a priori adherence to material causes to create an apparatus of investigation and set of concepts that produce material explanations, no matter how counterintuitive, no matter how mystifying to the uninitiated. Moreover, that materialism is absolute, for we cannot allow a Divine Foot in the door.[6]

After Voltaire, the bludgeoning club of materialism was taken up by Thomas Henry Huxley (1825-1895), the first great exponent of Darwin's theory of evolution. During his struggle to free British science from metaphysical influence, Huxley became an influential figure who brazenly advocated Darwin's work, defending it to great effect. As a result of materialists like Huxley, Darwinian evolution has become a common sense way of thinking for many.

Even today, those who oppose Darwinian evolution are often regarded as dimwitted or ignorant. As Richard Dawkins put it, "It is absolutely safe to say that if you meet somebody who claims not to believe in evolution, that person is ignorant, stupid or insane"[7] However, this kind of *ad hominem*, intimidating portrayal prevents scientists from voicing a theistic worldview. Consequently, they are forced to follow the groupthink mentality of atheists and evolutionists due to fear of derision from their counterparts, resulting in self-censorship and the suppression of honest intellectual debate.

After converting from atheism to Christianity, distinguished scientist Allan Sandage admitted, "Today the scientific community so scorns faith that there is a reluctance to reveal yourself as a believer, the opprobrium [criticism] is so severe."[8] If distinguished scientists like Sandage experienced this kind of repression, how many other scientists feel apprehensive about voicing alternative scientific explanations for human origins and the universe?

Although many have described Huxley as Darwin's bulldog, he at least honestly admitted that Darwin's theory could not prove evolution, but served the best available explanation for the origin of species. Well, since the time of Darwin, science has evolved (excuse the pun), bringing with it a number of revolutionary discoveries that support a theistic worldview.

One of the purposes of this book is to give readers an alternative best explanation, not only of the origin of species, but also for life itself. This book is not anti-science. Rather, it follows the scientific method by validating arguments with scientific, empirical and historical material. Be that as it may, people have different conceptions about science, some of which are misleading. One particular misconception is that science can prove something. Contrary to popular belief, there is no such thing as scientific proof. Science is based on the premise that any theory, no matter how widely accepted, could become invalid if new evidence emerges that falsifies it.

Karl Popper (1902-1994), probably the most important scientific philosopher of the twentieth century, asserted that science could not prove any knowledge claim. Popper developed the hypothetico-deductive model, the dominant scientific method in use today. This method involves deducing hypothetical statements from a given theory, then subjecting them to empirical (observable) testing. If these statements measure up to their own predictions, the theory is deemed valid, but if not, it is refuted and a new un-falsified theory is formed for testing. In essence, all science can do is support theory, not prove it with any certainty.

Another point to mention is that of objectivity. When scientists make scientific claims, they often include a tone of objectivity that implies their knowledge is factual (i.e., their minds are aligned with external reality). However, the problem with this particular view of reality is that it excludes subjective distortions, such as assumptions, biases and convictions—factors that cannot be completely eliminated from one's mind. It follows that one's observation of external reality can never be completely neutral, value free and objective.

To elucidate this point further, we return to the period of enlightenment where we find the German philosopher Immanuel Kant (1724-1804), arguably the greatest philosopher since Aristotle. According to Kant, there are subjective conditions in the human mind that presuppose our view of the world, and how we see it depends on the way our minds select, organize and interpret our experiences. Kant defined these *a priori* subjective conditions as conceptions of time, space and causality. He asserted that these conditions do not exist independently from ourselves, but are modes of perception in our minds, which define our experience of reality and the attributions we make. Hence, from a Kantian perspective, scientists (and everyone else for that matter) are incapable of holding an entirely objective view of the world.

What is often played out in the scientific world is a battle of differing worldviews. Have you ever wondered how scientists can look at the exact same data and arrive at completely different conclusions? This happens because our interpretations are tainted by unconscious assumptions about how we see ourselves and the world around us. Formed by deeply held beliefs, our assumptions not only give order to the world, but also inform us about how the world can go out of order, serving to wittingly or unwittingly block new ways of thinking and learning. This predicament explains why the battle is not between Christianity and science, but between two very different worldviews held by creationists and evolutionists, theists and atheists, etc. Oxford University Professor John Lennox put it best:

> There is a battle, between the worldview of theism and atheism, and there are scientists on both sides. Dawkins and co will tell everyone that the only rationally intelligent position to hold is atheism. I feel the exact opposite.[9]

This book is transparent about the Christian worldview, a view frequently denigrated and censored by the scientific community. Structured in a logical and coherent manner, it provides 101 reasons for believing that Christianity is a warranted worldview.

Supported with referenced scientific, historical and empirical material, this book begins with logical reasons for the existence of God. Subjects like human consciousness, objective morals, and the fallacy of atheism are addressed with arguments from famed philosophers. Their acceptance of Christianity implies an argument in the form, "I reckon all those wise men would not have believed if it were not true."

In the second part of this book, the case for creation and

intelligent design is presented. This case is underpinned by cosmological evidence and biological findings over the last 60 years, not available at the time Charles Darwin wrote his book, *On the Origin of Species* in 1859.

In part three, the historicity of Jesus, extra-Biblical evidence is provided. This evidence, along with assessments from Christian and non-Christian historians, corroborate New Testament records for the life, death and resurrection of Jesus Christ. The point here is that if Jesus actually existed and rose from the dead, should we not take His truth claims seriously?

Part four of this book sheds light on the differences between Christianity and all other main religions. Due to the vast theological disparities between them, this part dispels the myth that all religions lead to God, and at the same time refutes the claims of competing religions. The premise here is that not all religions are equal if they do not stand up to their own truth claims.

Part five of this book answers topical questions posed by critics and skeptics of Christianity: Who created God? Why does God allow human suffering? How can a loving God send people to hell? Important questions such as these are theologically answered to overcome the barriers that plague people's thinking toward the Christian faith.

In part six, a selection of narratives from prominent people about how they came to faith in Jesus Christ is provided. These stories richly illustrate their life-changing encounters with Christ and their personal experiences of Him. Many of the stories offered are from former atheists, making their claims all the more convincing, as most of them had no earlier socialization of Christian beliefs.

In part seven, the case for the reality of heaven and hell is presented. Supported with accounts from those who had near death experiences, this part offers empirical evidence for the existence of an afterlife. This is probably one of the most intriguing parts of the book, since these personal accounts (including those from atheists) confirm descriptions of heaven and hell recorded in the Bible.

In the final part of this book, conclusions are drawn from the key arguments presented and their main implications are discussed for thoughtful contemplation. The great Christian novelist C.S. Lewis noted, "Nearly everyone I know who has embraced Christianity in adult life has been influenced by what seemed to him to be at least probable arguments for Theism."[10]

When you read the arguments articulated in this book, it is my solemn hope you will construct your own verdict about the Christian faith, based on truth, not the culture of our times. Cultures change, but truth does not. It remains eternal.

PART I

Philosophical Arguments
for the Existence of God

Reason 1: The Existence of Objective Morals

The moral argument for the existence of God has been stated over centuries in a variety of different ways. One way of stating this argument is that if God does not exist, objective morals and duties do not exist; since objective morals and duties do exist, God therefore exists.[1] The point here is that because every rational person has an objective sense of what is right and wrong—good and evil—we appeal to a moral law, implying the existence of a transcendent moral lawgiver, God.

People commonly regard telling the truth as right and murder as wrong, or they feel kindness is good and torturing children is evil. Although ethical differences exist among cultures, virtues like courage and generosity and vices like cowardice and greed are universally accepted, implying the existence of a universal moral law within our conscience. While moral relativists (those who reject objective moral truths) argue that morality is based on a person's subjective opinions and choices, they are implying cruel acts like rape, murder, and child molestation are acceptable if they accord with one's own preferences. Since all civil societies regard these kinds of cruelties as unacceptable, moral relativism fails in its application and is therefore implausible. Two notable philosophers, Beckwith and Koukl, underscore this point: "Those who deny obvious moral rules—who say that murder and rape are morally benign ... have something wrong with them."[2]

1

But one could ask why a moral law necessitates a transcendent moral lawgiver. The answer is because no valid naturalistic alternative exists for the objective source of a moral law. This means the source has to be someone transcendent, all powerful, and morally pure—a definition that matches the Christian God. J.L. Mackie, a prominent atheist philosopher of the twentieth century, once said, "Moral properties constitute so odd a cluster of qualities and relations that they are most unlikely to have arisen in the ordinary course of events, without an all powerful god to create them."[3]

In Darwinian evolution, a stark contradiction exists. Darwin claimed, "There is no fundamental difference between man and the higher mammals in their mental faculties,"[4] yet humans explicitly differ from animals by their sense of objective morality. Even atheist evolutionists, such as George Gaylord Simpson who wrote, "Morals arise only in man,"[5] have acknowledged this difference.

While atheist evolutionists have attempted to bridge the chasm of morality between humans and animals, their naturalistic explanations fall short. What they fail to consider is that natural selection only operates on the basis of survival and reproduction, not on what is moral. As such, an evolutionary view of the world is one in which good and evil do not exist, as Richard Dawkins points out: "In a universe of blind physical forces and genetic replication...there is, at bottom, no design, no purpose, no evil and no good, nothing but blind, pitiless indifference."[6] Yet denying the existence of objective morality is akin to denying the objective reality of the physical world. It follows that Darwinian evolution is contradictory and fails to account for the existence of objective morals.

In conclusion, objective morals can only be plausibly explained by the existence of God, who created us in His own image with a moral law embedded in our conscience. As the apostle Paul points out, "The requirements of the law are written on their hearts, their consciences also bearing witness" (Romans 2:15).

Reason 2: The Origin of Human Consciousness

The argument from human consciousness takes the origin of our minds as evidence for God's existence. The argument can be stated in this way: The origin of human consciousness can only be reasonably explained through theism or naturalism; since naturalism provides no adequate explanation, theism is the best explanation.[7]

Although definitions of human consciousness abound, it can be defined as the mental awareness of our environment and of self, including our own thoughts, beliefs, feelings and choices.[8] While various neurobiologists claim some animals possess consciousness, this consciousness is limited to their awareness of sense data—what neurobiologist Gerald Edelman calls *primary consciousness*. In contrast, humans possess higher-order consciousness, allowing them to conceptualize their experiences and construct their own subjective views.[9] Humans are therefore unique because they possess the awareness to be an object to themselves (self-consciousness), to think about their own thinking (reflexive reasoning), and to philosophically choose a course of action[10]—characteristics that theologians claim belong to the human soul.[11]

The theistic explanation for human consciousness can be found in Genesis: "And the LORD God formed man of the dust of the ground, and breathed into his nostrils the breath [Spirit] of life; and man became a living soul" (Genesis 2:7 KJV). This account tells us the human soul (or mind) did not originate from physical matter but from the convergence of matter and God's life-giving Spirit. This idea implies that while the physical body and human mind interact, they are also distinct from each other, the body acting like a host for the mind. This distinction correlates with the mind-body dualism made famous by René Descartes who coined the dictum "I think, therefore I am."[12] Although opponents of dualism claim it is anti-scientific, Descartes's mind-body dualism is still dominant in today's mainstream conception of science, conveying the view that one can independently observe the natural world by the separation of you (the "knower") from the object (the "known").[13]

Numerous publications on human consciousness exist, yet none of them provide any conclusive naturalistic explanation for its development. Remarks from naturalists include "We believe that the emergence of consciousness is a skeleton in the closet of orthodox evolutionism,"[14] "Nobody has the slightest idea how anything material could be conscious,"[15] and "It remains biology's most profound riddle."[16] One of the starkest admissions from a naturalist about human consciousness comes from Steven Pinker, MIT Professor of Brain and Cognitive Sciences: "We are still clueless about how the brain represents the content of our thoughts and feelings."[17]

In his book, *Consciousness Explained*, Professor Daniel Dennett claims consciousness is an illusion, describing humans as soulless philosophical zombies who think they have consciousness.[18] However, Dennett's book received criticism by many of his contemporaries, some even dubbing it "Consciousness Explained Away" because Dennett refused to accept the undeniable existence of consciousness.[19]

Because naturalists have been flummoxed by the reality of human consciousness, some have consigned its origin to a "lucky accident,"[20] which is no explanation at all, while others have claimed consciousness to be "one of the greatest miracles."[21] But a miracle would surely require a miracle maker, the very entity naturalists are trying to refute. Since naturalism cannot adequately explain human consciousness, theism stands as the best explanation, warranting the existence of God.

Reason 3: The Argument from Human Conscience

As well as possessing consciousness, the human mind also has the psychic agency of conscience (or superego). According to psychoanalytic theory, the conscience works in conflict with our primeval human instincts, obligating us to do what is right by punishing misbehavior with feelings of guilt.[22] The argument from conscience is that our sense of moral obligation to be good and to do right is unique to humans and ultimately comes from a God who created us in His own image.

No matter how poorly heeded, in the depths of our souls is an intuitive inner voice compelling us to do what is noble. Yet many of us fail to obey this inner voice, a failure that can lead to guilt, repression and neurosis.[23] It follows that our own conscience convicts us of falling short of moral perfection, explaining why people often claim they are not perfect. This point accords with the writings of the apostle Paul: "For all have sinned and fall short of the glory of God [moral perfection]" (Romans 3:23). But when properly heeded, the human conscience leads us to God, so we can be "justified freely by His grace through the redemption that came by Christ Jesus" (Romans 3:24).

Although Charles Darwin recognized his theory would need to account for the origin of human conscience, he provided too simple an explanation involving an unspecified connection with intelligence.[24] However, psychoanalyst Sigmund Freud went further by claiming human conscience was acquired from processes that occurred in the primal horde—a primitive group of humans whose sons killed their tyrannical male fathers, which generated a great sense of guilt that was somehow passed on to their descendants.[25] However, many authors have fervently contested Freud's hypothesis, especially since it falls "outside the area of testability."[26] Psychotherapist Marjorie Rosenberg asserts that Freud's hypothesis is a myth dressed up as science, spread by followers who were not led by evidence, but by Freud's ability to dramatize his dogmas.[27]

Even today, the natural sciences provide no evidence-based explanation for how the human conscience could have evolved. Aside from psychological studies of conscience formation in children, and anthropological studies of shame and guilt, there are relatively few studies on conscience. Perhaps this is because each time that naturalists seek an evolutionary explanation, they experience a crisis of naturalistic fallacy, i.e., they misattribute natural properties to the metaphysical qualities of conscience.[28]

A recent study by neuroscientists at Oxford University found the region of the brain that supports the function of conscience (lateral frontal pole prefrontal cortex) is unique to humans, since it has no equivalent in macaque monkeys—our supposed closest relative.[29] This finding not only puts another question mark on Darwin's theory of common descent, but also confirms that humans are indeed morally unique from animals, supporting the theistic argument from conscience.

While atheists claim that God is dead, God's moral arbiter of the human soul—the conscience—is not. If we heed its absolute authority, not only will it guide us to act in a moral way, but it will also guide us to an absolute moral God.

Reason 4: The Ontological Argument

The greatest present day advocate of the ontological argument is Professor Alvin Plantinga, one of the world's leading analytic philosophers. Plantinga based his argument on the work of Anselm of Canterbury, but revised it by applying modal logic, i.e., deductive reasoning that expresses necessity and possibility. Plantinga's version also uses possible world semantics—a description of a possible reality, or a way the world could have been. According to Plantinga, God is a maximally great being who has both necessary existence and maximal excellence—defined as omniscience, omnipotence and moral perfection.[30] It is important to note that this definition of maximal excellence matches the Judeo-Christian God of the Bible. A simplified version of Plantinga's ontological argument is stated below:

1. It is possible that a maximally great being exists.
2. If it is possible that a maximally great being exists, then a maximally great being exists in some possible world.
3. If a maximally great being exists in some possible world, then it exists in every possible world.
4. If a maximally great being exists in every possible world, then it exists in the actual world.
5. Therefore, a maximally great being actually exists.

Although the ontological argument does not prove God's existence, it is logically sound, making belief in God a perfectly reasonable proposition. However, its application hangs on whether we think premise one is true. Since agnostics neither believe nor disbelieve in God, they would have to agree with the possibility that God exists. Even some of the most ardent atheists agree with this possibility. For instance, Richard Dawkins suggests, "The existence of God is a scientific hypothesis like any other."[31] In any case, to claim the impossibility for God's existence would be logically absurd, as that would imply having all knowledge about what is and what is not possible. Since humans are not all knowing, it follows that premise one of the argument is true, making its conclusion also true.

Despite the logic of Plantinga's argument, opponents typically object on the basis that just because it is possible for something to exist, it does not have to exist, citing a flying Pegasus or a unicorn as typical examples. However, examples like these do not apply to the ontological argument because their existence is not necessary. Remember, a maximally great being must have necessary existence, for if its existence were not necessary, it would not be so great!

Critics also oppose the argument by claiming the existence of a being in one possible world does not necessarily translate into every possible world. While that is true, what opponents overlook is that the ontological argument does not relate to just any being, but a maximally great being. By Plantinga's definition, if a maximally great being exists in one possible world, it must exist in every possible world, otherwise it would not be "maximally great." A flying Pegasus for example, may exist in some possible world but not in all of them, for its existence is possible but not necessary.

In conclusion, Plantinga's ontological argument is valid, not because it is possible for a being with maximal excellence (defined as all powerful, all knowing and all good) to exist, but for a maximally great being to exist (one that has maximal excellence and necessary existence). If it is possible that such a being exists, then it exists in every possible world. Since our world is one that exists from all possible worlds, God—a maximally great being—exists in our actual world.

Reason 5: The Existence of Abstract Objects

The thesis of this argument is that God provides the best explanation for the existence of abstract objects. In addition to concrete objects like humans, rocks and planets, there are abstract objects like numbers, sets and propositions. While abstract objects have a conceptual reality, they also have an objective reality and therefore, do not just exist in our minds.

Take for example, the mathematical proposition of $2 + 2 = 4$. Since this proposition is necessarily true and cannot be false, it exists as an objective reality. To state otherwise would mean this proposition is only true if we have knowledge of it in our minds. This form of realism is akin to platonism—the view that universal abstract objects exist independently of our rational activities, a view which holds widespread support among scientists, philosophers and mathematicians.[32] However, since God is a maximally great being who is the self-existent source of all reality, a modified form of platonism is put forward here, in that abstract objects are a causal reality.

If realism is true and abstract objects are part of causal reality, this realism begs the question: What is the metaphysical foundation for such objects? The theist has a plausible answer; they are grounded in the mind of God.[33] Professor Alvin Plantinga explains:

> It also seems plausible to think of numbers as dependent upon or even constituted by intellectual activity... But again, there are too many of them to arise as a result of human intellectual activity. We should therefore think of them as among God's ideas...the concepts of an unlimited mind.[34]

On such a view, universal abstract objects are tokens of God's divine ideas, capable of intellectual apprehension and multiple instantiation, i.e., producing specific applications.[35] Although there are arguments against this theistic explanation, these are generally nominalist (anti-realist).[36]

In reality, modern science provides no grounds for rejecting mathematical realism, especially when one considers the Quine-Putnam indispensability argument,[37] which gives good reasons to believe in the existence of mathematical objects. This point leaves us with the question of whether naturalism explains the existence of abstract objects? Simply answered, abstract reality does not support naturalism because metaphysical objects cannot arise from the physical, i.e., only the physical can arise from the physical.[38]

Although naturalists may argue that abstract objects do not require explanation because they are eternal, acausal and have necessary existence (a classical platonic view), theists could use this same premise for God's existence: that God neither requires explanation, for He too is eternal, acausal and has necessary existence.

Another point worthy of mention is the grave conflict between naturalism and mathematical realism—namely, the natural world of strictly natural processes runs counter to the metaphysical.[39] Yet, naturalists make metaphysical claims by using abstract objects whilst denying the metaphysical—an evident contradiction. It is therefore no surprise that many naturalists evade this contradiction by adopting nominalism (a belief that mathematical objects are mere names with no corresponding reality),[40] despite its philosophical limitations.[41]

In closing, theism has the advantage over naturalism for explaining abstract objects because theism can explain their existence, whereas naturalism cannot. It follows that theism provides the best explanation, since it gives a plausible metaphysical foundation for the reality of abstract objects.

Reason 6: The Existence of Eternal Truths

This argument is similar to the existence of abstract objects in that God is the best explanation for the existence of eternal truths. These include numerous mathematical, moral, natural and spiritual truths. Eternal truths can be defined as immutable and necessary absolutes which are so undeniable, proof of them is unnecessary.[42] For example, Descartes's dictum, "I think, therefore I am"[43] is an eternal truth requiring no proof for its existence. The very fact that Descartes was thinking showed he existed.

Throughout history, scientists, philosophers, artists and theologians have sought truth. In essence, people commonly and intuitively sense a prime reality beyond the veil of reason, from where they can grasp immutable truths that shed light on their souls. G. K. Chesterton sums up this point best: "Every true artist does feel, consciously or unconsciously, that he is touching transcendental truths; that his images are shadows of things seen through the veil."[44]

Just like abstract objects, eternal truths are objective. Although relativists claim there is no objective truth because people mentally construct truth from their own social environments,[45] a saying among trial lawyers refutes this claim: There is the plaintiff's truth, there is the defendant's truth, there is the jury's truth, and then there is the truth! Since relativists reject any independent arbiter of truth, they cannot validate their own claims—meaning their claims cannot be taken seriously.

Some of the world's foremost intellectuals such as Aristotle, Newton, Descartes and C.S. Lewis believed truth is discovered when our minds come into agreement with external reality, a principle known as the correspondence theory of truth. Accordingly, we do not construct truth; we apprehend it. If truth were merely derived from our temporal and changeable minds, it could not be relied upon as truth, since it would be prone to error. Eternal truth must derive from an eternal reality; a mind higher than our own: God's mind.

Although we possess finite minds, we are intuitively capable of recognizing truths, albeit in a partial sense. When we do apprehend them, we are delighted by their beauty, amazed by their splendor, enlightened by their wisdom and we rejoice in their justice. Now if truths like "the radii of the circle are equal" and "courage is better than cowardice," are always true irrespective of our knowledge of them, then they are greater than our intellect and independent of our minds. This point suggests that eternal truths ultimately point us to an immutable and eternal prime reality—a reality characterizing God. As Professor of Philosophy, Arthur Holmes eloquently put it, "All truth is God's truth."[46]

There is an indivisible link between eternal truths, our capability to recognize them, and God. When Jesus told Pontius Pilate, "Every one who is of the truth hears My voice" (John 18:37), He was not merely saying He spoke the truth, but that He is truth, for he said "I am the truth" (John 14:6). Thus, eternal truths not only bear witness to God's existence, but according to the Bible, they also lead us to understand that Jesus is the prime reality of truth.

Reason 7: The Argument from Desire

The Christian apologist C.S. Lewis, one of the foremost intellectuals of the twentieth century, made this argument famous. The thesis of the argument is that because all innate human desires correspond to real objects, our innate desire for God validates Him as a real object. Although this argument does not cogently point to the Christian God, it does support God's existence, warranting serious contemplation by skeptics.

Innate human desires are those that are natural and universal across a wide spectrum of cultures. The desire for food, drink, clothes, sleep, sex, beauty, companionship and knowledge are all examples of innate desires that relate to real objects. Since no one has ever found a case of an innate desire for a non-existent object,[47] a question for skeptics is, how likely is it that an innate desire for God is the one counterexample?

While skeptics claim there are many cases of people desiring non-existent things, innate desires should not be confused with artificial or psychologically contrived desires. Desires for superpowers, Aladdin's lamp or Shangri-La are not innate because these are motivated by external influences from culture, marketing, movies or fiction. Hence, the existence of contrived desires does not negate the thesis of the argument. What also cannot serve as a negation are examples of individuals who do not have a desire for God. After all, just because some people are asexual does not mean sex does not exist.

Throughout the ages, people in every known civilization have yearned for something beyond what this world can offer—the transcendent—the eternal. These people even include agnostics and atheists. For instance, agnostic Bertrand Russell once wrote, "The center of me is always and eternally a terrible pain—a curious wild pain—a searching for something beyond what the world contains."[48] Even famed atheist Aldous Huxley admitted, "There comes a time when one asks even of Shakespeare, even of Beethoven, is this all?"[49] The French philosopher Blaise Pascal, summed up this kind of eternal desire: "This infinite abyss [in man] can be filled only by an infinite and immutable object: in other words by God himself."[50] Another way of stating Pascal's point is that there is a God-shaped vacuum in every heart, which only God can fill.

It is important to mention that the argument from desire is not based on a teleological assumption—that is, presupposing the notion of design in the material world. On the contrary, this argument is based on empirical observations of real human experiences, which suggest people do not possess innate desires unless real objects exist that can satisfy them. A person desires companionship because companionship exists. A person desires food because food exists. Likewise, a person desires God because God exists. Although one could argue this syllogism is invalid because a desire for God does not correspond to the material world, C.S. Lewis explains, "If I find in myself a desire which no experience in this world can satisfy, the most probable explanation is that I was made for another world."[51] Lewis's explanation ultimately leads us to consider the Christian view, that we "were created by him, and for him" (Colossians 1:16 KJV). Unless we understand this point, our lives are unlikely to ever make sense.

Reason 8: The Argument from Beauty

Since we all desire beauty, this argument has particular intuitive strength. Whether evoked through art, literature, music or nature, our sense of beauty has been a motivating force for many a human endeavor. The argument from beauty is that our desire and experience of beauty can only be reasonably explained through theism, since naturalism provides no adequate explanation.

From a theistic view, beauty is seen as a property grounded in God, the divine creator of all things. Whether it be found in a crimson sunset, a glittering night sky, a gleaming smile, a quintessential poem, or the sound of Mozart, the beauty we experience signifies a world imbued with meaning and value by God as the primeval author of beauty. From this view, our desire for beauty and the feelings evoked by its tantalizing allure proceed from the reality that God is "the perfection of beauty" (Psalm 50:2) and we "were created by Him, and for Him" (Colossians 1:16 KJV).

Our aesthetic experiences of finite beauty in this world are a shadow of the transcendent and infinite beauty of another world (heaven), explaining why beauty has a powerful nostalgic ability to transport us beyond the physical. It is therefore of no surprise that people use metaphors such as heavenly, sublime, angelic and divine to describe their somewhat magical experiences of beauty. Although one could argue these metaphors are mere subjective qualities, from a psychoanalytic perspective they betray an unconscious longing for a truly transcendent reality. As C.S. Lewis stated: "Our longing to be reunited with something in the universe from which we now feel cut off…is no mere neurotic fancy, but the truest index of our real situation."[52] This theistic explanation for beauty not only provides a basis for the reality of beauty, but also for our aesthetic faculties and desires.

In contrast, naturalism provides no adequate explanation for our desire and experience of beauty. The cardinal difficulty with naturalism's impersonal and closed world of elementary particles and physical laws is that it cannot account for the existence of properties like consciousness, morality, truth and beauty.[53] Besides, why should an impersonal and meaningless universe care about beauty?

Naturalists argue that our basic aesthetic preferences evolved to enhance survival,[54] yet no specific naturalistic mechanism exists for the development of aesthetic faculties.[55] It is as though naturalists use evolution as a panacea—a get out of jail card for all things naturalism cannot explain. Professor of Philosophy, Anthony O'Hear rightly noted, "From a Darwinian perspective, truth, goodness, and beauty and our care for them are very hard to explain."[56] The conundrum naturalism faces is that beauty, much like morality, is irrelevant to natural selection, since it has no survival value. As such, naturalism has severe difficulties explaining the phenomenon of beauty. On the other hand, within a universe conceived by a benevolent creator, the reality of beauty and our experience of it are far less surprising.

In conclusion, theism constitutes an eminently more reasonable explanation for our desire, experience and rational understanding of beauty. When we see finite beauty as a derived quality grounded in God Himself, it will draw our aesthetic attention to the infinite beauty of heaven. As F.R. Tennant wrote: "God reveals himself...in many ways; and some men enter his Temple by Gate Beautiful."[57]

Reason 9: The Argument from Reason

The thesis of this argument is that theism provides the best explanation for valid human reasoning, since naturalism undermines the rational basis for proper logical inferences. Although this argument was first given by Arthur Balfour in his 1914 Gifford Lectures, a more widely read version came from C.S. Lewis, who claimed naturalism is self-refuting because it is incompatible with reason—the very faculty humans depend on to believe in naturalism.[58]

People generally trust in their reasoning faculties to make truth claims. By observing the natural world through our senses, we make logical inferences about reality. Unlike a material object such as a rock or plant, an inference is immaterial because it involves the reasoning process of the mind—the deduction of logical relations between propositions from things observed.

The conundrum naturalists face is that a world wholly restricted to the operation of physical laws and physical properties does not support metaphysical entities like propositions and logical inferences. In other words, non-conscious material forces working by chance within the closed box of nature do not produce conscious, rational thinking minds. This conundrum poses serious questions for naturalists in the form: How can the laws of physics direct the brain to rationally deduce the premises of an argument? How do irrational physical properties produce rational thoughts?

If however naturalism were true, our thoughts would be governed by irrational physical properties—meaning, we should not trust our capacity to reason, including our arguments for naturalism. Thus, naturalists face an inescapable double bind; naturalism not only refutes itself, but also renders the claims from naturalists untrustworthy. What is all the more astonishing is naturalists admit to this double bind. For instance, in his book *Possible Worlds*, the famous naturalist J.B.S Haldane stated, "If my mental processes are determined wholly by motions of atoms in my brain, I have no reason to suppose that my beliefs are true…and hence I have no reason for supposing my brain to be composed of atoms."[59]

Naturalists unaccustomed with this argument will invariably appeal to Charles Darwin at this point. But even Darwin admitted:

> With me the horrid doubt always arises whether the convictions of man's mind, which has been developed from the mind of the lower animals, are of any value or at all trustworthy. Would any one trust in the convictions of a monkey's mind, if there are any convictions in such a mind?[60]

In effect, Darwin's question strikes another blow against naturalism because without valid human reasoning, no science can be deemed true. In light of this argument, naturalists must concede that their beliefs in naturalism are not held on rational grounds.

In conclusion, human reasoning lends greater credibility to theism than naturalism. For our truth claims to be valid, there must be an acceptance of something outside the physical world to account for our reasoning faculties, namely God. A theistic worldview asserts the universe is a rational place because it was designed by a rational being. On this point, C.S. Lewis leaves us with some final thoughts:

> Supposing there was no intelligence behind the universe, no creative mind. In that case, nobody designed my brain for the purpose of thinking... Unless I believe in God, I cannot believe in thought: so I can never use thought to disbelieve in God.[61]

Reason 10: The Argument from Miracles

Occurrences of miracles, including those recorded in the Bible, have long been taken as arguments for the existence of God. However, since the enlightenment era, there has been a strong rejection of miracles, largely influenced by the views of British philosopher David Hume. As a naturalist, Hume famously defined a miracle as "a violation of the laws of nature," claiming no matter how strong the evidence was for a miracle, it is always more rational to reject a miracle than to believe it because of "uniform experience."[62]

In his book *Miracles*, C.S. Lewis gives a brazen affirmation of the supernatural, where he not only refutes naturalism (as explained in the previous argument), but also deals with the premises of Hume's reasoning against miracles. Lewis asserts:

> Unfortunately, we know the experience against them [miracles] to be uniform only if we know that all the reports of them are false. And we know all the reports are false only if we know already that miracles have never occurred. In fact, we are arguing in a circle.[63]

By exposing Hume's circular reasoning, Lewis successfully refutes Hume's premise of "uniform" experience. Lewis also challenges Hume's concept of "experience" by addressing the issue of interpretation. According to Immanuel Kant, we cannot directly know *noumena* (things as they are), because of subjective conditions in the human mind.[64] This means experience is not detached from interpretation, because what we gain from experience is determined by our presuppositions. By addressing the issue of interpretation, Lewis exposes Hume's presupposition against miracles—meaning, if one is locked into a worldview that excludes the miraculous, then miracles will never be observed.

Another premise of Hume's is his definition of a miracle as "a violation of the laws of nature."[65] Professor of Science and Religion at the University of Oxford, Alister McGrath, rightly questions Hume's meaning of natural laws. He argues that if laws of nature are propositions of natural regularities, they would not be violated by a miracle, as they were not "laws" in the first place.[66] On this point, another definition of a miracle is warranted. Unlike Hume who defines a miracle in observational terms, Lewis defines it in theological terms: "An interference with nature by supernatural power."[67] This definition not only evades Hume's premise of what a miracle is, but also allows for a wider interpretation of what a miracle could be. For some, it might be winning the lottery just before the house is repossessed, and for others, an immediate recovery from a terminal illness. Miracles do not therefore necessarily break laws of nature, but work within the normal course of nature.[68] After all, if God created the natural universe, could He not also supernaturally work within it?

In closing, let us ask: Do Hume's views deliver a knockout blow to the phenomena of miracles? Certainly not. Lewis not only shows us how Hume's reasoning is circular, but also exposes Hume's naturalistic presupposition of excluding miracles on the basis of uniform experience. And since our experiences of nature are open to interpretation, they cannot be offered as evidence against miracles, no matter how many miracles we do not see. As Lewis alludes, miracles are like pinholes in the cloth of uniform experience. Just because we find no pinholes in one part of the cloth, does not mean there are no pinholes elsewhere in the cloth.

Reason 11: The Argument from Religious Experience

Throughout history, many people from different cultures have testified to having religious experiences. These are typically ineffable and range from people experiencing miracles to their sensing a power or presence beyond themselves, which they attribute to divine agency. The argument espoused here is that religious experiences constitute evidence for God's existence, since more probably than not people have experienced something that exists.

A leading proponent of this empirical argument is Richard Swinburne, Professor of Philosophy at the University of Oxford. In his book *The Existence of God*,[69] Professor Swinburne invokes two principles that make it reasonable to accept religious experiences as evidence for God's existence. The first is the principle of credulity: in the absence of counter evidence, if something appears to be the case, it should be taken as the case. The second is the principle of testimony: in the absence of special considerations, the experiences of others are probably as they report them to be. As such, unless there are counter evidences and special considerations, we should accept the reality of religious experiences.

Although Swinburne defends his argument to great effect, it is not without criticism. Critics argue that because religious experiences are subjective, they cannot be used as objective evidence. However, from a Kantian perspective, one can argue that because all human experiences are subjective, no experience can be regarded as objective, including the non-religious type. Since it would be incredulous to reject all experiences of any kind, the particular experiences we accept as reality have more to do with whether they fit our worldview than with any objective criteria.

Another objection to Swinburne's argument is that principles of credulity and testimony should only apply to ordinary events, and since religious experiences are extraordinary, they require a greater burden of proof. Although this objection might apply to one case of religious experience, when there are multiple testimonies from different people with similar religious experiences, the combined cases constitute an increased burden of proof, making the reality of their experiences of God more probable than not.

In his book *The Future of an Illusion*, Sigmund Freud claimed religion is a delusion, serving as a kind of narcotic to repress the existential fears and anxieties people sense from an uncertain world.[70] This view has been echoed by others, including Professor Stephen Hawking who claims, "There is no heaven…that is a fairy story for people afraid of the dark."[71] In response, Professor John Lennox retorted, "Atheism is a fairy story for people afraid of the light."[72] Hence, one cannot be so quick to glibly dismiss theism, since arguments exist for both atheism and theism.

What seems to tip the balance in favor of theism though, is the enormous amount of empirical accounts from people with religious experiences.[73] Whilst it would be impossible to investigate each account for the purpose of this argument, they nevertheless constitute evidence. Swinburne suggests that each empirical account should not be treated in isolation, but as part of a collective whole.[74] In other words, when one considers the mass of empirical evidence that exists, each account increases the probability that God exists. As Swinburne states, "The testimony of many witnesses to experiences apparently of God…is in that case sufficient to make theism overall probable."[75]

Reason 12: The Common Consent Argument

For thousands of years, people from almost every culture have commonly believed in God. While this belief may not appeal to some as evidence for God's existence, the argument here is that belief in God is a perfectly reasonable proposition, since it is doubtful there would be such widespread belief in an entity that does not exist.[76]

Skeptics typically seek to refute this argument by claiming a common belief in God is an unsubstantiated assertion, since there are many who do not believe in God, including Pygmy tribes in Africa who have no identifiable gods. To address this point, much published research can be relied upon. For instance, a recent survey by WIN Gallup International found that 63% of people in the world were theists, compared to 11% atheists.[77] Hence, one can confidently assert that theism is commonplace across the world.

Another criticism of the common consent argument is that it epitomizes a bandwagon fallacy—meaning, a proposition is not always true just because many people believe it. But how conceivable is it that billions of theists are all wrong? Such a collective error appears unlikely unless someone can demonstrate they are all suffering from collective delusion or psychosis. Rather, there is something to be said about the state of mind of those who cast aside the reality of God's existence. The famed psychotherapist Carl Jung once noted about the many hundreds of patients he treated: "It is safe to say that every one of them fell ill because he had lost that which the living religions of every age have given their followers."[78] Conversely, there are many lucid reasons for a common belief in God, which include religious experience, logical reasoning, innate human desire, and arguments from science. As Bernard Boedder wrote, "The consent of nations in the recognition of God must be deemed the voice of universal reason yielding to compelling evidence of truth."[79]

While inconsistencies exist between religions, the central purpose of this argument has not been to contend for one religion over another, but to simply assert that theism is perfectly reasonable. Now if one were to take the common consent argument further, one could deduce Christianity as the more plausible religion, since it is the largest religion in the world with 2.2 billion Christian followers.[80]

Although it seems odd that sheer popularity may somehow constitute evidence for truth, when taken with other arguments in this book, Christianity can be relied upon as a warranted belief. Even Sir Anthony Flew, a man once described as the world's most notorious atheist, conceded:

> I think that the Christian religion is the one religion that most clearly deserves to be honored and respected whether or not its claim to be a divine revelation is true. There is nothing like the combination of a charismatic figure like Jesus and a first-class intellectual like St. Paul...If you're wanting Omnipotence to set up a religion, this is the one to beat.[81]

Reason 13: Pascal's Wager

For those still not entirely convinced of God's existence, this next argument by Blaise Pascal is worthy of consideration. Known as Pascal's wager, the argument invites others to consider the gains and losses of believing in whether God exists. According to Pascal, even if there is a small chance the Christian God exists, it is better to believe in Him than not, because the payoffs are infinitely in favour.[82] Thus, his wager offers a pragmatic reason for believing in the Christian God, as summarized below:

1. If God exists and you believe in Him, you will be rewarded with eternal life in heaven; an eternal gain.
2. If God exists and you do not believe in Him, you will be condemned to hell; an eternal loss.
3. If God does not exist and you believe in Him, you will lose little or nothing; a finite loss.
4. If God does not exist and you do not believe in Him, you will gain little or nothing; a finite gain.

According to this wager, if you believe in God, you have an eternal gain or finite loss; but if you disbelieve him, you have an eternal loss or finite gain. Since the possible outcome of believing in God is infinitely greater than disbelieving, the rational choice is to believe in God. Whilst this argument has been criticized for promoting narcissism (i.e., selfish gain), it provides an incentive to seek the Christian God—to motivate the skeptic to pray, "God, I'm not sure if You exist, but if You do, help me to believe." This is quite an honest way to pray and is similar to the way one man in the Bible prayed, when he asked Jesus, "Help me overcome my unbelief" (Mark 9:24).

An objection to this argument is that beliefs are not chosen, but formed on the basis of evidence. However, Pascal's wager merely prescribes the consequences for believing or disbelieving in God, based on Christian theology. The logic behind the wager invites us to use our reason by philosophically choosing a course of action, which even God Himself encourages: "Come now, and let us reason together" (Isaiah 1:18 KJV).

The wager has also been criticized for coercing belief, but this was not Pascal's aim. Pascale essentially argued that if a benevolent Christian God exists, He rightly deserves our faith and worship.

And by not believing in him, we risk committing the greatest injustice. Although the Bible clearly depicts the consequence for disbelieving in God, this is not God's intended outcome, for He sent Jesus, His only born Son to atone for our sins on the cross—to make a way for us to spend eternity with Him in heaven. The only requirement He asks from us is to believe in Him. As C.S. Lewis rightly noted, "One must keep on pointing out that Christianity is a statement which…if true, is of infinite importance."[83]

In summary, Pascal's wager gives us two main outcomes: If we choose to believe in the Christian God and He does not exist, we lose nothing; but if we disbelieve and He does exist, we lose everything—God, heaven, eternity and an infinite reward. In essence, if you place your wager on God and you win, you win everything; but if you lose, you lose nothing. One should therefore ask, "Where should I place my bet?"

PART II

The Case for Creation and Intelligent Design

Reason 14: The Universe Had a Beginning

Cosmology is the branch of science involved with studying the origin, development and fate of the universe (or cosmos). The universe is commonly defined as the entirety of space-time, energy and matter, including all planets, stars and galaxies.[1]

Throughout recorded human history, the origin and state of the universe has been the subject of much debate. From Hindus in the fifteenth century BC, ancient Greek philosophers in the fourth century BC, to cosmologists in the early twentieth century, a common theory held was that the universe is eternal. However, this theory was undermined in 1929 after cosmologists Edwin Hubble and Milton Humason published their findings from research carried out at Mount Wilson Observatory, Los Angeles.

By carefully measuring the Doppler shift (redshifts of light showing increased wave lengths) of several galaxies, Hubble discovered the universe was rapidly expanding. As other scientists measured its rate of expansion, they were able to determine the age of the universe by calculating when all galaxies were condensed into one place.[2] Hubble's findings led to the discovery that the universe was not eternal, but had a beginning. This discovery formed the basis of the Big Bang theory—the idea that the universe began with an extreme eruption of energy at a single moment in time and has been expanding ever since.[3]

In an attempt to refute the Big Bang, in the mid 1900s,

physicists Hermann Bondi, Thomas Gold and Fred Hoyle developed an alternative theory called Steady State. This theory combined concepts of an eternal and expanding universe with the existence of matter maintaining a constant average density.[4] Although Steady State theory attracted interest, its credibility began to diminish when astronomers discovered quasars, highly luminous cores of distant galaxies. These quasars showed the universe was not homogeneous (did not look the same at any given point in time), as Steady State predicted. The final death knell of Steady State theory came in 1964 by astronomers Arno Penzias and Robert Wilson. Using a large twenty-foot antenna they detected cosmic microwave background radiation (CMBR), i.e., thermal radiation left over from the Big Bang.[5]

Cosmological evidence strongly shows that the universe came into existence from a finite point in time, and nothing existed prior to its beginning. This evidence parallels the Biblical record of creation, "In the beginning, God created the heavens and the earth" (Genesis 1:1). If the universe were eternal, no cause for its existence would be necessary. But precisely because it has a beginning, the age old question remains: "Why is there something rather than nothing?" Even today, scientists have no evidence-based answers to this question.

Since the universe demands a cause beyond itself, the best explanation would be a timeless, metaphysical and supremely powerful cause. It so happens that the God of the Bible fits this description, for He is eternal,[6] supernatural[7] and all powerful.[8]

Reason 15: The Big Bang—Evidence of Creation

The Big Bang denotes the beginning of the universe, and is the prevailing cosmological model among scientists today.[9] According to this model, the universe began from a highly compressed point of extreme density and temperature, then rapidly expanded before cooling off. This process allowed nuclei to produce atoms (nucleosynthesis), which in turn coalesced to form stars and galaxies, etc.[10]

Scientists claim that if the Big Bang occurred, there would be observable fluctuations in cosmic microwave background radiation (CMBR). These fluctuations are small initial irregularities (finger-prints of creation), remnants of the early uniform universe that later developed into the cosmic structures we see today. Evidence of these fluctuations would by far, provide the most important confirmation of the Big Bang.[11]

In 1989, NASA launched a satellite called COBE (cosmic background explorer) to search for evidence of these CMBR fluctuations. After more than two years of observation and analysis involving over 1000 researchers, findings showed the existence of precise fluctuations that enabled galaxies to form.[12] These findings were so critical and spectacular, the NASA leader for COBE and Nobel Laureate, George Smoot remarked, "What we have found is evidence for the birth of the universe...If you're religious, it's like looking at God."[13] Smoot later said, "There is no doubt that a parallel exists between the Big Bang as an event and the Christian notion of creation from nothing."[14]

What adds further weight to the Big Bang model is Einstein's theory of general relativity, which shows that gravity, space-time, energy and matter are inseparably linked. Although physicists believe Einstein's theory is incomplete, results from many experiments and observations over the last century have shown it to be remarkably accurate.[15] His general theory of relativity is highly suggestive of a cosmic singularity—a point of density and space-time curvature where time had a beginning.[16]

When Einstein initially developed his theory in 1917, it predicted the universe was expanding. But because Einstein thought the universe was stable (the current thinking at the time), he added a "cosmological constant" (or fudge factor), forcing his equations to yield a static universe. Later, Einstein admitted that adding this constant was a mistake, calling it his "biggest blunder."[17] Before Einstein passed away in April 1955, he gave an interview where he stated, "I want to know how God created this world...I want to know his thoughts."[18] Although Einstein never claimed to be a Christian, he explicitly recognized God's hand in creation.

Among the sacred manuscripts of all major religions, only the Bible describes what scientists have discovered. In the Old Testament, God says, "My own hands stretched out the heavens" (Isaiah 45:12). Notice the phrase "stretched out." This verse, which denotes the concept of an expanding universe, was written nearly three thousand years before scientists like Einstein and Hubble discovered it. Now that is truly worth contemplating on.

Reason 16: If the Universe Had a Beginning, It Must Have a Beginner

The Big Bang model describes a universe created from a point of singularity. This point is elucidated by Professor Steven Weinberg, a Nobel laureate in High Energy Physics (a field of science dealing with the early universe):

> At about one-hundredth of a second [before expansion], the earliest time about which we can speak with any confidence, the temperature of the universe was about a hundred thousand million (10^{11}) degrees Centigrade. This is much hotter than in the center of even the hottest star.[19]

Weinberg notes that, as matter rushed apart in this explosion, "The universe was filled with light."[20] This particular description unnervingly matches the Biblical record of creation, "And God said, 'Let there be light,' and there was light" (Genesis 1:3).

On such a model, the universe originates *ex nihilo* (out of nothing). As Professor John Barrow from Cambridge University put it, "If the Universe originated at such a singularity, we would truly have a creation ex nihilo."[21] This conclusion is extremely disturbing for atheists because they cannot provide any evidence-based explanations for how the universe began from nothing. It is no wonder Stephen Hawking admitted, "Many people do not like the idea that time has a beginning, probably because it smacks of divine intervention."[22]

Although some scientists have put forward alternative models (e.g., steady state, oscillating universe, multi-verse, quantum gravity), these naturalistic (no God) alternatives all have theoretical or observational difficulties. As Oxford Professor John Lennox put it: "Trying to avoid the evidence that is visible to all for the existence of a divine intelligence behind nature, atheist scientists are forced to ascribe creative powers to less and less credible candidates."[23]

In light of the universe's origin *ex nihilo*, one is forced to conclude that if the universe had a beginning, it must have a supernatural, transcendent beginner. In other words, the universe must have a metaphysical cause outside of space-time. This view is much more consistent with a belief in a divine creator (God), than it is with a materialistic worldview espoused by atheists.

Surprisingly, countless outstanding scientists, including Michael Faraday, Galileo Galilei, William Kelvin, Guglielmo Marconi, Isaac Newton, Louis Pasteur and Edmund Whittaker, believed that God created the universe. In the words of Arno Penzias, the 1978 Nobel Prize recipient in physics, "The best data we have (concerning the Big Bang) are exactly what I would have predicted, had I nothing to go on but the five books of Moses, the Psalms, the Bible as a whole."[24]

Reason 17: The Uncaused First Cause

Because the law of causality requires every material effect to have an adequate cause,[25] it is logical to argue that the universe must have been caused. This logic follows Kalam's cosmological argument:

Whatever begins to exist must have a cause; the universe began to exist; therefore, the universe had a cause.[26]

Although Kalam's argument has been the subject of criticism, these criticisms are based on assumptions involving no causal principle, no Big Bang, and the existence of infinities. The problem however, is that these assumptions not only defy rational laws of physics, but also the most current evidence supporting the Big Bang—the beginning of space-time, energy and matter. Furthermore, there is no valid argument for the universe evolving from a prior state, because science shows there was no prior state.

The cause of the universe can only be explained as a transcendent first cause outside the universe itself. On this basis, it is understandable that naturalists often become flummoxed in finding a materialistic cause, since they would have to attribute the cause of universe to a supernatural phenomenon. Surprisingly, atheist scientists occasionally make this attribution. For example, the famed British astronomer Sir Fred Hoyle noted, "A common sense interpretation of the facts suggests that a super intellect has monkeyed with physics, as well as with chemistry and biology."[27]

Whilst some scientists are intellectually honest enough to attribute the Big Bang to a supernatural deity, a common response from ardent atheists comes in the satirical form, 'If God created the universe, who created God?' A simple answer is that laws of science are limited to observing natural, not supernatural phenomena. Hence, this question is outside the realm of what science can answer. Besides, the God of the Bible is both uncreated and uncaused, rendering the above question illogical.

Over many centuries, scientists and philosophers have recognized the need for an uncaused first cause of the universe. For instance, in *Physics*[28] Aristotle asserts the initial cause of motion must have been an entity that is not itself in motion, i.e., an unmoved prime mover. Although opponents of first cause reasoning argue that it involves special pleading, this reasoning is warranted because cosmological evidence shows the universe originated *ex nihilo*. Hence, like petulant children we can keep asking "Why?" but in the end, the answer is either "we don't know" or "God made it so." What we really should be asking is what are the attributes of this God? The Bible says God is loving,[29] holy,[30] gracious,[31] omnipresent,[32] omniscient,[33] omnipotent,[34] eternal[35] and invisible.[36]

But some may ask, "If He's invisible, how can I believe in Him?" In the New Testament, the apostle Paul declares, "Christ is the visible image of the invisible God. He existed before anything was created and is supreme over all creation, for through Him God created everything in the heavenly realms and on earth" (Colossians 1:15-16). This record explicitly tells us that God is visibly personified in Christ, as the uncaused first cause of the universe.

Reason 18: Hawking's Imaginary Time Is a Little Too Imaginary

In his book *A Brief History of Time*, Professor Stephen Hawking uses the concept of imaginary time to propose the universe could have naturally created itself.[37] By refuting the idea of a supernatural first cause, Hawking creates an argument for not believing in God.

Based on quantum theory of gravity (a synthesis of general relativity with the uncertainty principle), Hawking suggests that imaginary time is just as real as the "real-time" in which we live. By conflating space with imaginary time, he proposes the existence of a boundary-less (infinite) space-time prior to the Big Bang.[38] In effect, Hawking proposes the Big Bang singularity happened in real-time, but was derived from gravitational effects acting within imaginary space-time. Although Hawking admits his hypothesis is un-falsified (untested), in his later book *The Grand Design*, he makes the positive assertion, "Because there is a law like gravity, the universe can and will create itself out of nothing."[39]

Although Hawking's assertion may resonate with a skeptic public, Professor John Lennox gives a critical rebuttal. He claims, "To presuppose the existence of the universe to account for its own existence sounds like something out of Alice in Wonderland, not science."[40] Lennox goes on to argue that Hawking's hypothesis holds illogical and contradictory assumptions.

The first assumption is that gravity existed in a state of "nothing." Since gravity is not "nothing" in its truest sense, Hawking is claiming the universe created itself from both something and nothing—an evident contradiction. Even if his meaning of "nothing" is aligned with the concept of a quantum vacuum, this is not distinctly "nothing."

The second assumption is that in Hawking's imaginary space-time, the total energy is zero, a value he makes explicit in his later book *The Grand Design*. However, the problem with this assumption is that in imaginary space-time, there would be no energy from which gravity could borrow to create a body of mass. As Lennox put it, "Could all this be just a little too 'much ado about nothing?'"[41]

The third assumption is that the law of gravity can actually create something. On this point, Hawking is attributing a somewhat magical ability to physical laws. Physical laws do not create anything, but are merely universal rules that describe or predict what happens under certain conditions.[42] To illustrate this further, suppose we replace the universe with a jet engine. Could physical laws alone manifestly create the engine? No. Physical laws simply describe how the jet engine works, which means Hawking is misattributing creative agency to the laws of physics.

The final assumption is that the universe can "create itself." To illustrate the logical fallacy of this assumption, Lennox explains: "If, therefore, we say 'X creates X,' we imply that we are presupposing the existence of X in order to account for the existence of X."[43] Since Hawking begins with what he is trying to end with, he is guilty of circular reasoning.

In conclusion, Hawking's hypothesis that the universe created itself cannot be relied upon. He is implicitly asking us to choose between God and physical laws, which is analogous to choosing Frank Whittle or physical laws to create the turbojet engine. In Lennox's own words, "What this all goes to show is that nonsense remains nonsense, even when talked about by world-famous scientists."[44]

Reason 19: The Fine-Tuning of the Universe

The fine-tuning of the universe is the proposition that because fundamental physical constants have such narrow parameters, life would not exist if any one of these constants had slightly different values. According to cosmologist and agnostic Paul Davies, there are 40 precisely-tuned fundamental physical constants.[45] Examples include the speed of light, Planck constant, gravitational constant, charge of the electron, proton-neutron mass ratio and permeability of vacuum.

To give an idea of their importance, if protons were slightly heavier than neutrons, atoms would not exist.[46] Similarly, if the charge of the electron were any different, stars would not have been able to burn hydrogen and helium, yielding no chemistry for life.[47] Although opinions differ among scientists as to how finely tuned these life-permitting constants are, some require infinitesimally precise tuning. Professor Steven Weinberg elucidates this point:

> One constant does seem to require an incredible fine-tuning: it is the vacuum energy, or cosmological constant....the existence of life of any kind seems to require a cancellation between different contributions to the vacuum energy, accurate to about 120 decimal places.[48]

Since many constants have been discovered over the last 40 years, Davies suggests the majority of cosmologists agree that the universe is "fine-tuned for life."[49] Some physicists go further, by arguing the precise tuning of so many constants is evidence that the universe was intentionally created for life. Harvard-educated NASA astrophysicist John A. O'Keefe asserts, "If the universe had not been made with the most exacting precision we could never have come into existence. It is my view that these circumstances indicate the universe was created for man to live in."[50]

O'Keefe's worldview is consistent with the Biblical view: "He who created the heavens, He is God; He who fashioned and made the earth, He founded it; He did not create it to be empty, but formed it to be inhabited" (Isaiah 45:18). Those relying on fine-tuning as evidence for Biblical creation are often accused of employing the anthropic principle. This principle states that because we exist, we are biased toward selecting properties to satisfy the conditions for our own existence. However, using the anthropic principle to refute fine-tuning backfires when one considers that none of us can remove ourselves as observers of our own universe. On this basis, all scientists who provide explanations for our existence fall prey to the anthropic principle, in one variant form or another.

Although we can all make specific claims about our existence, without observational evidence our claims are mere conjectures. Considering the scientific evidence of nature's many life-permitting constants, the argument that our universe is finely tuned for life on earth is beyond question.

Reason 20: The Insurmountable Odds of Chance

The fine-tuning of nature's constants must have been evident in the initial conditions of the universe, otherwise we would not be present to discuss the subject.[51] With reference to how accurately organized these initial conditions were, Oxford Professor of Mathematics, Roger Penrose (one of Stephen Hawking's collaborators) states:

The Creator's aim must have been, namely to an accuracy of one part in 10, to the power of 10, to the power of 123. This is an extraordinary figure. One could not possibly even write the number down in full, in the ordinary denary notation... Even if we were to write a '0' on each separate proton and on each separate neutron in the entire universe—and we could throw in all the other particles for good measure—we should fall far short of writing down the figure needed.[52]

In probability theory, odds of less than 1 in 10 to the power of 50 are considered zero-probability.[53] Since Penrose's number is more than a trillion, trillion, trillion times more than that, the odds of the universe existing by random chance can be regarded as impossible. The implication of such insurmountable odds is that it takes more faith to believe the universe exists by chance, than to believe in a divine creator. Unsurprisingly, the August 1997 issue of *Science* (a prestigious peer-reviewed journal) featured the article, "Science and God: A Warming Trend?" Here is an excerpt:

The fact that the universe exhibits many features that foster organic life—such as precisely those physical constants that result in planets and long-lived stars—also has led some scientists to speculate that some divine influence may be present.[54]

The number of scientists, many of them prestigious, who believe God divinely tuned the universe for life is growing. For instance, cosmologist and distinguished emeritus Professor Edward R. Harrison states, "Our finely tuned universe was designed by God specifically for inhabitation by life."[55] Another is Allan Sandage, an influential astronomer of the twentieth century:

I find it quite improbable that such order came out of chaos. There has to be some organizing principle. God to me is a mystery but is the explanation for the miracle of existence, why there is something instead of nothing.[56]

Moreover, Nobel laureate, William D. Phillips asserts, "Exceptional fine-tuning of the conditions of the universe for the development of life suggest that an intelligent Creator is responsible."[57]

One of the most prestigious scientists today is Professor George Ellis, who co-authored *The Large Scale Structure of Space-Time* with Stephen Hawking. Ellis claims, "Amazing fine tuning occurs in the laws that make this [complex functioning of life] possible. Realization of the complexity of what is accomplished makes it very difficult not to use the word 'miraculous.'"[58] In the book *Quantum Cosmology and the Laws of Nature*, Ellis explicitly refers to the cause of this miraculous accomplishment: "God is the creator and sustainer of the universe and of humankind, transcending the universe but immanent in it."[59]

In view of the impossible odds of the universe existing by accident, we must ask ourselves: "Which cause is more likely, blind chance or God's design?"

Reason 21: God or Multiverse

Since the evidence of fine-tuning suggests a designing intelligence, atheists resort to ideas with no evidence. One such idea is the multiverse hypothesis. Its proposition is that if enough universes exist, there is an increased probability of one of them (namely ours) has all of nature's constants falling by chance into a highly narrow life-permitting range. It is therefore understandable that proponents of a multiverse often use it as a scientific theory to explain away God.

The multiverse hypothesis could be plausible if it were not

for the fact that no observational evidence exists for it.[60] Even multiverse proponent Brian Greene admits no direct evidence exists: "As of today, we are far from crossing this threshold."[61] Furthermore, distinguished Professor of Complex Systems, George Ellis, claims multiverse theory (M-Theory) is "untestable," posing a blow to its validity.[62] Another damaging blow comes from famed mathematical physicist, Roger Penrose. Commenting on a talk show in 2010, Penrose remarked, "What is referred to as M-Theory isn't even a theory, it's a collection of ideas, hopes, aspirations..."[63]

Given that M-Theory is metaphysical and not subject to observation, its proponents can be justifiably accused of abandoning evidentialism (beliefs resting on evidence) to explore their atheistic presuppositions. As physicist and atheist Steven Weinberg pointed out, "If you discovered a really impressive fine tuning... I think you'd be really left with only two explanations: a benevolent designer or a multiverse."[64] Professor Bernard Carr made this point more explicit when he remarked, "If you don't want God, you'd better have a multiverse."[65] Drawing from Weinberg and Carr, naturalists who posit M-Theory as a quasi-fact do so because it supports their *a priori* (presupposed) rejection of God's existence.

A chief proponent of M-Theory is Professor of Physics, Alexander Vilenkin. He takes the concept of a multiverse to another level by proposing an eternal inflation model of infinite universes.[66] His model dramatically depicts an infinite amount of galaxies and worlds that have an infinite past, with an infinite number of people with your name who may be reading this book right now. Aside from its speculative nature, this particular multiverse hypothesis faces a potentially grave problem. Put simply, if our world is one of an infinite number, we should be observing an infinite number of highly unusual events in our own universe. These could include time travellers arriving here through wormholes and visitations from flying unicorns or spaghetti monsters through collisions with other universes. The fact we do not observe such events strongly disconfirms the infinite multiverse hypothesis.[67]

Since M-Theory cannot be considered a valid explanation for fine-tuning, according to Weinberg, one is forced to rely on the alternative—a benevolent designer. But one could argue this conclusion is a matter of faith not science. Agnostic Paul Davies answers this point:

> In the end it boils down to a question of belief...if we cannot visit the other universes or experience them directly, their possible existence must remain just as much a matter of faith as belief in God...the seemingly miraculous concurrence of numerical values that nature has assigned to her fundamental constants must remain the most compelling evidence for an element of cosmic design.[68]

This conclusion has obvious theological implications, because if the universe was designed, it requires an intelligent designer. And who best fits this description? God, of course.

Reason 22: If the Universe Was Designed, It Must Have a Designer

Although naturalists characterize design advocates as a fanatical fringe group, an impressive array of notable scientists view the fine-tuning and complexity of the universe as evidence of intelligent design (ID). The main premise of ID theory is that complex features of the universe and living matter are best explained by an intelligent cause (or force), not by an undirected random process.[69]

Many Nobel laureate scientists advocate a form of ID. What they all have in common is that their field of science led them to conclude the universe (and life) is a product of ID. One such scientist is the famed theoretical physicist and agnostic Max Planck, who won the 1918 Nobel Prize for his work on quantum theory. As the originator of quantum physics, Planck made this remarkable statement in a speech on The Nature of Matter in 1944 in Florence, Italy:

> All matter originates and exists only by virtue of a force which brings the particle of an atom to vibration and holds this most minute solar system of the atom together. We must assume behind this force the existence of a conscious and intelligent mind. This mind is the matrix of all matter.[70]

Incidentally, Planck's finding correlates with the New Testament scripture: "In Him (Christ) all things hold together" (Colossians 1:17). Another acclaimed scientist who supports ID is theoretical physicist Brian Josephson, who won the 1973 Nobel Prize for his discovery of a quantum super-current. In a lecture he delivered to the Cambridge Physics Society in 2008,' he stated, "Intelligent design is real. Intelligent design is rejected just because it's part of the scientific culture that it cannot be true, you must not talk about it."[71]

Each year, evidence emerges that supports ID, but as Josephson alludes, naturalists resist it. The problem for them is that acceptance of design implies the existence of a designer. This reasoning follows Paley's teleological argument, illustrated in his watchmaker analogy: The complex functionality and design of a watch necessitates a designer; since the cosmos exhibits complex functionality and design, it necessitates a cosmic designer.[72] Regardless of how dissimilar natural objects are to a watch, Paley's argument implies that because natural objects exhibit complex properties and principles, they reliably indicate design and thus warrant an intelligent designer.

Whilst not an ID advocate, Professor Steven Weinberg

acknowledges, "If we were to see the hand of the designer anywhere, it would be in the fundamental principles, the final laws of nature, the book of rules that govern all natural phenomena."[73] His acknowledgment resonates with the writings of the Psalmist: "The heavens declare the glory of God; the skies proclaim the work of his hands" (Psalm 19:1).

Unfortunately, to admit the existence of a designer would be anathema to many naturalists, since it opens the door to divine agency. Dr. Scott Todd, an immunologist from Kansas University addresses this point well: "Even if all the data point to an intelligent designer, such a hypothesis is excluded from science because it is not naturalistic."[74] This point suggests that even when evidence strongly supports ID, naturalists rule it out because of their dogmatic philosophical assumptions. Should not all scientists follow the evidence wherever it may lead, no matter how counter-intuitive? Since cosmological evidence indicates design, it follows there must be a designer.

Reason 23: The Complex Design of Life

In addition to evidence of design in the fine-tuning and complexity of the universe, there is also evidence of design in molecular biology. A cell is the basic unit of life, and all living organisms are composed of one cell (unicellular) or more (multicellular). In multicellular organisms like humans, specific types of cells are bound together to create the tissue, organs and systems required for them to function.[75] To give a sense of how complex humans are, an adult human body has 37.2 trillion cells made up of 200 different types. If these cells were lined up end to end, the line would circle the earth almost 19 times.[76]

But how do living cells assemble themselves to form an organism? DNA (Deoxyribose Nucleic Acid) is made up of molecules that reside in each cell. It holds genetic instructions for the assembly of proteins, i.e., building blocks of life responsible for the function and anatomical features of all living organisms.[77] Although DNA was discovered in 1869 by biochemist Friedrich Miescher, it was not until 1953 that biologists James Watson and Francis Crick discovered the structure of DNA.

This biological discovery is probably the most important over the last 100 years because it answered a fundamental mystery—namely, how genetic information is stored inside a cell, and how it is inherited from one generation to the next. Watson and Crick found that DNA has a highly complex three-dimensional, double-helical structure that functions as a storing and copying mechanism for genetic material.[78] This structure entails the specific pairing of four base chemicals: Adenine (A), Thymine (T), Cytosine (C) and Guanine (G), which are bonded together along two long strands that are coiled like a twisted ladder (double helix). These base pairs are interlocked like rungs on a ladder, which only occur if their characteristics are compatible (e.g., G–C and A–T), acting like a digital code.[79] The linear sequence of these four bases is what determines the DNA's information (or genetic code), which in the language of the cell, instructs it how to make proteins.[80]

Watson and Crick also discovered that these two strands are held together by hydrogen bonds, allowing them to unzip for replication. This replication process is carried out by various enzymes acting on the DNA to unwind it, read and copy its information to produce more DNA. A similar process known as transcription uses a DNA strand as a template for the production of RNA, a single-stranded nucleic acid that carries coded information from the DNA to the protein synthesizing machinery of the cell.[81]

The point being made here is that the intricate assemblies of living systems, along with the complex information storage, retrieval and copying mechanism of DNA, could not have occurred through an undirected random process. Rather, these living systems indicate an ultra-complex design directed by intelligence.

Although some scientists argue that natural selection and random genetic mutations (alterations in DNA) can produce design-like structures, they have no valid explanations for the origin of DNA. According to ID advocate Dr. Stephen Meyer, no plausible theory even exists for the origin of genetic information required to build the first living cell through biochemical evolution.[82]

This predicament begs several questions in the form: Where did DNA's four-character code (A-T-C-G) come from? Who or what programmed the sequence of this code to produce information? How did the cell's complex information processing system arise? Francis Crick gives us a clue:

> The DNA molecule is the most efficient information storage system in the entire universe. The immensity of complex, coded and precisely sequenced information is absolutely staggering. The DNA evidence speaks of intelligent, information-bearing design.[83]

Reason 24: The Complex Language of DNA

Molecular scientists and researchers accept that DNA is a complex language—the language of life itself.[84] After Watson and Crick discovered the structure of DNA in 1953, other molecular biologists deciphered how specific DNA sequences instruct the manufacture of proteins within cells for life to exist. Crick played an integral role in this development through his famous "Sequence Hypothesis," purporting that proteins are built in accordance with the sequence of four chemical bases (A-T-C-G), functioning like a four-character code.[85]

Similar to the way the order of letters in the alphabet form words to convey a particular message, sequences of chemical bases along the strand of a DNA molecule convey precise instructions. This means DNA possesses the same sequence-specific features characterizing languages, linguistic texts and computer codes.[86] Even Richard Dawkins acknowledged, "The machine code of the genes is uncannily computerlike."[87] Bill Gates, the founder of Microsoft also noted, "DNA is like a computer program, but far, far more advanced than any software we've created."[88]

Furthermore, the information storage capacity of DNA is so enormous it exceeds any other known system. For instance, the human genome which weighs less than a few thousand millionths of a gram contains 3.2 billion base pairs (genetic letters), equivalent to more than 12 sets of The Encyclopedia Britannica, an astonishing 384 volumes.[89] Michael Denton explains, "The information necessary to specify the design of all the species of organisms which have ever existed on the planet…could be held in a teaspoon and there would still be room left for all the information in every book ever written."[90]

In a bid to show common ancestry, evolutionists claim that human DNA is 98% similar to that of great apes.[91] However, what evolutionists fail to consider is that because there are 3.2 billion genetic letters in the human genome, a shortfall of just 2% equates to 64 million letters—1000 average size books of information. It follows that an intelligent designer is a very plausible explanation for the origin of species.

The famed British Professor Anthony Flew who championed atheism for more than half a century, defended evolution. However, in keeping with his commitment to follow the evidence wherever it leads, in 2004 he announced to the world his belief in the existence of God after examining DNA evidence. In an interview, Flew explains, "The findings of more than 50 years of DNA research have provided materials for a new and enormously powerful argument to design."[92]

Although Darwinists propose that DNA sequences are a product of an evolutionary process, their proposal is like saying letters of the alphabet could randomly sequence themselves into a great work of literature. Information scientist, Professor Werner Gitt argues:

> There is no known law of nature, no known process and no known sequence of events which can cause information to originate by itself in matter...All experiences indicate that a thinking being voluntarily exercising his own free will, cognition and creativity, is required.[93]

The implication of Gitt's argument is that DNA information originated from a conscious, mental activity rather than a strictly material cause. Although evolutionists are still applying nineteenth century Darwinian thinking to 21st century science, it is not working. A more warranted explanation for the source of DNA's complex language is that a personal, super-intelligent being devised it.

Reason 25: High-tech in Low Life

In the nineteenth century, the cell could only be viewed as a glob of plasma, a black box that scientists could not fathom. However, due to advances in microscopy over the last 50 years, the black box has been opened, revealing a cell filled with high-tech machinery. These advances also reveal that information in DNA and RNA is only part of the cell's complex information processing system. The following illustration gives an insight into the advanced nanotechnology inside the cell, exceeding our own technological systems in their complexity, design and information storage capacity.[94]

At the heart of every cell is DNA, containing assembly instructions to build all the cells in an organism. In a process known as transcription, molecular machinery first unwinds a segment of DNA to expose the biological instructions needed to assemble protein molecules. Other machinery then copies these instructions to form a molecule known as mRNA. When transcription is complete, mRNA enters through the nuclear pore complex—the gatekeeper of the cell's nucleus, carrying with it the biological instructions copied from DNA. The mRNA strand is then directed to a two part molecular factory called a ribosome, where it attaches itself for translation, i.e., the process of creating proteins.[95]

Inside the ribosome, a molecular assembly line builds sequence-specific chains of amino acids (polypeptides), in accordance with precise biological instructions contained in the mRNA. These amino acids arrive from other parts of the cell and their sequence determines the type of protein to be manufactured. When the polypeptide chain is finished, it is escorted to a barrel shaped machine (chaperonin), where it is folded into a precise three-dimensional shape, critical for its function. After the polypeptide is folded into a protein, it is escorted by another molecular machine to the exact location where it is needed.[96]

This illustration demonstrates that the exquisite machinery, information processing and complex organization of the cell could not have been derived by evolution (purposeless chance), but by specified design. In relation to the molecular apparatus inside the cell, Professor Dean Kenyon remarked:

> This is absolutely mind-boggling, to perceive at this scale of science, such a finely tuned apparatus that bears the marks of intelligent design and manufacture. And we have the details of an immensely complex molecular realm of genetic information and processing, and it's exactly this new realm of molecular genetics where we see the most compelling evidence of design on the earth.[97]

Can Darwin's theory of evolution account for the enormously

complex machinery of life within the cell? No. The nanotechnology inside the cell is so highly specified and calibrated, it is inconceivable to think it was derived by random chance. Moreover, if you search the scientific literature on evolution, there is an unnerving silence on the origin of molecular machines.[98] A more plausible explanation is that a supremely intelligent creator designed them. The Psalmist described this point well when he claimed, "For you created my inmost being; you knit me together in my mother's womb" (Psalm 139:13).

Reason 26: Neo-Darwinism Debunked

Based on data from genetic research, evolutionists in the 1900s developed a modern theory of evolution known as Neo-Darwinism, often used to repudiate the Biblical account of creation. Neo-Darwinism suggests that all species evolved from a common ancestor (a single origin of life on earth) by natural selection acting on random genetic mutations (variations in DNA) acquired by inheritance.[99]

The problem with Neo-Darwinism is that random mutations have never been observed to add the kind of complex, functional genetic information required for large-scale evolution.[100] Even award winning biologist, Professor Lynn Margulis argues, "Many biologists claim they know for sure that random mutation (purposeless chance) is the source of inherited variation that generates new species of life…'No!' I say."[101]

For the development of novel, complex body plans and biological features, evolution from the first organism requires a random process for forming new DNA information within the cell. This process is analogous to saying that a great work of literature like Moby Dick could emerge from lesser pre-existing books, if enough random typos or swapping of letters occurred along the way. The argument taken here is that only with intelligent guidance can meaningful sentences and paragraphs be formed, the same applying to genetic information.

In discussing this argument, the meaning of *information* must be clearly defined. Neo-Darwinists often refer to information theorist Claude Shannon's generous definition, which includes density, lengths, variations and noise. From this perspective, garbled and functionless DNA sequences (caused by genetic mutations) can be seen to increase genetic or biological information within the cell. However, when genetic information is defined as a specified, complex and functional sequence of DNA (the type required for large-scale evolution), the information produced by mutations is zero.[102]

When providing examples of how mutations produce new information, Neo-Darwinists invariably cite new traits caused by changes in existing information—that is, variations of the same genes (alleles) as can be seen in tailless cats and white-coated lab mice. However, these examples do not justify the kind of mechanism Darwinian evolution requires.

What Neo-Darwinism essentially requires is a mechanism for developing substantively new biological functionality. Although Neo-Darwinists cite gene duplication (a piece of DNA abnormally copied one or more times) as a mechanism for adding biological information, this type of mutation can negatively alter the function of the resulting protein. When an organism has extra copies of a specific gene, it may not be able to control the expression of that gene, resulting in loss of function.[103] The truth is, the majority of genetic mutations that produce noticeable effects are recessive, leading to a loss of biological information and function.[104] That is not to say mutations cannot sometimes have beneficial outcomes for an organism, like antibiotic resistance in bacteria, but this kind of outcome is a form of adaptation within an existing species group.

The real issue Neo-Darwinists frequently overlook is the conflict between random mutation and ultra-complexity. To get from a single cell organism to a complex multi-cellular organism (like a human), there must be a mechanism for adding new genetic information to make vital organs, eyes, arms and legs, etc. On this point, Margulis and Sagan assert, "Mutation accumulation does not lead to new species or even to new organs or tissues."[105]

In conclusion, Neo-Darwinism cannot stand as a theory for large-scale evolution. Can genetic mutations create new biological information in DNA? Yes, in a Shannon sense, but not the kind necessary for producing novel, complex biological features. It follows that Neo-Darwinism is incapable of refuting the Biblical account of creation—that is, all living organisms originate from specific acts of divine creation by God.

Reason 27: The Fallacy of Darwinian Evolution

British naturalist and geologist, Charles Darwin, devised the theory of evolution by natural selection. He proposed that all animal and plant species commonly descended by the natural selection of slight modifications that increased their ability to adapt, survive and reproduce.[106] Even today, many in the scientific community and the general public, regard Darwin's theory (albeit in a modified form) as a scientific fact.

Since Darwin's theory undermines the Genesis account of divine creation, atheists employ Darwinian evolution as confirming evidence of their *a priori* rejection of God's existence. Although theistic evolutionists attempt to reconcile Darwinism with creationism, this position undermines the infallibility of scripture—that is to say, if the Bible is fallible in one part, it is fallible in another. In Genesis chapter one, God clearly informs us that He created a rich diversity of living plants and animals "according to their kind," meaning, they were created as mature species ready to reproduce. God also explicitly tells us that He created the first fully formed human being, not from an ape-like creature, but in his own image from natural elements within the ground, then "breathed into his nostrils the breath of life" (Genesis 2:7).

While critics of creationism prefer Darwin's account of the origin of species, some may not be aware that Darwin did not propose his theory as fact, but as "a provisional hypothesis or speculation."[107] While studies confirm microevolution, i.e., small-scale adaptation such as insects developing resistance to pesticides, evolutionists incorrectly generalize these studies to support macroevolution, i.e., large-scale evolutionary change such as dinosaurs becoming birds.

In 1980, approximately 150 of the world's leading evolutionary scientists gathered at the University of Chicago for a historic conference entitled Macroevolution. Roger Lewin, a Prize winning science writer, reported the conclusion of the conference in his peer-reviewed article, *Evolutionary Theory under Fire*: "The central question of the Chicago conference was whether the mechanisms underlying microevolution can be extrapolated to explain the phenomena of macroevolution...the answer can be given as a clear, No."[108]

Scientists understand that hundreds, even thousands of mutations are required to produce the biological step changes needed for a new animal order to evolve. The argument here is that genetic mutations observed in microevolution cannot produce the complex biological functions and features organisms require for macroevolution. Evidence from recent discoveries in molecular biology support this argument and are plunging Darwinian evolution into crisis. In his peer-reviewed article, molecular biologist Douglas Axe calculated that biological features with more than six mutations are unlikely to give any benefit, even when given a waiting time of the entire history of the earth, some 4.54 billion years.[109] In other words, Darwinian evolution is incapable of producing the multi-mutation features organisms require for complex adaptations.

An empirical study by Gauger et al. in 2010 found that when

only two mutations were required to restore function to a bacterial gene, the Darwinian mechanism failed, meaning the gene could not be repaired to regain its fitness.[110] This finding corroborates another peer-reviewed paper by Professor Michael Behe who discovered that bacteria and viruses tend to lose function when they undergo biological modifications at a molecular level.[111]

In conclusion, these studies along with others (too many to mention here), cast grave doubt on Darwin's theory. While critics of creationism will have their own counter arguments, the take home message of molecular research is that Darwinian evolution is at best, uncertain and at worst, fallacious. In contrast, the Genesis account of creation is one of the richest doctrines in the Bible. It reveals that God created us with meaning and purpose, a stark contrast to a life of purposeless chance that Darwinism entails.

Reason 28: Irreducible Complexity

Another argument for the fallacy of Darwinian evolution is the irreducible complexity of biological systems. Consisting of five parts (a platform, a spring, a hammer, a catch and a holding bar), a mousetrap is an elementary example of an irreducibly complex system. What makes it irreducibly complex is that the absence of any one of its five interdependent parts renders it useless. As such, all five of its components are simultaneously needed for it to exist. In his book *Darwin's Black Box*, Michael Behe argues that irreducibly complex systems like the blood-clotting cascade, immune system and bacterial flagellum, could not have evolved from simpler systems. This is because all their components are instantaneously required for them to exist.[112]

For example, the flagellum is a molecular machine made of proteins on a submicroscopic scale. As an appendage to a bacterial cell, it functions like a locomotive, enabling the cell to move through aqueous environments. Its components include a propeller; a hook; and a motor consisting of rotors, bushings, and a drive shaft.

The motor is plugged into the bacterial cell's membrane from where it draws power by an electrochemical gradient (a mismatch of hydrogen ions). Spinning at up to 20,000 rpm, its motor can be switched in either a clockwise or counterclockwise direction through the use of transduction circuitry, allowing the flagellum to guide the bacterial cell to find food and evade enemies.[113]

Since all of the flagellum's components are simultaneously required for it to exist, it typifies an irreducibly complex system. The flagellum defies evolution, since no Darwinian mechanism exists for producing such a biological system in one fell swoop.[114] Although evolutionists argue the flagellum randomly evolved through pathways like exaptation (existing structures co-opted for new functions), scaffolding (initial proteins that degenerate after use) and successive gene duplications,[115] these explanations trivialize the sophistication and elegance of the flagellum.[116] As previously discussed, genetic mutations tend to reduce biological functionality.[117] Exaptation and scaffolding are also inadequate explanations because multiple proteins from other cells would have to break free and randomly coalesce to form a new complex system.[118]

Both Darwin and his early critics recognized that if biological features could not be accounted for by gradual modifications, natural selection would be falsified. Charles Darwin admitted, "If it could be demonstrated that any complex organ existed, which could not possibly have been formed by numerous, successive, slight modifications, my theory would absolutely break down."[119] Since the bacterial flagellum is an irreducibly complex biological system that is unlikely to have evolved from slight modifications, its existence undermines Darwinian evolution.

The flagellum signifies a biochemical engineering marvel—something designed rather than something evolved.[120] Since it has fantastically intricate features at a molecular level, the flagellum's miniaturized functionality is nothing short of the kind of design seen in nanotechnology. Thus, the most plausible explanation for the origin of irreducibly complex systems like the flagellum is that they were intelligently designed, necessitating the existence of an intelligent designer. Although Darwinists contend the appearance of design is illusory, ID theorists argue that living systems look designed because they actually were designed. This argument supports the notion that a supremely intelligent God designed and created living systems as purported in the Bible: "For you [God] created all things, and by your will they existed and were created" (Revelations 4:11).

Reason 29: Cambrian Explosion:
The Animal World's Big Bang

The Cambrian explosion is a term used by scientists to describe an event that reportedly occurred around 542 million years ago when new animal species suddenly appeared over a relatively short period of time. In fact, almost every major animal group (phyla) from the fossil record (including those that are extinct), appear in the Cambrian rock layer.[121] To add to this point, evolutionary biologist Professor Jeffrey Levinton asserts that fossils in rock layers above the Cambrian show no new or different body plans to those in the Cambrian layer.[122] In contrast, the only fossils found from pre-Cambrian rock layers consist of bacteria, algae, soft worms and single cell organisms.[123]

So what does this all mean? It means the Cambrian event defies Darwinian evolution because natural selection calls for slow, incremental modifications by common descent. Even Charles Darwin knew about the scarcity of transitional (intermediate) species from pre-Cambrian to Cambrian creatures,[124] but hoped transitional fossils would eventually show up over time. Unfortunately for Darwin, over 150 years have passed and no pre-Cambrian fossils have been identified as ancestral to Cambrian phyla,[125] a problem known as the Cambrian conundrum.

So why does the Cambrian fossil record show an abrupt

appearance of so many phyla with no prior ancestry? Although scientists have attempted to answer this conundrum, there is no generally accepted explanation.[126] Some evolutionary scientists speculate that Cambrian phyla evolved as far back as 800 million years ago,[127] but the fossil record does not support this view.[128] Hence, scientists have no credible answers to explain the Cambrian explosion from an evolutionary perspective. To underscore this point, evolutionary biologists Erwin and Davidson concluded that the origin of Cambrian phyla could not be explained by any proposed theory of micro or macroevolution.[129]

An alternative explanation is that the sudden appearance of forty major animal groups with no prior ancestry is precisely what one would expect if an omnipotent creator had constructed animal life over a short time. Moreover, the Cambrian explosion fits the Genesis account of creation, in which God suddenly created a diversity of species: "God created the great creatures of the sea and every living thing with which the water teems and that moves about in it, according to their kinds, and every winged bird" then "God made the wild animals according to their kinds, the livestock according to their kinds and all the creatures that move along the ground" (Genesis 1:21-25). In other words, in the same way God initiated the cosmological Big Bang, He also initiated the animal world's big bang.

Reason 30: Gaps in the Fossil Record

Gaps in the fossil record resulting from missing intermediate fossils between species, has been a longstanding problem for evolutionary theory. Because Charles Darwin proposed that new species descended from other pre-existing species, it follows that an enormous number of intermediate fossils should exist.

Awkwardly for evolutionists, from the thousands of species identified in the fossil record, only a tiny fraction appear to be candidates for intermediate forms. The famous paleontologist Stephen Jay Gould wrote:

> The absence of fossil evidence for intermediary stages between major transitions in organic design, indeed our inability, even in our imagination, to construct functional intermediates in many cases, has been a persistent and nagging problem for gradualistic accounts of evolution.[130]

Even Darwin acknowledged the lack of intermediate fossils, describing it as "the most obvious and gravest objection which can be urged against my theory."[131] Like escape artists, Darwin and his exponents attempt to remove themselves from this dilemma by invoking the argument of an extremely imperfect fossil record. However, this argument has lost credibility in the last few decades.

Despite its imperfections, paleontologists widely maintain the fossil record provides adequate documentation of past species.[132] Some paleontologists go further by claiming, "The gaps we see reflect real events in life's history not the artefact of a poor fossil record."[133] The lack of fossil evidence supporting evolution has led some paleontologists and anthropologists to make false claims of intermediate fossil discoveries. Well-documented examples include:

- Bone fragments proclaimed in 1912 as the missing link between apes and humans (i.e. Piltdown man) were exposed as a fraud in 1953 when found to consist of a human cranium and the jawbone of an orangutan.[134]
- A tooth in 1922 gave inspiration to the *Hesperopithecus haroldcookii* (i.e., Nebraska man), was later found to belong to a wild pig.[135]
- The 1959 discovery of a skull that inspired the *Zinjanthropus boisei* (i.e., nutcracker man) was dismissed

after further analyses showed it was not a direct ancestor to modern humans.[136]

- Although the bone fragments of a *Ramapithecus*, discovered in 1964, was considered to be a direct ancestor of modern humans; in 1976 it was found to be ancestral to the orangutan.[137]

- A feathered fossil from China dubbed *Archaeoraptor liaoningensis* (i.e., Piltdown chicken), was heralded in 1999 as the missing link between dinosaurs and birds, but was later exposed as one of the largest hoaxes in history when found to be a forgery.[138]

The above examples demonstrate that in paleontology, things are not always as they seem. According to Professor Lubenow, even legitimate fossil discoveries provide no evidence for intermediary links, especially between humans and other species, which are "more in the imagination of paleoanthropologists than in the fossils themselves."[139] After 25 years of research, Lubenow concludes:

> There is simply no viable scientific explanation of modern humans in an evolutionary model. When humans reject the authority of God's Word and the historicity of the Genesis account of human creation, it should not surprise us that more than 100 years of secular research into human origins has yielded no reliable answers.[140]

PART III

The Historicity of Jesus

Reason 31: The Existence of Jesus

No serious historian doubts the existence of Jesus. Although Biblical scholars differ on His beliefs and teachings, there is almost universal consensus among historians that Jesus existed.[1] Richard Burridge, Professor of Biblical Interpretation at King's College, wrote "There are those who argue that Jesus is a figment of the Church's imagination, that there never was a Jesus at all. I have to say that I do not know any respectable critical scholar who says that anymore."[2]

In addition to the eyewitness gospel accounts in the New Testament, there are many apocryphal texts, dating back to the first centuries. All of these ancient manuscripts account for the life, death and resurrection of Jesus. Even though Biblical scholars regard these manuscripts as sufficient evidence, some critics dismiss them because they are not extra-Biblical—meaning, they are not historical writings from outside the Bible. However, what critics fail to realize is that there is more extra-Biblical evidence for the existence of Jesus, than for any other historical figure from the same period and place.[3]

The extra-Biblical evidence for Jesus includes a plethora of non-Christian historical writers and sources such as Thallus, Phlegon, Josephus, Tacitus, Suetonius, Celsus, Lucian and the Jewish *Talmud*. For example, Josephus, a respected first century Jewish historian made two references to the Biblical Jesus in his work, *Antiquities of the Jews* (AD 93-94); and Tacitus, regarded by many as one of the finest historians of ancient Rome, referred to

Christ's execution by Pontius Pilate in his *Annals* (AD 116). Hence, one can confidently assert the existence of Jesus is as much a matter of fact as the existence of any other ancient historical figure. Even atheist Michael Grant, the eminent Cambridge historian agrees on this point: "We can no more reject Jesus' existence than we can reject the existence of a mass of pagan personages whose reality as historical figures is never questioned."[4]

While historians differ on their constructed portrayals of Jesus, many agree on a number of details about him and his followers—namely, He was a Galilean, He was baptized by John the Baptist, He called disciples, His ministry was confined to Galilee and Judea, He was crucified by the Romans near Jerusalem, and His disciples continued after his death.[5] Thus, Jesus not only existed, but also carried out many things historians are certain of.

Reason 32: The Uniqueness of Jesus

Among all religions in the world, Christianity stands as unique because it stems from the uniqueness of its founder, Jesus Christ. Whether we believe them or not, the eyewitness accounts of the synoptic gospels provide the clearest insights of the uniqueness of Jesus—His virgin birth, divinity, virtues, truth claims, miracles, crucifixion, resurrection, and ascension into heaven.

From conception to ascension, Jesus lived a supernaturally empowered existence, fulfilling hundreds of Messianic prophecies from the Old Testament, foretold centuries before his birth. Their fulfillment alone makes Jesus unique. Isaiah 7:14 predicted how He would be born, Micah 5:2 predicted where He would be born, Genesis 49:10 predicted His lineage from the Tribe of Judah, 2 Samuel 7:12 predicted He would be a son of David, Zechariah 12:10 predicted His crucifixion, and Psalm 16:10 predicted He would rise from the dead.

Although some have placed Jesus alongside other religious leaders, Jesus stands out from among them by His claim of being

God in human flesh. For instance, when He said, "Before Abraham was born, I AM" (John 8:58) He was claiming to be Yahweh—the God of Moses, and by calling Himself the "Son of Man," (Luke 19:10), He was identifying with human flesh. By becoming a man, Jesus was able to fully identify with the pains and struggles of human experience, without ever losing His identity as God.

Another unique feature is that no other religious leader in human history performed the miracles He did. According to the eyewitness account of John's gospel, Jesus turned water into wine, healed the dying son of a royal official, made a crippled man walk, fed 5000 with just five loaves and two fishes, walked on water, made a blind man see, and raised Lazarus from the dead. Whilst critical historians attempt to explain these events as myth, prominent scholar Marcus Borg states, "On historical grounds it is virtually indisputable that Jesus was a healer."[6] His greatest miracle was His own resurrection from the dead. After the Jews delivered Jesus to Pontius Pilate, the Bible says He was crucified for our sins; then after having been laid in a tomb for three days, He victoriously rose from the dead as savior of the world.

Among the 107 billion people who have ever walked the earth, the person, life and work of Jesus Christ stands out as one of a kind. Author Max Lucado exquisitely sums up the uniqueness of Jesus:

> What do we do with such a person? We applaud men for doing good things. We enshrine God for doing great things. But when a man does God things? One thing is for certain, we can't ignore him. Why would we want to? If these moments are factual, if the claim of Christ is actual, then he was, at once, man and God. There he was, the single most significant person who ever lived.[7]

Reason 33: The Historical Impact of Jesus

Jesus was truly a man without equal, whose impact changed the way we live and think today. While there have been many battles, conquests and scientific discoveries in eras past, none of them have influenced human history more than a powerful personality. The historian Thomas Carlyle wrote, "The history of the world is but the biography of great men,"[8] and none of them was more influential than Jesus Christ.

Jesus wrote no book, yet more books have been written about Him than about any other person. Jesus opened no hospital, yet Christians like St Basil of Caesarea and members of the Benedictine Order, built the first hospitals to show the compassion of Christ. Jesus was no scientist, yet Christian scientists like Galileo Galileo, Johannes Kepler and Sir Isaac Newton, laid the foundation of modern science in their pursuit to understand the creation of Christ. Jesus was no philosopher, yet Christian philosophers like Immanuel Kant, René Descartes and Sir Francis Bacon influenced the enlightenment in their quest to know the wisdom of Christ. Jesus opened no school, yet world-leading universities like Harvard, Yale, Princeton, and Oxford were founded by Christian clergymen to advance the knowledge of Christ. Jesus led no human rights movement, yet Christian politicians like Abraham Lincoln and William Wilberforce, pioneered the abolition of slavery because they believed every person was valued by Christ. Jesus opened no orphanage, yet Christian philanthropists like George Mueller and Thomas Barnardo opened children's homes in the name of Christ. This list could include many other Christian pioneers who shaped the world because of Christ's influence on their lives.

Although Jesus's earthly ministry spanned a mere three and a half years, His legacy continues to reverberate across the world. Even today, the Bible is still the best selling book of all time with over five billion copies sold.[9] Furthermore, according to a large data-driven study in 2014,[10] Jesus ranks as the most significant figure in human history. What can be said about such a historic figure? During an interview, Albert Einstein commented, "I am a Jew, but I am enthralled by the luminous figure of the Nazarene."[11] When asked if he accepted the historical existence of Jesus, Einstein replied, "Unquestionably. No one can read the Gospels without feeling the actual presence of Jesus. His personality pulsates in every word. No myth is filled with such life."[12]

The historical impact of Jesus Christ demands a verdict. Surely, no myth can make such a colossal impact. No quip can dispose of his legacy, no matter how artful. His impact alone testifies of who He claimed to be. Son of the divine. Son of God.

Reason 34: The Divinity of Jesus

Without question, Jesus is the most controversial figure that ever lived. Perhaps the most controversial claim He made, and the most central, is that He was the Son of God. However, this claim should not be understood in the same context of a human father and son. God did not marry or physically mate with a woman. Rather, the Bible states the Virgin Mary conceived by the power of the Holy Spirit so that God could manifest Himself in human form.[13] In essence, Jesus was claiming to be God the Son.

Some critics argue that Jesus did not explicitly claim to be the Son of God. This is simply not true. One example is when the Jews attempted to stone Jesus for claiming, "I and the Father are one," he asked them, "Do you accuse me of blasphemy because I said, 'I am God's Son?'" (John 10:36). Another example is in Matthew 16:15-17. When Jesus asked his disciples, "Who do you say I am?" Peter answered, "You are the Messiah, the Son of the living God." Instead of contesting Peter's claim, Jesus affirmed it by replying, "Blessed are you, Simon son of Jonah, for this was not revealed to you by flesh and blood, but by my Father in heaven."

In his book *Mere Christianity*, C.S. Lewis makes a compelling case for the divinity of Jesus. He argues that Jesus could only have claimed divinity if he was a lunatic, liar or Lord, an argument known as the trilemma. This argument excludes the possibility of Jesus being a mere "great moral teacher,"[14] because no human making such divine claims could be deemed rational or morally reliable. In other words, Jesus's claim to divinity was so outlandish, there is no escape from this trilemma; you must either dismiss Him as mad or bad, or accept Him as God. Lewis concludes, "Now it seems to me obvious that He was neither a lunatic nor a fiend: and consequently, however strange or terrifying or unlikely it may seem, I have to accept the view that He was and is God."[15]

Lewis's trilemma argument has been criticized by various opponents, but none of them provide any convincing counter arguments. For example, New Testament scholar Bart Ehrman asserts a fourth option, legend.[16] However, since a legend is based on myth, this option can be dismissed based on the existence, uniqueness and historical impact of Jesus (the first three arguments of this chapter). Lewis also dismissed the idea that the gospel accounts were legends: "I have read a great deal of legend and I am quite clear that they are not the same sort of thing."[17]

Another argument against the divine claims of Jesus is that the gospels have been misinterpreted. However, this too can be refuted, for there are too many accounts of Jesus claiming divinity to be misinterpreted. In fact, there are 12 such accounts in the gospels. In any case, Jesus's claim to divinity was the precise reason why the Jewish leaders wanted him dead.[18] It follows that the divinity of Jesus cannot be easily refuted, as one would have to assert he was mad or bad, deluded or evil. Since there is nothing in the eyewitness gospels that cast these aspersions, it is reasonable to deduce that Jesus was and is the Son of God.

Reason 35: The Virtuosity of Jesus

The argument here is that the virtuous character of Jesus corresponds with His claim to divinity. No other historical figure exemplified the virtuosity of Jesus. He showed temperance in temptation, humility in washing the disciples feet, kindness in blessing children, compassion in healing the sick, courage when facing His enemies, patience with His accusers, diligence in doing His Father's will, forgiveness toward those who crucified him, and love by giving His life for humanity. There has never been anyone so virtuous as Jesus Christ. As the Scottish theologian, Oswald Chambers put it, "The dearest friend on earth is a mere shadow compared to Jesus Christ."[19]

Whether it be Napoleon, Muhammad, William Shakespeare or Abraham Lincoln, every other historical figure had moral flaws. In contrast, the gospels give no indication that Jesus had any moral shortcomings. He never acted in haste. He never harmed anyone. He never yielded to pride. He never reneged on his word. He never turned down a sincere request, and never lusted for women, money or fame. Even when others intended to crown Him as King, He "withdrew again to a mountain by himself" (John 6:15). Christ's character sets the highest moral standard. His golden rule, "Do to others as you would have them do to you" (Luke 6:31), embodies the essence of universal morality, and has been used as a moral maxim in the fields of psychology, philosophy, sociology, and economics.

The moral character of Jesus was so great that when He challenged His enemies with the question, "Can any of you prove me guilty of sin?" (John 8:46), He was met with total silence. His bold 2000-year-old question still beckons an answer today. Even after the chief priests delivered Jesus to Pontius Pilate for claiming to be the Son of God, after careful examination Pilate concluded, "I find no fault in him" (John 19:6 KJV).

Can you find any fault with Jesus? If not, then you too must conclude that He was faultless. The flawless, moral character of Jesus epitomizes Him as a perfect human being, and at the same time, exemplifies His divinity. Even the Centurion who assisted in Christ's crucifixion claimed, "Surely he was the Son of God" (Matthew 27:54).

Reason 36: The Sinlessness of Jesus

Since God is best defined as a maximally great being who is morally perfect (without sin), the argument here is the sinlessness of Jesus affirms His divinity as the Son of God. Although Jesus was also human and subject to temptation like any other man, those who knew Him best—His disciples—unequivocally claimed He was sinless. For example, Peter asserted, "He committed no sin, and no deceit was found in his mouth" (1 Peter 2:22), and John proclaimed, "in him is no sin" (1 John 3:5).

Bible critics have argued the disciples were biased in claiming Jesus was sinless. Yet, what is most interesting is that even Christ's enemies thought He was sinless. For instance, after having betrayed Jesus for thirty pieces of silver, Judas Iscariot confessed, "I have betrayed innocent blood" (Matthew 27:4). Moreover, when members of the highest court in ancient Jerusalem; the Sanhedrin, looked for evidence against Jesus, "They did not find any" (Mark 14:55). It follows that affirmations like these from hostile witnesses attest to the sinlessness of Christ.

Bible critics also claim instances in the gospels where Jesus implicitly sinned. However, their claims do not stand the test of critical investigation. For instance, one claim is that Jesus sinned in the temple when he angrily overturned the tables of the moneychangers. Conversely, this incident illustrates righteous indignation than a fit of rage, since Jesus was displeased that His Father's house had been turned into "a den of thieves" (Matthew 21:13 KJV).

Another instance in which critics claim Jesus sinned was when He allegedly repudiated the fifth commandment by demanding that His followers hate their parents.[20] However, by studying the context of what Jesus said, one can interpret that He simply required his followers to love him more than their own families, even more than they loved their own selves.[21] After all, if Jesus were God, this requirement would have been consistent with the first commandment: "Love the Lord your God with all your heart and with all your soul and with all your mind" (Matthew 22:37). Besides, Matthew 15:4 says that Jesus clearly upheld the fifth commandment when He exhorted the Pharisees to "Honor your father and mother." Hence, critics who claim Jesus sinned lack a hermeneutic understanding of the Bible; that is to say, they are not interpreting Biblical texts in the proper socio-historical context.

Because none of us is morally perfect, we all know what it is like to sin. When we tell a lie, hold a grudge, cheat or steal, our consciences convict us of guilt. While sins like pride, arrogance and greed are subtler, they nonetheless constitute moral failures. Unlike us, Jesus never sinned. As such, He alone was qualified to vicariously atone for our sins on the cross, so "everyone who believes in Him receives forgiveness of sins through His name" (Acts 10:43). Amazingly, not only is Jesus without sin, but He also forgives sin.

Reason 37: The Forgiveness of Jesus

Another reason to believe Jesus was divine is that He forgave people of their sins. In Judaism, only God can forgive sins.[22] So, when Jesus forgave sins, the Jewish leaders clearly understood He was claiming equality with God, something they regarded as blasphemy because they rejected His deity. An example of this situation can be found in Luke 5:20-21: "When Jesus saw their faith, he said, 'Friend, your sins are forgiven.' The Pharisees and the teachers of the law began thinking to themselves, 'Who is this fellow who speaks blasphemy? Who can forgive sins but God alone?'"

The act of forgiving people of their sins sets Jesus apart from any other historical figure. Neither Muhammad, Buddha, nor the writers of the Hindu *Vedas* ever claimed to forgive people of their sins. Whilst we all have the capacity to forgive those who have wronged us, only God has the power to forgive sins because sin is a transgression of God's moral law. Since we have all broken God's moral law (the ten commandments) in one way or another, e.g., "Thou shalt have no other gods before me," "Thou shalt not take the name of the Lord thy God in vain," "Thou shalt not commit adultery" (Exodus 20:1-17 KJV), all of us need God's forgiveness. So by forgiving sins, not only did Jesus give people assurance of salvation, but He also exercised a divine right reserved only for God Himself, a view shared by various Biblical scholars.[23]

Critics challenge Jesus's divine right to forgive sins by claiming Old Testament figures such as prophets and priests forgave sins. However, there is no firm Biblical evidence to support this claim.[24] Critics also argue that Jesus delegated authority to His disciples to forgive sins, commonly citing John 20:23: "If you forgive anyone's sins, their sins are forgiven" (John 20:23). Their point is that if Jesus delegated this authority to mere mortals, then perhaps God had also delegated authority to Jesus as a mortal. What these critics fail to consider is that Jesus made this statement in relation to sending His disciples to preach the gospel, meaning if people believed their message, the disciples could affirm their sins were forgiven by God. In no way did Jesus mean that others beside Himself had the authority to forgive sins, as this would violate the core gospel message: "Everyone who believes in Him [Jesus] receives forgiveness of sins through His name" (Acts 10:43).

In closing, Jesus had the authority to forgive sins because He was divine. The Jewish leaders knew exactly whom He claimed to be when He practiced the forgiveness of sins. But instead of recognizing Jesus as their Messiah, they accused Him of blasphemy, despite the many miracles He did. Now if Jesus were guilty of blasphemy, surely God would never have granted Him the power to do such miracles.

Reason 38: The Miracles of Jesus

The many miracles Jesus wrought affirm His deity as the Son of God. According to the eyewitness accounts of the gospel writers, Jesus turned water into wine, walked on water, fed thousands with a few loaves and fishes, made the deaf to hear, the mute to speak, the blind to see, the cripples to walk, and even the dead to rise. No other person in human history performed the miracles Jesus did, which serve as confirmation of His divine message and nature. According to the apostle John, "Jesus performed many other signs in the presence of his disciples, which are not recorded in this book. But these are written that you may believe that Jesus is the Messiah, the Son of God, and that by believing you may have life in His name" (John 20:30).

Although critics allege the miracles of Jesus were myth not fact, even rabbinical writings of the Jewish *Talmud* attest to His miracles. The record of Jesus's trial in Sanhedrin 43a states that Jesus was executed for practicing "sorcery,"[25] implying His supernatural deeds were genuine because illusions were not punishable by death. This allegation of sorcery against Jesus is also found in the Bible: "Jesus was driving out a demon that was mute. When the demon left, the man who had been mute spoke, and the crowd was amazed. But some of them said, 'By Beelzebul, the prince of demons, he is driving out demons'" (Luke 11:14-15). However, Jesus refuted this allegation by telling them, "If Satan is divided against himself, how can his kingdom stand? I say this because you claim that I drive out demons by Beelzebul" (Luke 11:18).

Additional independent evidence for the miracles of Jesus comes from Josephus, the credible first century Jewish Historian. In his *Testimonium Flavianum*, Josephus wrote,

> About this time arose Jesus, a wise man, if indeed
> one ought to call him a man, for he was a maker of

miraculous works, a teacher of human beings who receive the truth with pleasure, and he won over both many Jews and also many from the Gentiles. This one was the Christ.[26]

While the authenticity of this passage has been questioned, a strong majority of scholars agree that its vocabulary and style matches that of Josephus. Professor Louis Feldman is an eminent scholar whose work on Josephus is highly regarded among academics. He reported that between 1937 and 1980, 39 out of 52 scholars who vigorously reviewed Josephus's *Testimonium Flavianum*, found portions of it to be authentic.[27]

Independent and multiple attestations such as these lend much credibility to the miracles of Jesus. Furthermore, the followers and large crowds that Jesus attracted also bear witness to the miraculous feats He performed. As Professor Mark Saucy put it, "Jesus's messianic identity was revealed by His miracles" and "there is little doubt the crowds considered Jesus a prophet because of His miracles."[28]

Reason 39: The Followers of Jesus

One reason to believe the claims of Jesus is that His followers were willing to die spreading the gospel message. Philip was beheaded by hostile Jews after evangelizing in Phrygia, Peter was crucified upside down by the Romans, James was beheaded in Jerusalem after refusing to deny Christ, Andrew was hanged in Achaia after preaching Christ's resurrection to the Scythians and Thracians, Thomas was impaled with a spear during his missionary trip to India, and Bartholomew was whipped to death in Armenia after spreading the gospel in Asia. In fact, all the original apostles except John suffered martyrdom.

Would these followers have left their families to preach the gospel and suffer gruesome deaths if it were a lie? That would be highly improbable. Although critics claim the early disciples went to such lengths because they had been proselytized, they had every reason to abandon their faith after Jesus was buried in a tomb. Rather, it makes more sense that the apostles remained faithful in preaching the gospel message precisely because Jesus was resurrected. Why would they die for a lie?

Although Jesus predicted His resurrection, His disciples did not understand what He was saying. Even when Mary Magdalene informed them Jesus was risen, the Bible says "they did not believe it" (Mark 16:11), refuting the argument that they were projecting their own unconscious wishes. In fact, they only believed Jesus was risen after He physically appeared to them: "Later Jesus appeared to the eleven as they were eating; he rebuked them for their lack of faith and their stubborn refusal to believe those who had seen him after he had risen" (Mark 16:14).

The original apostles were not alone in sacrificing their lives to spread the truth of the gospel. According to Plinius Secundus, the second century Roman governor, early Christians were people who loved the truth at any cost. In his letter to the Roman Emperor Trajan, Secundus stated:

> The method I have observed towards those who have been denounced to me as Christians is this: I interrogated them whether they were Christians; if they confessed it I repeated the question twice again, adding the threat of capital punishment; if they still persevered, I ordered them to be executed.[29]

For centuries, Christians have often braved torture and death to follow Christ. Recently, four Iraqi children under 15 years of age were beheaded for their Christian faith. According to Andrew White, Vicar of Baghdad, Islamic State militants gave them the choice to convert to Islam or die. The children's response was, "No, we love Yesua (the Iraqi name for Jesus), we have always loved Yesua, we have always followed Yesua."[30] What would drive such children to make an unwavering stand for Jesus in the face of certain death? Only an authentic salvation experience of the risen Christ.

Reason 40: The Salvation of Jesus

The argument here is that Jesus is the only person in history to atone for the sins of humanity. From all the great religious leaders of the world, only Jesus claimed to be savior of the world and sacrificed Himself on the cross as reparation for humanity's sins.

Although other religious leaders taught moral principles, none of them did anything about humanity's sin problem. Teaching, at best, invites us to be moral, but is not in itself efficacious. Like a mirror, it can show us when our face is dirty, but it can never wash our face. Jesus alone promised to wash us from our sins by His own blood. On the night before His crucifixion, He told His disciples, "This is my blood of the new testament, which is shed for many for the remission of sins" (Matthew 26:28 KJV). As the sinless Son of God, He alone was worthy to vicariously atone for our moral failures. Jesus stepped out of eternity into time to save us—to pay a debt He did not owe because we owed a debt we could not pay. There is no greater demonstration of God's grace than the finished work of Christ's cross.

The cross of Jesus is the timeless intersection where immortality met mortality, where sinlessness met sin. It represents a divine exchange in which Jesus traded places with us. He took our unrighteousness so we could receive His righteousness; He took our shame so we could receive His glory; He took our punishment so we could receive His reward; He took our sickness so we could receive His healing; He took our curse so we could receive His blessing; He took our death so we could receive His eternal life. In effect, Jesus saved us in every way we could be saved.

It was not the jeers of the Jews that crucified Jesus, nor was it the nails of the Roman soldiers. It was our sin that crucified Jesus. Christ's crucifixion was God's plan before time began. To the Romans, the cross was their gruesome method of execution; but to God, the cross was His method of salvation. Outside of Christ's cross, there is no hope in this world. Those who reject the atonement of Jesus's death on the cross are rejecting the only means for their salvation. On this point, the apostle Paul wrote, "For the message of the cross is foolishness to those who are perishing, but to us who are being saved it is the power of God" (1 Corinthians 1:18).

What can we say about such salvation? No greater love can be found in history than the sacrificial death of Jesus on the cross. Neither Buddha, Muhammad, the writers of the Hindu *Vedas*, nor any other religious figure died for the sins of the world. No other went to the cross to save us. Motivated by love, Jesus knew all along He was born to die. Before His crucifixion, He told his disciples: "Greater love hath no man than this, that a man lay down his life for his friends" (John 15:13 KJV). Although crucified 2000 years ago, His sacrifice still beckons a response today. What will yours be?

Reason 41: The Crucifixion of Jesus

The atonement Jesus made for us on the cross is one of the central claims of the gospel in the New Testament. Although the canon of the New Testament is a credible historical document, critics attempt to subvert the gospel by claiming there is insufficient evidence outside of the Bible to corroborate Christ's crucifixion. However, nothing can be further from the truth. As a matter of fact, multiple extra Biblical sources exist for the crucifixion of Christ.

One independent non-Biblical source for the crucifixion is the credible first century Roman Historian Tacitus. In his *Annals* (15.44), which have been subject to much scholarly analysis, he wrote "Christus [Christ in Latin]...suffered the extreme penalty during the reign of Tiberius at the hands of one of our procurators, Pontius Pilate."[31] Another independent source is Josephus, a respected first century Jewish historian. In his *Antiquities of the Jews* (18.63-64), Josephus noted "At this time there was a wise man named Jesus...Pilate condemned him to be crucified and to die."[32]

Lucian of Samosata was a second century author and skeptic of Christianity. He wrote, "The Christians, you know, worship a man to this day—the distinguished personage who introduced their novel rites, and was crucified on that account."[33] The Jewish *Talmud* in (Sanhedrin 43a) also speaks of the execution of Jesus: "On the eve of the Passover they hung Yeshu the Notzri [Jesus the Nazarene]."[34] Finally, Mara bar-Serapion, an Assyrian Stoic philosopher implicitly refers to the death of Jesus in a letter he wrote to his son in AD 73: "What advantage did the Jews gain from executing their wise King? It was just after that their kingdom was abolished."[35]

Although not every independent source explicitly refers to Christ's execution by crucifixion, this kind of capital punishment was customary during ancient Rome.[36] Hence, one can be certain beyond any reasonable doubt that Jesus was indeed crucified. Contrary to popular belief, those crucified did not die from blood loss but from asphyxiation, as they could no longer hold themselves up to breath. They experienced excruciating pain as they pushed on their nailed feet, and pulled on their pierced hands to support themselves, until they were exhausted. The point here is that Jesus could not have survived crucifixion. Besides, the Romans were very good at eliminating any possibility of survival.

The Bible states that after Jesus died, Joseph from Arimathea took His body and "laid it in his new tomb...and he rolled a large stone against the door of the tomb" (Matthew 27:60). However, after three days something remarkable happened, something that would define the course of history forever. Jesus rose from the dead.

Reason 42: The Resurrection of Jesus

The greatest evidence for the deity of Jesus was His own resurrection from the dead. Jesus consistently predicted He would rise from the dead, and when Jewish leaders asked Him for a sign to prove it, He answered, "For as Jonah was three days and three nights in the belly of a huge fish, so the Son of Man will be three days and three nights in the heart of the earth" (Matthew 12:40). In essence, Jesus was saying His own resurrection would validate His claim as the Messiah—Son of God.

Critics understandably question the resurrection of Jesus from the dead. However, historical evidence supports it. Even acclaimed atheist Sir Antony Flew said, "The evidence for the resurrection is better than for claimed miracles in any other religion. It's outstandingly different in quality and quantity."[37] Professors Gary Habermas and Michael Licona have put together a strong case for the resurrection of Jesus, using a minimal facts argument. This approach minimizes the facts to what all historical scholars claim on the subject, even skeptical ones. These facts are 1) Jesus died by crucifixion, 2) the disciples experienced post-resurrection appearances of Jesus, 3) James the skeptical brother of Jesus became a believer, and 4) Paul the church persecutor dramatically changed to a preacher of the resurrection.[38]

What further strengthens the minimal facts argument is that it meets the criteria historians use to conclude whether a certain event occurred, such as evidence from independent multiple sources, attestations from skeptics or opponents, eyewitness accounts, and early testimonies as these are less likely to be the result of legendary development. Even though the eyewitness gospels were written between 20 to 40 years after the resurrection of Jesus, they constitute evidence because many historians consider them a credible source of evidence in the study of antiquity. For example, Luke the gospel writer and author of the book of Acts, provides copious historical data that has been corroborated by independent historical sources.[39]

Even more astonishing is that atheist historians like Gerd Lüdemann accept that the earliest disciples had experiences of Jesus after His resurrection. Lüdemann concludes, "It may be taken as historically certain that Peter and the disciples had experiences after Jesus's death in which Jesus appeared to them as the risen Christ."[40] In closing, Jesus's resurrection is the only valid explanation for why the original disciples were willing to go to their deaths proclaiming He had risen, despite having every disposition to the contrary. Now if the resurrection is a fact, Jesus rightly deserves to be believed upon and worshipped as the Son of God.

Reason 43: The Messianic Jesus

The Old Testament or Hebrew Bible is a collection of 39 books written by 30 different authors up to 1400 years before the birth of Christ. Many of these authors never knew each other. Yet, a central theme addressed by them was the coming of the Messiah, providing detailed predictions or prophecies that could identify him. The argument here is that Jesus's fulfillment of these prophecies validates His identity as the Messiah—Son of God.

Most people's lives are chronicled after they have lived, but what makes the life of Jesus profoundly unique is that His was chronicled centuries before He lived on earth. Bible scholar Josh McDowell documented 333 Messianic prophecies in the Old Testament, many of which contain predictive details regarding the birth, life, death and resurrection of the Messiah.[41] While space prohibits listing all these prophecies, examples include His virgin birth,[42] His place of birth in Bethlehem,[43] His progeny from Abraham and King David,[44] His miracles,[45] His entrance into Jerusalem riding on a donkey,[46] His betrayal by a close friend for thirty pieces of silver,[47] His rejection by the Jews,[48] His physical suffering,[49] crucifixion,[50] resurrection,[51] and ascension into heaven.[52] Predictive prophecies such as these were given by Old Testament prophets as an efficient mechanism for recognizing the Messiah, all of which were fulfilled by Jesus.

Due to the accuracy in which Jesus fulfilled Messianic prophecy, some critics have suggested He could have been a masterful imposter who manipulated events to appear as the Messiah. Whilst it is possible for a mere man to have manipulated half a dozen or so events, like riding on a donkey into Jerusalem or making a friend betray him, many prophecies were far beyond any human control. Pre-arranging the identity of His own ancestors, His place of birth, the price for His own betrayal, the precise method of His own suffering and execution, not to mention His own resurrection, would have been humanly impossible. It follows that the quantity and quality of Messianic prophecies fulfilled by Jesus clearly demonstrate His identity as the Son of God. It is no wonder the apostles often appealed to Christ's fulfillment of Messianic prophecy as evidence for His deity. Even Jesus used Messianic prophecy after His resurrection to convince the early disciples of His identity: "And beginning with Moses and all the Prophets, he explained to them what was said in all the Scriptures concerning himself" (Luke 24:27).

It is nothing short of miraculous for so many authors to accurately predict hundreds of details about the life of Jesus centuries before His birth. In conclusion, only God, a maximally great being with divine foreknowledge and power, could have fulfilled all these Messianic prophecies in the person of Jesus Christ.

Reason 44: The Mathematical Case for Jesus

A final confirmation that validates the deity of Jesus is the insurmountable odds of one man fulfilling 333 Messianic prophecies. Even though it might be possible for someone to fulfill several prophecies, the chance of one person fulfilling all of these is impossible. That is because the more prophecies are made about the future, and the more detail they contain, the less likely their fulfillment will be.

Using mathematical probabilities, Emeritus Professor Peter Stoner of Westmont College calculated that no human being in history could have fulfilled all the major Messianic prophecies by chance.[53] His calculation involved 600 university students who carefully considered all the factors in relation to just 48 predictive Messianic prophecies. Students discussed each prophecy at length and took into consideration the likelihood of manipulating the fulfillment of each particular prediction. Their calculation was so conservative that there was unanimous agreement, even among the most skeptical students. However, Professor Stoner made their calculations even more conservative, and submitted his final figures for review to a committee at the American Scientific Affiliation. Upon examination, the committee verified that his calculation was dependable and accurate in regard to the scientific material presented.[54]

Professor Stoner concluded that the mathematical probability of one person fulfilling 48 Messianic prophecies by chance was one in 10 to the power of 157. To give you an idea of how large this figure is, consider there are 10 to the power of 78 atoms in the entire known universe.[55] For the purpose of this argument, envision a duplicate universe with the same number of atoms. The sum total of atoms in both universes would equal 10 to the power of 156. Now imagine that one of these atoms was painted red and hidden among the mass of remaining atoms. The odds of one person fulfilling just 48 Messianic prophecies by chance would be like trying to find one red atom among a whole mass of atoms within two universes—an impossibility. It is important to note that had Professor Stoner based his calculation on all Messianic prophecies, the impossibility would have been even greater.

What this all means is that by any standard of calculation,

Jesus's fulfillment of Messianic prophecies cannot be attributed to coincidence, blind chance, or a lucky accident. The only possible explanation is that His fulfillment of them was by divine agency. In conclusion, Stoner's calculation is irrefutable evidence the Judeo-Christian God exists and that Jesus is who He claimed to be—the Messiah—God incarnate and savior of the world.

PART IV

Comparing Christianity
with Other Religions

Reason 45: Key Differences Between Christianity and Islam

Because Islam is regarded as a monotheistic and Abrahamic religion like Christianity, some have gone to the extent of claiming both religions lead to the same God. But nothing can be further from the truth. Perhaps the most important difference between the two religions is that the Quran—Islam's central text written by Muhammad, denies the divinity of Jesus.[1] In essence, Islam denies the notion that Jesus was God incarnate, asserting He was merely the messenger of Allah. This difference alone makes Christianity and Islam irreconcilable.

Jesus said, "If you do not believe that I am He, you will die in your sins" (John 8:24). When Jesus referred to Himself as "I am," He was identifying with the God of Israel, as revealed to Moses. When Moses asked God for His name during the burning bush episode, He answered, "I AM WHO I AM" (Exodus 3:14), which is the derivative of Yahweh, the Hebrew name for God. Jesus's use of this name is further evidenced when the Jews attempted to stone Him for blasphemy after He told them "before Abraham was born, I am!" (John 8:58). Thus, believing in Jesus means believing He is God in human form (God the Son), and any deviation from this belief is a denial of God Himself. The apostle John made this point clear when he wrote, "No one who denies the Son has the Father; whoever acknowledges the Son has the Father also" (1 John 2:23).

Another key difference between Christianity and Islam is the

Quran denies the crucifixion and resurrection of Jesus.[2] Whether Muslims believe another person was crucified in the place of Jesus (substitution theory), or that Christ somehow survived the rigors of crucifixion (swoon theory), or escaped it and ascended to heaven (ascension theory), each of these theories deny the crucifixion, death and resurrection of Jesus—fundamental tenets of Christianity. It follows that not only is the Quran in direct conflict with the Bible, but is also in conflict with empirical and historical evidence.[3]

Christianity and Islam are not two sides of the same coin, but opposite sides of a vast canyon with no hope of any connecting bridge. In reality, the chasm between the two is so enormous that belief in one occludes belief in the other. Since belief in Christ's divinity, crucifixion and resurrection are prerequisites for salvation,[4] it is difficult to see how anyone accepting the claims of Muhammad can be saved.

Reason 46: Comparing Jesus and Muhammad

Since the claims of Christ and Muhammad are in conflict, exploring critical differences between them could help determine who should be believed. To assist in comparing the two, their main differences are summarized below:

- The Bible says Jesus was sinless;[5] the Quran says Muhammad was sinful.[6]
- Jesus claimed to be divine;[7] Muhammad claimed to be a mere man.[8]
- Jesus claimed to be the savior of the world;[9] Muhammad claimed to be a mere messenger.[10]
- Jesus claimed to hear directly from God the Father;[11] Muhammad claimed to hear from an angel.[12]
- Jesus claimed God loves everyone;[13] Muhammad claimed Allah only loves Muslim believers.[14]

- According to the Bible, Jesus healed multitudes;[15] according to the Quran, Muhammad healed no one.[16]

- Jesus never married;[17] Muhammad had multiple wives, sex slaves, and married a six year old girl.[18]

- Jesus forgave a woman caught in adultery;[19] Muhammad commanded a woman to be stoned for adultery.[20]

- Jesus condemned violence and killed no one;[21] Muhammad condoned violence and killed others.[22]

- Jesus preached love and forgiveness;[23] Muhammad preached hate and intolerance.[24]

- Jesus died for the sins of the world;[25] Muhammad died for his own sins.[26]

- Jesus rose from the dead;[27] Muhammad remained dead.[28]

- Jesus fulfilled Biblical prophecy;[29] Muhammad fulfilled no Biblical prophecy.[30]

The above comparisons demonstrate that Muhammad was inferior to Jesus in every respect, which begs the question why anyone would believe him over Jesus. Muslims revere Muhammad as the greatest prophet, but Jesus demonstrated greater power, authority, morality and miracles. Unlike Jesus, Muhammad never claimed to be divine, nor did he make the blind to see, the deaf to hear, the lame to walk or the dead to rise. In fact, the Quran describes Muhammad as a messenger without a sign,[31] the Quran being the only overt miracle attributed to him.[32] Expecting others to believe Muhammad's writings simply because he wrote the Quran, is a circular argument that offers no independent confirmation of his truth claims.

Reason 47: The Bible and the Quran

Whilst similarities exist between the Bible and the Quran,[33] their theological differences are vast.[34] Though each book espouses the existence of only one God,[35] they differ in doctrine, including the nature and identity of God. Hence, nobody can reasonably claim the two books refer to the same God.

The Bible describes God as a triune being who manifests Himself in three persons: the Father, Son and Holy Spirit.[36] This doctrine is central to Christianity, distinguishing it from all other major religions. The following Bible verse epitomizes the trinity: "For there are three that bear record in heaven, the Father, the Word [Jesus], and the Holy Ghost: and these three are one" (1 John 5:7 KJV). When Jesus was baptized, the Bible gives us a glimpse of all three persons of the trinity in action: "As soon as Jesus was baptized, He went up out of the water. At that moment heaven was opened, and He saw the Spirit of God descending like a dove and alighting on Him. And a voice from heaven said, 'This is my Son, whom I love; with Him I am well pleased'" (Matthew 3:16-17).

In contrast, the Quran describes God as a Unitarian being and spurns the existence of a triune God.[37] As such, the Quran categorically rejects the God of the Bible. Furthermore, the Quran's explicit denial of Jesus as the Son of God[38] makes Islam an anti-Christ religion, especially since it curses Christians and condemns worshippers of Jesus to hell.[39]

Another distinction between the Bible and the Quran is its teaching about the Fatherhood of God. The Bible says God is our heavenly Father, a notion denied in the Quran,[40] which instructs Muslims to rebuke Christians and Jews for claiming God is their Father.[41] Perhaps the most overlooked difference between the two books is that not a single verse in the New Testament incites violence toward others, whilst over 100 such verses exist in the Quran.[42] These Quranic verses typically direct Muslims to commit brutal acts, including beheadings and crucifixions, toward non-Muslims. These verses depict a deity who is not so loving, peaceful and merciful as claimed in other Quranic passages,[43] casting grave questions about the Quran's consistency and cogency.

In essence, the Bible and the Quran are not merely different, but antithetical. The Bible contains 66 books written by 40 different authors over 1500 years. It is a coherent historical masterpiece, backed up by archaeological and extra-Biblical evidence.[44] Although the Bible addresses many themes, its main focus is on one man—the Messiah, and contains 333 predictive prophecies confirming His identity as Jesus.[45] In contrast, the Quran was written by one author over twenty three years and contains no predictive prophecies.[46] As to which book is more warranted, that is a question one can answer with great certainty in light of the above comparisons.

Reason 48: Comparing Christianity and Hinduism

With no single founder, Hinduism is currently the third largest religion in the world with approximately one billion followers, mostly located in India.[47] Hinduism is not only considered to be the world's oldest religion, but also the most complex and polytheistic, involving the worship of 330 million deities or manifestations of the supreme god, which many Hindu's call Brahman.[48]

Unlike Christianity where God is personal and knowable, Brahman is impersonal and unknowable,[49] an evident barrier for someone seeking to know God and cultivate a personal relationship with Him. What makes Hinduism even more paradoxical is that Brahman has three principal deities: Brahma, the creator; Vishnu, the preserver; and Shiva, the destroyer.[50] The obvious difficulty with this theology is that the function of Shiva runs counter to the function of Brahma and Vishnu, exposing a schizoid element to the nature of Brahman. In contrast, the Bible reveals perfect unity within the Godhead. Although the Christian God exists in three persons (the Father, Son and Holy Spirit), they are in essence one being and in complete harmony with one another.[51]

Another difference is that Christianity relies on one central text (the Bible), while Hinduism relies on many texts such as the *Vedas, Upanishads, Puranas, Mahabharata* and the *Ramayana*.[52] It is no wonder that contradictions run amok among these texts.

For example, in the *Bhagavata Purana*, Krishna is regarded as the supreme god,[53] but in the *Mahabharata* text, Krishna is just one of the several incarnations of Vishnu.[54] Conversely, in the *Shiva Purana*, Shiva is regarded as the supreme god,[55] whilst *Atharvaveda* (the fourth *Veda*) claims Brahma is the supreme god.[56] These contentions create confusion and a sharp inconsistency among authors, undermining the veracity of their claims. Besides, narratives from these texts depict deities with competing personalities who strive with each other, promoting incredulity toward Hinduism.

Another issue with Hinduism is that its three principal deities do not discriminate between good and evil, since they afford boons to demons who worship them even when they know these demons will eventually cause trouble.[57] In contrast, the Bible tells us that Jesus never aided demons, but cast them out from people and healed all those oppressed of the devil.[58]

Perhaps one way to view Hinduism is a fusion of various beliefs, myths and folklore among indigenous Indians and the Aryans who migrated to India from central Asia.[59] Though this fusion enabled a colorful religious mythology, interwoven with India's rich history and culture, it unfortunately generated a pluralism of conflicting narratives and philosophies. For this reason, Hinduism cannot be seen as a logically consistent belief system.

Reason 49: Key Differences between Christianity and Hinduism

Differences between Hinduism and Christianity are so considerable that one could not possibly list them all here. However, to aid a broader understanding of their competing claims, important differences are listed below (some of which are mentioned in the previous reason):

- Christianity has an identifiable origin in the person of Jesus Christ;[60] Hinduism has no identifiable single origin.[61]
- Christianity teaches Jesus is the only way to God;[62] Hinduism teaches all religions (despite their contradictions) lead to one supreme god.[63]
- In Christianity, God is personal and knowable;[64] in Hinduism, god is impersonal and unknowable.[65]
- Christianity has only one God;[66] Hinduism has 330 million gods.[67]
- The Christian God loves people;[68] some Hindu gods kill people.[69]
- The Christian God forgives sins;[70] Hindu gods do not forgive sins.[71]
- Christianity teaches humans only live once on this earth;[72] Hinduism teaches life is a continuous cycle of rebirths (reincarnation).[73]
- In Christianity, empirical experience is real;[74] in Hinduism, empirical experience is illusory (maya).[75]
- In Christianity, truth is objective;[76] in Hinduism, truth is subjective.[77]
- Christianity promotes equality;[78] Hinduism promotes inequality.[79]
- In Christianity, women are equal to men;[80] in Hinduism, women are inferior to men.[81]
- Biblical creationism is supported by science;[82] Hindu creationism conflicts with science.[83]
- The Bible is theologically consistent;[84] Hindu texts are theologically inconsistent.[85]
- In Christianity, salvation is by grace through faith in Jesus Christ;[86] in Hinduism, salvation (moksha) is merited by works.[87]
- Christians know they are saved;[88] Hindus do not know if they are saved, or ever will be saved (achieve moksha).[89]

These differences show Hinduism is far less rational and morally appealing than Christianity. For example, Christianity teaches all people are equal, but Hinduism promotes discrimination. In the *Manusmriti*, (a Hindu legal text),[90] four castes (varnas) are prescribed in society, each with their own duties based on the body part of Brahma they represent.[91] The Brahmins who represent his mouth, are high class members of society (e.g., scholars, priests and teachers), whilst the Shudras who represent Brahma's feet, are low class manual workers. With such social inequality, Hinduism faces many grave doubts about its truth claims.

Reason 50: The Fallacy of Hinduism

Perhaps the most alarming fallacy of Hinduism is the inherent immorality within its ancient beliefs and customs. Hindu traditions and mythological narratives promote a wide range of present-day vices, from racism and rape to burning widows and child sacrifice. As such, it is difficult to see how Hinduism can be regarded as a morally defensible religion.

According to the *Bhagavad Gita*,[92] the caste system is an intrinsic fact of life, implying one's caste is determined by birth.[93] Whilst discrimination against lower castes is illegal in India, the horrors of the Hindu caste system are alive today. For instance, Dalits (known as "untouchables") are considered so unworthy that they typically perform impure jobs such as removing dead carcasses from roads and cleaning human waste from sewers by hand.[94] Dalits not only live in abject poverty, but also face discrimination, violence and rape with impunity.[95] Since Hindus believe people are born into their castes based on karma (what they did in their previous lives), higher castes refrain from helping Dalits, creating a system of slavery.[96]

For centuries, a particular inhumane Hindu tradition was suttee. This involved burning widows alive on the funeral pyres of their deceased husbands, and the first Sanskrit reference to this practice is found in the *Mahabharata*.[97] Suttee was often committed voluntarily, but if the widow refused, she was sometimes thrown into the fire by the mob who gathered to watch her burn. Although never widely practiced, this tradition was seen as the epitome of womanly devotion by some Brahmins and has been linked to the myth of Sati, the Hindu goddess who immolated herself after her father insulted her husband Shiva.[98] Fortunately, the British outlawed suttee in 1829, although remote instances of it still occur.[99]

Another barbaric Hindu tradition criminalized by the British is human sacrifice, which includes the slaying of children to appease Hindu gods. These sacrifices were performed in relation to the worship of Shakti (the supreme mother goddess of Shaktism),[100] and Kali (the blood thirsty goddess of death).[101] Although this Hindu tradition diminished from the early period of modernity,[102] various reports suggest human sacrifices are still being performed in tribal parts of India.[103] According to the police in Khurja, dozens of human sacrifices were performed by Kali worshippers in 2006.[104] Also, after investigating allegations of human sacrifice in 2015, police in Madurai found the skeletal remains of four persons (including a child) in a quarry.[105]

Whilst it is fair to say many Hindus do not formally practice the caste system or the barbaric traditions of suttee and human sacrifice, these aspects of Hinduism reveal the inherent social injustice and immorality at its root. In conclusion, Hindu traditions lead one to seriously doubt the moral integrity of Hinduism and its foundational texts.

Reason 51: Comparing Christianity and Buddhism

Born in India as a Hindu prince some 2500 years ago, Siddhārtha Gautama (Buddha) was an ascetic sage whose teachings founded Buddhism. Since Gautama had a Hindu background, it is of no surprise that similarities exist between Buddhism and

Hinduism—namely, the practice of meditation, belief in maya, karma and reincarnation.[106] However, one particular difference with Buddhism is that none of Buddha's teachings make any reference to the existence of God, making it implicitly non-theistic.[107] This point explains why atheists and agnostics find Buddhism attractive, with various reports suggesting it is the fastest growing philosophical religion in the West.[108]

Although Buddha rejected the notion that the universe was conceived by a divine creator, he gave no explanation for its origins because he deemed the issue irrelevant to the cessation of suffering (nirvana).[109] As a matter of fact, Buddha remained mostly silent on the subject of origins, which begs the question of how seriously Buddhism can be taken as a coherent belief. In contrast, the Bible provides an account of creation that is supported by both cosmological and scientific evidence.[110]

While some ethical similarities exist between Buddhism and Christianity (like equality, and the pursuit of wisdom and compassion), vast differences exist between Buddha and Christ. Although Buddha taught compassion as a cardinal virtue,[111] he fell short of it because he abandoned his wife and child to live a monastic life in pursuit of self-enlightenment and liberation from suffering.[112] Unlike Buddha, Christ epitomized the virtue of compassion in every way. Rather than escape suffering, He embraced it by ultimately sacrificing Himself on the cross.[113]

A particular aspect of Buddhism that runs counter to Christianity is the notion of reincarnation. This notion is problematic in a number of ways. First, although some case studies show anecdotal evidence for reincarnation, no verifiable scientific evidence exists from hypothesis testing.[114] Second, since Buddha rejected the permanence of the human soul,[115] it is difficult to see how one's self could transmigrate (move) into another body. Third, Buddhism implicitly denies belief in a moral supreme being, leaving the whole question unanswered of who determines a person's karma. Fourth, the idea that sentient beings are punished for actions they cannot remember renders karma morally indefensible. Finally, similar to moksha (in Hinduism), nirvana in Buddhism is an eternal state where one's reincarnation ends, except that it extends to the termination of one's own existence.[116] A final outcome of Buddhism, disappearing into nothingness, is hardly a prospect most people would look forward to.

In conclusion, Buddha borrowed concepts from Hinduism to construct his own philosophy of life. Whilst his philosophy is a welcome departure from the Hindu caste system, it is nonetheless unsupported by science and fails to stand up to logical enquiry.

Reason 52: Key Differences Between Christianity and Buddhism

Some ecumenically minded Christians and Buddhists have attempted to merge Christianity and Buddhism. However, these attempts typically gloss over irreconcilable differences, making their unification extremely problematic. These irreconcilable differences include:

- Christianity is monotheistic;[117] Buddhism is agnostic.[118]
- In Christianity, belief in a personal creator is central;[119] in Buddhism, belief in a personal creator is unnecessary.[120]
- In Christianity, belief in Jesus is necessary for salvation;[121] in Buddhism, belief in Jesus is unnecessary for salvation (nirvana).[122]
- Christianity rejects reincarnation;[123] Buddhism teaches reincarnation.[124]
- Christianity emphasizes salvation by grace through faith;[125] Buddhism emphasizes salvation by enlightenment through meditative works.[126]
- Christians focus on becoming Christlike;[127] Buddhists focus on becoming like the Buddha.[128]

- In Christianity, humans have a soul;[129] in Buddhism, humans do not have a soul (anatta).[130]
- In Christianity, Christ died for the forgiveness of our sins;[131] in Buddhism, there is no forgiveness of sins.[132]
- The Bible condemns the use of meditative objects (idols and statues);[133] Buddhism allows the use of meditative objects.[134]
- In Christianity, humankind is inherently evil;[135] in Buddhism, humankind is merely ignorant (avijja).[136]
- The goal in Christianity is to love and follow Christ;[137] the goal in Buddhism is enlightenment and liberation from suffering (nirvana).[138]
- In Christianity, following Jesus gives us eternal life;[139] in Buddhism, following Buddha gives us the cessation of life (nirvana).[140]

Not only do the above differences reveal that Christianity and Buddhism are mutually incompatible, but they also expose shortcomings in Buddhist philosophy. Buddhism offers no redemption, no forgiveness and no assurance of salvation. In contrast, Christ offers all of these, including the promise of eternal life through a personal relationship with Him.[141]

Perhaps the most disturbing aspect of Buddhism is the goal of attaining nirvana, because it ultimately means the extinction of self. Unlike Buddha, Christ taught that we do have souls and if we put our trust in Him, our souls will ascend to live eternally with Him in heaven after our physical bodies die. Not only is Christ's offer of salvation more appealing than Buddha's, but it also has greater credibility, since Christ conquered death and lives forevermore.

Reason 53: Comparing Christianity and Chinese Folk Religion

With an estimated 400 million followers, Chinese folk (or popular) religion is the largest religious tradition in China.

Even non-religious Chinese are adherents of Chinese folk religion.[142] Though difficult to define, this tradition stems from beliefs embedded in Chinese culture, merged with aspects of Confucianism, Taoism and Buddhism. Its practices include a mixture of ancestral principles, the veneration of ancestors, spirit mediumship, sacrificial rituals and the worship of multiple gods like deities of nature, city gods, and cultural heroes featured in Chinese mythology.[143]

The difficulty with Chinese folk religion is that it is heavily imbued with magic, ghosts and superstitions that are irreconcilable with scientific reasoning and empirical evidence. Even the communist government of China rendered Chinese folk religion a feudal superstition, unworthy of formal recognition.[144] Although the Chinese government's stance is not in itself an arbiter for truth, it nevertheless underscores the point that this religion is wrapped in myth and folklore. For instance, it includes the belief that all natural bodies are capable of attaining supernatural attributes, and advocates animism; i.e., the idea that plants and inanimate objects (like rocks and trees) have a living soul. Since none of these beliefs are grounded in any kind of observational science, it is no wonder many struggle to accept the claims of Chinese folk religion.

In contrast, the claims of Christianity have been scientifically, empirically and historically corroborated. As mentioned in earlier parts of this book, discoveries such as the Big Bang, Cambrian explosion, and the historical evidence for the crucifixion and resurrection of Jesus all point to a Christian faith that is reasonable and verifiable.

Unlike Chinese folk religion with its multiplicity of gods, the Bible unequivocally states there is one God, and that everything else from the stars in the sky to the grains of sand on the beach was created by Him.[145] Furthermore, the God of the Bible forbids the worship of anything other than Himself,[146] since He alone is the creator of all things.

Whilst there are many differences between Chinese folk religion and Christianity, the key differentiator is, "For God so loved the world that He gave His one and only Son, that whoever believes in Him shall not perish but have eternal life" (John 3:16). This is a message of supreme love and hope. It tells us we do not need to rely on magic or ritual sacrifices for salvation, but on the sacrifice of Jesus on the cross, who alone redeemed us from sin to restore us in fellowship with Himself, a holy God.

Reason 54: Comparing Christianity and Shintoism

Shinto in Japanese means 'the way of the gods.' It is the native faith of the Japanese people and dates as far back as the sixth century. Although Shintoism ranks alongside Buddhism as Japan's major religion, it is akin to Chinese folk religion in that it is both polytheistic and animist.[147] Another point to mention is that Shintoism is rarely practiced outside of Japan because it teaches no other land is divine but Japan.[148]

Alongside the doctrine of Japan being the country of the gods, Shintoism also teaches that Japanese people are of divine descent, elevating them above other nations in importance. This kind of jingoism undermines the legitimacy of Shintoism, as one could argue that such doctrines are myths, designed to promote a sense of ultra-nationalism and imperialism. This sense of patriotism was especially useful in forging political unity during Japan's long and turbulent wartime history.

What is perhaps most disturbing about Shintoism is its concept of kami—spirits that are worshipped in heaven and earth. At the top of the divine hierarchy is the sun goddess, Amaterasu, followed by good and evil deities, including Japanese emperors. According to traditional Shinto belief, the emperor is a direct descendent of the kami who gave birth to Japan, and therefore can be worshipped as a divine being.[149] For instance, the late Shōwa emperor (Hirohito) was venerated as a god during the twentieth century, and even today his portrait exists at the grand shrine of Ise where worshippers gather from all over Japan. Such Shinto doctrines and practices have led to the criticism that Shintoism is nothing more than an imperial cult, focused on generating blind obedience from its followers.[150]

In contrast to Shinto beliefs, the Bible teaches no human is worthy of worship, for all have broken God's moral law.[151] As a consequence, all require God's forgiveness, an absolution that cannot be provided by Shinto rituals of purification, but through the precious blood of Christ who was sacrificed for our sins.[152] As such, salvation is by grace through faith in God's one and only Son,[153] not something that can be attained by ceremonial acts designed to appease kami.

Moreover, the Bible teaches that our allegiance must rise above our family and nation, to God Himself in the person of Jesus Christ—not through "the way of the Gods," but through Christ who said "I am the way, the truth and the life" (John 14:6). Furthermore, unlike Christianity, Shintoism has no founder, no canonical scriptures, no authoritative set of beliefs and no moral absolutes. Factors such as these make accepting Shintoism difficult and beg the question of how it remained dominant in Japan for so long. Perhaps the answer lies in its cultural capital, providing an identity with a strong sense of security and national origins among the Japanese people.

Reason 55: Comparing Christianity and Sikhism

Originating in the Punjab region of south Asia 500 years ago, Sikhism is currently the fifth largest religion in the world with an estimated 25 million followers. Sikhs follow the teachings of its founder, Guru Nanak, along with nine other successive Gurus whose beliefs include unity, equality, selfless service, social justice and meditation, as well as the belief that there is only one creator.[154]

Interestingly, Sikhism originated out of Hinduism, since its founder was raised a Hindu and belonged to the Sant tradition, a movement heavily influenced by the Vaishnava bhakti people (worshippers of the god Vishnu). However, Sikhism eventually separated to become a monotheistic religion in its own right, but maintained various Hindu concepts like maya, karma, reincarnation and moksha.[155] Sikhism can therefore be thought of as a religion inspired by Hindu thought, although differences apply.

Whilst Christianity and Sikhism are both monotheistic, acute disparities exist between the two. In Christianity, God is represented in the person of Jesus Christ, but in Sikhism, God is formless and shapeless. Sikhism also teaches both good and evil come from God, while Christianity teaches only good comes from God.[156] Hence, not only do they differ in terms of their identity of God, but also on the nature of God. As such, Sikhism's dualistic good-evil nature of God poses a dilemma: if evil comes from God, one would be resisting God if one resisted evil. Yet, without resisting evil, how could one follow good Sikh beliefs like equality, selfless service and social justice? As one can see, this good-evil dualism of God is paradoxical.

Unlike Sikhism, the Bible is very clear on the nature of God. James 1:17 says, "Every good and perfect gift is from above, coming down from the Father of the heavenly lights, who does not change like shifting shadows." Another point of difference is that Sikhism rejects Christ as the only way to God, because it asserts all religions are equally valid. But how can this assertion be true when all religions have opposing truth claims?

Perhaps the most important point of difference is that Sikhs have no assurance of salvation, for they are taught to engage in an almost endless cycle of good works before they can be free from reincarnation. In fact, Guru Granth Sahib taught that Sikhs go through 8.4 million reincarnations of different species before merging with God.[157] Conversely, Jesus promised that whoever believes in Him as the Son of God will receive eternal life.[158] Jesus's offer of salvation is a free gift, paid for by His own sacrifice on the cross. And the best part is that it's available now, not in 8.4 million lifetimes.

Reason 56: Comparing Christianity and Judaism

Judaism is the oldest monotheistic religion, dating back to the patriarch Abraham who was born circa 1800 BC.[159] As the Jewish religion, Judaism has a close relationship with Christianity, since both regard the Old Testament (the Tanakh) to be divinely inspired, and both teach the God of Israel (Yahweh) to be the one true God, who alone is omnipotent, omniscient and omnipresent.

While there are many areas of agreement between Christianity and Judaism, the all-important difference is in the identity of Jesus Christ. Christianity teaches that Jesus is the Messiah, Son of God, but followers of Judaism do not recognize Him as such, despite Jesus's fulfillment of all Messianic prophecies in the Tanakh. Because of their failure to accept Jesus as the Messiah, adherents of Judaism continue to practice the Law of Moses and other Jewish customs like circumcision, rituals of purification and the observation of holy days in the hope of attaining salvation by their own works.

Christianity teaches that Jesus perfectly fulfilled all the requirements of Mosaic law, something no other person has ever done or can do, then sacrificed Himself in atonement for our sins.[160] As a result, those who believe in Jesus become justified by God's grace; that is, they receive the righteousness of God by faith.[161] What this all means is that 2000 years ago God established a New Testament with humankind, not through the blood of animals, but through the blood of His own Son. This explains why on the night before his crucifixion, Jesus told His disciples, "This is my blood of the new testament, which is shed for many for the remission of sins" (Matthew 26:28 KJV).

Jesus never scolded His fellow Jews for believing in the God of

Abraham and Moses, but rather for rejecting His identity as the anointed one whom the prophets foretold.[162] Although many Jews still reject Jesus, the Bible says that one day there will be a great awakening among Jews, who will accept Jesus as their promised Messiah.[163]

In conclusion, Christianity has superseded Judaism. God's moral law under Judaism only served to convict us of sin, making us realize we have all fallen short of the Ten Commandments. The Old Testament served to underscore our need for salvation through Jesus Christ alone.[164]

In essence, no one can be saved by following Judaism, but by following Christ. By giving us a new covenant, God actually made it easier for us to know Him. Instead of obeying a plethora of commands under Judaism, there is but one command in the New Testament: "And this is His commandment, that we should believe on the name of His Son Jesus Christ, and love one another" (1 John 3:23 KJV). Since love does not steal, kill or harm others, love is the fulfillment of God's moral law. Hence, by believing in Jesus as God's only Son and by loving one another, we are made right with God and receive everlasting life. Christianity does not get any simpler than that!

PART V

Answers to Critics of Christianity

Reason 57: If God Exists, Why Does He Allow Human Suffering?

This question is one of the most frequently asked, and is perhaps the most difficult to answer. One way of answering it is as follows: for God to eliminate suffering, He would have to eliminate evil; to eliminate evil, He would have to eliminate moral choice; to eliminate moral choice, He would have to eliminate free will and to eliminate free will, He would have to eliminate humans. Since God does not wish to destroy the human race,[1] He must allow suffering as a consequence of the evil choices humans make.

It is granted that suffering does not only include people inflicting evil upon one another, but can also involve diseases and natural disasters (subjects which are dealt with later on in this chapter). However, research shows that more people suffer from human conflicts than from any other cause. In the past 100 years, over twenty times more people died from war and government oppression, than from natural disasters, like earthquakes and storms.[2] This statistic alone should help us realize the boundless extent of human depravity.

But you might ask, why does God allow us to inflict such evil upon each other? To answer this question, one must understand creation. The Bible says that when God created humans, He did not create automatons, but sovereign agents in charge of governing the earth. God told the first humans, Adam and Eve, "Be fruitful, and multiply, and replenish the earth, and subdue it: and have dominion" (Genesis 1:28 KJV). In reality, they had so much freedom that God only gave them one moral law: "You must not eat from the tree of the knowledge of good and evil, for when you eat from it you will certainly die" (Genesis 2:16-17). This passage implies that God initially created humans to be immortal, with the capacity to do only good. But should they disobey His moral law, God warned they would also have the capacity to do evil and lose their immortality. This situation is exactly what happened, as recorded in Genesis chapter three.

Contrary to what skeptics claim, God is not some celestial dictator who seeks to control everything we do. If He were, He would have taken control by now and imposed peace on earth by force. But using force to make us obey Him is not in God's nature, since He bequeathed us free will. As much as it grieves God to look upon our own suffering, He gave us freedom to obey and to rebel—to choose good and evil. But this kind of freedom comes with a caveat: as long as people continue to choose evil, human suffering will continue.

Reason 58: If God Cares, Why Does He Allow People to Starve?

Critics argue that if God exists, he is unjust for allowing people to starve. The assumption here is that it is somehow incumbent on God to solve humanity's problems. Could an omnipotent God feed all the starving people in the world? Clearly, yes, but the argument here is that it is not His responsibility to do so. It is ours.

As previously mentioned in this book, when God created human beings He endowed them with responsibility to govern this world—an act of delegation He cannot rescind. On this basis, it is our civic duty to share and care for one another, so there can be equality; so one person's abundance could meet another's lack. This kind of social responsibility follows Christ's golden rule: "Do to others as you would have them do to you" (Luke 6:31). John the Baptist underscored this responsibility when he told the crowds, "Anyone who has two shirts should share with the one who has none, and anyone who has food should do the same" (Luke 3:11). In light of our social responsibility to help one another, the question we should be asking is, why are we allowing people to starve?

Some argue that because of an increasing world population (of over seven billion), there is not enough food to feed everybody, especially considering the impact of climate change on farming. This argument is simply not true. According to various research studies, the world already produces enough food to feed everyone, with some reports suggesting there is enough to feed ten billion people.[3] This means world hunger is not caused by food scarcity, but by poverty and inequality.[4] According to one study, about one billion malnourished people exist in the world,[5] while almost two billion people are obese,[6] a ratio of two obese people to one hungry person.

So what does this all mean? It means that instead of being socially responsible over the use of natural resources, individuals and institutions are wasting food, mismanaging resources, and acting in greed. God is not responsible for our narcissism and corrupt behavior. God already showed us He cared by sending His one and only Son two thousand years ago to redeem us from the effects of sin. It is now up to us to make a difference.

Throughout the entire church age, God has led Christians to help alleviate world hunger. Currently, Christian organizations like Compassion International, World Vision, Feed the Hungry, and Samaritan's Purse, alongside other humanitarian agencies, are feeding the hungry. But if the majority of us continue to ignore the plight of the hungry, the number of starving people will only increase.

Reason 59: If God is All Powerful, Why Doesn't He Heal Everyone?

The Bible records a considerable number of healings and miracles, especially in the four gospels and the book of Acts. Even up to the present day, believers around the world continue to offer testimonies of divine healing, with many defying the bounds of possibility. Yet, some argue that because not everybody gets healed, God is impotent.

To better understand why God does not always heal, we must examine the healing ministry of Jesus. Although Jesus performed many astonishing miracles, including raising Lazarus from the dead, He only healed a few people in His hometown of Nazareth. Why? Because of their unbelief.[7] Does this situation mean God is only capable of healing some sicknesses? No, it simply means that faith in Christ is a prerequisite to receiving divine healing. While it is true that not all believers get healed, this predicament does not undermine the existence of an all powerful God, nor does it imply a person's malady is always the result of unbelief. After all, Paul the apostle pleaded with the Lord three times to be healed of his "thorn in the flesh," but the Lord's response was, "My grace is sufficient for you, for my power is made perfect in weakness" (2 Corinthians 12:9). Paul's response shows God's grace is available in the midst of sickness, helping us to endure as Jesus endured the cross.

Sickness is a consequence of the decay that began after Adam's original sin. When Adam rebelled (committed treason) against God, he lost access to God's divine life and became mortal, a condition we inherited as members of the human race. In turn, the entropy (decline) in our physical bodies ensued as an effect of being separated from God's divine life. Sickness, aging and death are all part of this entropy. Although God sent a savior to redeem us from sin, salvation from the entire effects of sin will not be realized until Christians receive the full redemption of their physical bodies after Christ's return.

The great hope of the Christian faith is that the afflictions of this life cannot be compared with the glories that follow.[8] When a believer loses a limb, he or she has God's promise of future wholeness. When a believer is in pain, he or she has God's assurance of perfect peace. As such, it is better to enter heaven maimed and become eternally whole, than to enter hell whole and become eternally maimed.

In his book *The Mystery of the Cross*, Alistair McGrath eloquently notes: "God is active and present in his world, quite independently of whether we experience him as being so. Experience declared that God was absent from Calvary, only to have its verdict humiliatingly overturned on the third day."[9] One day, perfect healing will come, not as a result of believers demanding it now, but when they receive their full redemption in Christ—the promise of a resurrected body.[10]

Reason 60: If God is All Knowing, How Can Free Will Exist?

The subject of free will can be incredibly complex, not helped by misunderstandings about God's sovereignty and omniscience. Critics argue that if God is sovereign over all creation and knows all things, then free will is illusory because God predetermines all our choices. However, this argument is flawed for two reasons. First, God and man are both sovereign—meaning, one cannot undermine the other. Second, divine foreknowledge does not necessitate predetermination.

Just because God has all knowledge, critics mistakenly attribute situations to His control over them. Consider the analogy of a thermometer. A thermometer reads the temperature but cannot change it. Likewise, meteorologists predict weather patterns but cannot change them. So it is with God in terms of the choices we make. He foresees all our choices but allows us to freely make them, a view supported in scripture.[11]

Free will does not stop becoming free will just because God knows the future. Take for example my ten your old daughter. Because I know she loves pasta, I know she will choose it above any other food on the menu. Did I determine that choice for her? Not at all. Even if I told her to choose something else on the menu, she will still choose the pasta. How do I know? Because I know her better than she knows herself. God is the same with us. As a loving heavenly father, He attempts to guide our decision making, but we ultimately have the free will to choose. Even when our choices are bad, including grave offences like rape and murder, God does not control them. Thus, omniscience and free will are not incompatible. It is a logical fallacy to claim otherwise.

So why is God all knowing? Because He would not be a maximally great being without omniscience. He is the one who brought the universe into existence with all that would occur. The Bible says His understanding is unsearchable;[12] He knows the end from the beginning;[13] He knew us before we were born;[14] He knows our words before we speak them,[15] and nothing in all creation is hidden from His sight.[16] Does that mean He sits idly by as an uninvolved deity? Certainly not. Even before Adam brought sin and entropy into the world, God planned our salvation by choosing to send His only Son to atone for our sins.[17] As enigmatic as this sounds, it is nonetheless true. How do we know? Because Jesus fulfilled that plan at the cross of Calvary. Now God is waiting for you to choose Jesus.

Even though an omniscient God already knows what you will choose, the Bible says He is "not willing that any should perish, but that all should come to repentance" (2 Peter 3:9). The important point being made here is that the decision is yours not God's. Repentance involves an act of your will. It involves you turning from sin and coming to Jesus, to accept who He is and what He did for you at the cross. Although God loves you, like a perfect gentleman He will not force you. Why? Because you have free will.

Reason 61: Why Did God Create Man Knowing He Would Sin?

This is a profound question and worthy of a response. While many ask this question to try and undermine God's omniscience or goodness, the answer surprisingly underlines God's amazing grace, love and mercy.

God could have created man without free will. But doing so would have meant him only functioning within the bounds of a set of commands, much like a computer program. Instead, God created a human, a unique being capable of self-consciousness, who could think about his own thinking and philosophically choose a course of action. God could have also created a garden without any forbidden fruit. But again, that would have resulted in Adam existing within an environment where disobedience was not possible—similar to having no free will. Hence, for meaningful obedience to exist, the choice of disobedience had to also exist.

God had every right to destroy Adam after he sinned, since He warned Adam of the penalty for committing treason; i.e., death.[18] Instead, God manifested His great mercy by allowing both Adam and Eve to physically live. God even made coverings for them to hide their shame.[19] Knowing the entire human race would inherit Adam and Eve's fallen nature, God put in place a redemptive plan to demonstrate His amazing love: "But God demonstrates His own love for us in this: While we were still sinners, Christ died for us" (Romans 5:8). So by allowing man to sin, God showed His grace by sending Jesus to eternally restore us into right relationship with Himself. It follows that without the fall of man, God could never have demonstrated the greatest act of love in history—Christ's death on the cross.

If you find this answer unconvincing, consider the following: if God did not create man because of his future rebellion, you too would not exist. By analogy, parents have no guarantees their children will love them or never rebel against them. Yet, the possibility of losing them does not stop parents having children. Why? The poet Alfred Lord Tennyson answers this point: "Tis better to have loved and lost than never to have loved at all."[20]

Despite us all being such undeserving sinners, God shows His love by giving us life; eyes to see the sunrise; ears to hear the birds sing; noses to smell fresh green meadows, and taste buds to sense sizzling flavors. But while God is love, He is also our judge. His very nature demands perfect love and perfect justice. Knowing every sin we would ever commit, God sent Jesus to suffer the penalty for our sins upon an unspeakably cruel cross.

All God requires from us is to turn from sin and put our trust in Jesus. By doing so, God can legally dismiss our case, much like acquitting a death row convict. Such grace is too glorious to fully comprehend; such love, too wonderful to pass. Now what will you do? Will you rebel like Adam, or accept God's free gift of eternal life?

Reason 62: Why Did God Create Satan Knowing He Would Rebel?

This question reveals a significant misconception—namely, that God created Satan. The Bible unequivocally states that God created Lucifer, and only after committing high treason did Lucifer become the Devil and Satan. This is an important point because it shows that God is not the author of evil. Neither is God responsible for Lucifer's evil choices, since Lucifer had free will.

The Bible says that God created Lucifer as a covering cherub (a beautifully winged celestial being), an archangel who stood beside the throne of God. Whilst God created all the angels, Lucifer was different in that he was perfectly created, flawless in beauty, excellent in wisdom and possessing great musical ability.[21] But something dramatic happened.

Lucifer became proud of his beauty. He coveted the worship that belonged to God alone. Lucifer wanted God's throne for himself and as a result, committed the worst kind of treason, drawing a third of the angels into rebellion.[22] After his failed coup d'état, he was banished from the kingdom of God and subsequently became the Devil, while his fallen angels became demons, all of whom are primeval enemies of God.

In the Bible Satan is described as the devourer, deceiver and destroyer.[23] Jesus called him the first murderer and father of lies.[24] In essence, Satan is evil and the author of it. Seeing that Satan cannot defeat God, his venom is directed at the human race; people created in the image and likeness of God. That is why Satan surreptitiously tempted Eve in the garden, deceiving her into eating the forbidden fruit, leading to Adam's fall.[25]

This above narrative begs the question: Why did God create Lucifer knowing he would become evil? So a choice between good and evil could exist. Good is defined by who God is, and evil is defined by who Satan is. The Christian worldview is that good and evil, right and wrong, originate from outside of us as distinct objective realities.

The kind of world God wants is one in which love is at the center. But for love to have its fullest expression, people must have the free will to love. Yet, free will is only possible when wrong choices are allowed, and rebellion is one of those choices.

In essence, God allowed Satan so that men and women would have a free choice between good and evil, and for the consequences of those choices to become manifest. This explanation turns the whole question of why God allows evil on its head, by placing the focus on why we allow evil. Because, like Satan, we too are in rebellion against God.

The whole human race could stop evil tomorrow by simply choosing God. Choosing God is principally a choice of good over evil, love over hate, righteousness over sin; a choice made by the most sacred gift of all—free will. Now that is a gift neither God nor Satan can control, but only you!

Reason 63: Why Do Bad Things Happen to Good People?

Although some people ask this question to make better sense of the suffering of innocents, skeptics use this question to argue God does not exist, or that He is not so good and all powerful after all. Whatever the case, there are two ways of answering this question.

The first answer is to say there are no good people. The Bible makes it abundantly clear that everyone is tainted by sin: "There is no one righteous, not even one...for all have sinned and fall short of the glory of God" (Romans 3:10, 23). Since no one is good, it follows that bad things happen to all people. Whilst this answer circumvents the question, it leaves one feeling dissatisfied because we all know of decent people who have fallen prey to some undeserving, unexplained misfortune.

The second answer relates to the effects of sin. When Adam sinned, he allowed evil into the world, which produced all kinds of indiscriminate consequences like murder, rape, theft, social injustice and war. To illustrate the effects of sin, imagine a hand grenade exploding in a crowd. Although everyone hears it, some people are hit by its shrapnel, while others are not. Sin works in a similar way. Some, even seemingly good people, are more affected by its consequences than others.

The unpredictable effect of sin applies to natural disasters. According to the second law of thermodynamics,[26] everything in the universe is subject to entropy. With the exception of human expansion of the greenhouse effect,[27] tsunamis, earthquakes, hurricanes and mudslides are all part of our naturally decaying universe. When natural disasters strike, they affect people indiscriminately, making us realize how tenuous life is— prompting us to think about eternity. Losing a loved one is cruel.

Yet, the prospect of eternity means God is able to one day restore that life and provide us with an explanation, including final justice.

On the other hand, naturalists believe in a purposeless universe—that there is no meaning to our existence, no hope in our suffering, and no redeeming gain from our pain. In contrast, Christians have the promise that God works all things, even calamity, together for good in their lives.[28] Does this mean God orchestrates evil to teach us a lesson? No, it simply means that for those who put their trust in Jesus, God can manifest His goodness and grace, even in the midst of great evil.

If we lived in a utopian world without pain or suffering, what kind of world would it be? It may not be as you think. No suffering would require no compassion; no wrong would require no mercy; no danger would require no bravery; and no struggle would require no forbearance. In other words, suffering helps us to affirm eternal values. So when bad things happen, we should look upon them as opportunities to express enduring virtues, love being the greatest of them all.

Reason 64: How Can a Loving God Send People to Hell?

Contrary to popular opinion, God does not send anybody to hell. His desire is for everyone to be saved and come to the knowledge of the truth.[29] But if we reject Christ's sacrifice for our sin, we are rejecting God's mercy, leaving no other alternative but divine judgment in which "the wages of sin is death" (Romans 6:23). So by rejecting Christ, we are sealing our own eternal fate in hell, not because God chose that fate but because we did.

God did everything He could to save us from hell without violating our free will. Man sinned against his creator, joined the likes of Satan in rebellion, committed hellish evil (e.g., incest, rape, murder and genocide) for thousands of years, yet God still loved man enough to save him from eternal doom. How?

Jesus came to earth in the form of a man and suffered for

every sin we ever committed.[30] But you might say, "I am a good person. I don't lie, cheat, steal or kill, nor have I been unfaithful to my partner." Even if you did not commit any of these things, none of them comes close to the gravest sin of all—rejecting Jesus who was crucified for you.

Imagine a perfect judge who delivers faultless justice every time, a judge who is supremely intelligent, completely fair, totally impartial, morally flawless, and not out to get you. You might think relying on a judge like this would guarantee you perfect justice. But that is precisely the problem. God is that judge and His justice exposes man's inadequacy. Under His moral law, nobody measures up; everyone is guilty.

You might think you have not broken God's moral law, but one way or another, you have fallen short, even in your deepest thoughts. Jesus said, "Anyone who looks at a woman lustfully has already committed adultery with her in his heart" (Matthew 5:28). God sees our hearts and His verdict is "The heart is deceitful above all things, and desperately wicked" (Jeremiah 17:9 KJV). We thus find ourselves under God's justice, where nobody is good enough; nobody deserves to go to heaven. But God gave us a way out: the cross.

The cross of Jesus is the intersection where divine justice met divine love. It is the place where God executed justice on us by pouring out His wrath on Jesus. At the cross, God showed His love for us by making Jesus suffer the penalty we deserved. So by accepting Christ, we are choosing mercy instead of judgment.

The gospel message is simple: there is no other means for our salvation outside of Jesus. There is no divine clemency outside of the cross. This is an unchangeable truth. You can jump from a tall building while shouting 'God is love,' but gravity will still kill you. You can reject the gospel while claiming "God is love," but the fires of hell will still burn you. When you reject the message of the cross, you are choosing divine judgment instead of mercy, and the penalty is eternal death in hell.

Reason 65: Is God Against Gays?

God is not against gays. Jesus loves sinners but hates their sin. He loves murderers but hates murder; He loves thieves but hates theft; He loves liars but hates lies; and He loves homosexuals but hates homosexuality. In truth, God hates sin much like a father hates a rattlesnake threatening the life of his child. Why? Because sin is evil and God hates evil.[31] But how do we know God loves sinners? Because "While we were still sinners, Christ died for us" (Romans 5:8).

Whilst some claim that homosexuality is not sinful, many scriptural references condemn homosexuality or same sex relationships. In the Old Testament, God explicitly warns us against certain types of sexual sin, including homosexuality: "Do not have sexual relations with a man as one does with a woman; that is detestable" (Leviticus 18:22). In the New Testament, even more explicit references exist. Romans 1:26-27 says:

> God gave them over to shameful lusts. Even their women exchanged natural sexual relations for unnatural ones. In the same way the men also abandoned natural relations with women and were inflamed with lust for one another. Men committed shameful acts with other men.

Despite these scriptural references, some argue that one can be a Christian and a practicing gay. This however, is an oxymoron. The Bible explicitly tell us that those who practice homosexuality, including other types of sin, will not inherit the kingdom of God. 1 Corinthians 6:9-10 says:

> Do not be deceived: Neither the sexually immoral nor idolaters nor adulterers nor men who have sex with men nor thieves nor the greedy nor

drunkards nor slanderers nor swindlers will
inherit the kingdom of God.

Those who practice sinful lifestyles cannot therefore call
themselves Christians. Even worse, they cannot experience God's
salvation. And without salvation, there is only the prospect of
eternal damnation.

The mark of a real Christian is someone who follows Christ.
As Jesus said, "Whoever wants to be my disciple must deny
themselves and take up their cross and follow me" (Matthew
16:24). Being a Christian means living a Christ-centered life. To
illustrate this point, when "Christ" is removed from the word
"Christian," only the letters 'i-a-n' remain, an acronym for "I am
nothing."

But what did Jesus mean when He said His disciples must "take
up their cross"? The apostle Paul tells us: "Those who belong to
Christ Jesus have crucified the flesh with its passions and desires"
(Galatians 5:24). This means those who are Christ's are people
who resist their sinful instincts to pursue a godly life. So although
God is not against gays, He commands, "All people everywhere
to repent" (Acts 17:30). In essence, God loves homosexuals, but
hates homosexuality. And like any other sin, it must be nailed to
the cross.

Reason 66: If God is Good, Why Did He Kill People in the Bible?

This question requires a longer response than usual, especially
since God did in fact destroy multitudes of people according to the
Old Testament. An important point to clarify is that killing and
murder are not synonymous. Killing can be lawful but murder
is not. For instance, the death penalty is legal in some civilized
countries, and homicide is justified in certain circumstances; e.g.,
to protect oneself or others from a lethal threat.[32] So when the

Old Testament records God killing people, this does not mean He murdered them.

Critics argue that God contradicts Himself because He commands us not to kill, yet He killed. To address this point, one must revert to the original Hebrew text. Although the King James Bible renders the sixth commandment as "Thou shalt not kill" (Exodus 20:13), the Hebrew word for "kill" (ratsach) actually means "murder." For this reason, most Bible versions translate the sixth commandment as "You shall not murder." In any case, if anyone can be justified in taking a life, it is God, for He alone is able to fully restore that life.

Although God is a loving creator, some feel perplexed when reading Old Testament narratives of God showing His wrath. Critics capitalize on these narratives by claiming love and anger cannot coexist. But this is not true. If you caught someone in the act of raping your loved one, you would naturally feel angry, perhaps even react with violence to protect the one you love. Why? Because you love that person. Therefore, love and anger can coexist.

To better understand the different contexts of God's wrath, we shall examine three Biblical narratives. The first is the universal flood during the time of Noah. Before the great flood, the Bible says every person's intentions were exceedingly wicked and violence had permeated the earth,[33] refuting the notion that God drowned innocent people. Besides, it took Noah 100 years to build the ark, and since he was a preacher of righteousness, people had sufficient warning to change their behaviors, indicating the patience of God. Although the flood shows God's severity, it also shows His mercy, in that He saved humanity from complete extinction by not destroying Noah and his family.

Another narrative used by critics is the destruction of Sodom and Gomorrah. What is often overlooked is that these two cities were filled with great evil and debauchery.[34] Furthermore, before destroying them, God sent two angels to save righteous Lot and his family, signifying the salvation of God.

Our final narrative is how Israel took possession of the land of Canaan. Although critics question how a loving God condones the destruction of an entire nation, the Bible states the Canaanites were engaged in witchcraft, bestiality, extreme cruelty, and even burned their children to death in sacrifice to pagan gods.[35] Besides, God gave them 400 years to repent before commanding the Israelites to destroy them. Another important point is that before destroying their enemies, God instructed Israel to make a conciliatory offer of peace and only to engage in warfare after this offer was rejected.[36]

Biblical narratives like these indicate a number of themes— namely, God is holy and requires righteousness; God warns people to change their behaviors; God's judgment is in response to unrepentant sin; and God saves innocent people from destruction. So, do narratives like these throw God's goodness into question? No. On the contrary, they depict Him as a merciful and moral God whose judgment only falls after people have been given fair warning to repent. This point leads to the question: Have we chosen to accept God's offer of salvation in Christ Jesus? If not, we too will face God's wrath on the judgment day. Ultimately, God's pattern of judgment will be repeated at Christ's second coming, when He returns to judge the world a final time.[37]

Reason 67: If God Created the Universe, Who Created God?

People who ask this question have not grasped the definition of the Judeo-Christian God. The God of the Bible is the uncreated, eternal and transcendent creator of the universe. He existed before anything else existed. He needs no creator because He is a maximally great being who has both necessary existence and maximal excellence defined as omniscience, omnipotence and moral perfection.[38]

Despite this definition of God, skeptics continue to ask the question of who created God. Perhaps this is because they have a Hindu like concept of God, where gods beget gods. Alternatively, it could be because in the age of science in which we live, there is an obsession with causation, leading people to make endless correlations of cause and effect among variables to better understand the world. However, God exists beyond our world. He operates outside the boundaries of science and physical laws. Science concerns the examination of natural phenomena, not of the supernatural; the observation of the material world, not of the immaterial. Hence, enquiry into the nature of a supernatural God is beyond the limits of modern science and any scientific attempt to show His non-existence is illogical.

Because the Judeo-Christian God exists outside of space-time with no beginning or end, asking who created Him is absurd. It is akin to asking, "To whom is the bachelor married?" The answer is no one. Asking whether God has a cause, is like asking whether there is such a thing as a squared circle. Let us therefore dispense with such a question, for in the words of David Hume, it is "mere sophistry and illusion."[39]

Reason 68: Did God Literally Create the Universe in Six Days?

Debates on the six-day creation account in Genesis have been ongoing since the enlightenment, possibly earlier. These debates typically hinge on whether the six-day creation account is literal or figurative; whether each day represents 24 hours or a longer period. The position taken here is that the Genesis account is reliable and accurate. What is questionable however, is our understanding of it. Thus, whether God literary created the universe in six 24 hour days or not is a moot point. The seminal point is that God created the universe and everything in it.

Young earth creationists insist the universe was created in six days and that each day in the creation account cannot be interpreted as anything other than 24 hours in length. The implication of this argument is that the Universe is circa 6,000 years old because the Biblical timeline of Adam and Eve date back to circa 4000 BC. This understanding of creation is commonly known as the fundamentalist view. The downside of this view is that it is not consistent with scientific studies, which place the age of the earth at 4.5 billion years, and the age of the entire universe at 13.8 billion years.[40]

On the other hand, old earth creationists argue that the universe could be billions of years old because the Bible does not tell us when the Universe was created. They argue that "yom," the Hebrew word for "day," has a broad range of meanings, and is used throughout the Bible to refer to 24-hour solar days or longer periods; e.g., years and ages. This perspective of creation is known as the progressive view. Although this view could be plausible, these prolonged days would have to be extremely long (hundreds of millions of years) to fit with what scientists accept as the age of the universe.

Another view taken by old earth creationists is that God created the world we see today, but not the entire universe, in six literal days. For instance, Genesis 1:1 (KJV) says, "In the beginning God created the heavens and the earth." But verse two says, "And the earth was without form, and void; and darkness was upon the face of the deep." While verse one tells us that God created the universe, verse two says the earth was still formless and empty of organic life. A significant point to note is the six creation days in Genesis do not begin until verse three, which means the universe could have been created billions of years before God began shaping our earth and creating the life forms we see today. This view of creation is known as the gap theory and does not conflict with scientific studies on the age of the universe.

Each view listed here does not conflict with the six-day creation account in Genesis. What differs however, is our understanding of creation. Whichever view you take, the fundamentalist, progressive or gap view, none of them undermine the inerrancy of scripture.

Reason 69: Can God Create a Heavy Rock He Cannot Lift?

Whilst this seems a rather peculiar question, it typifies the kinds of paradoxical questions atheists use in their attempt to prove God's non-existence. Needless to say, this question belongs in the logically absurd category, along with questions such as "Can God create a squared circle?" Whilst God can do anything, the argument here is that he will not do anything that violates His own word, character or logic.

Now if God cannot create a rock He cannot lift, critics will argue that God is impotent. But if the answer is yes, critics will again accuse God of impotence because He cannot lift it. Either way, the answer is designed to show God is not all powerful as the Bible claims, and therefore does not exist. However, contradictory questions like this do not prove anything. They are akin to asking, "What does the color yellow taste like?" and "Can a pentagon have eight sides?" Obviously, colors do not have taste and a pentagon only has five sides. To think otherwise would be logically fallacious. In the same token, God will not be logically inconsistent or do anything self-contradictory.

Using paradoxical questions and challenges to try to prove God's non-existence is self-refuting. Although inexperienced atheists typically use such questions, most intelligent atheists stopped using them long ago, since they do nothing to generate an omnipotence paradox (an omnipotent entity with limited ability).

The immensely influential philosopher and doctor of the church, St Thomas Aquinas, dealt with the omnipotence paradox when he wrote, "Whatever implies being and nonbeing simultaneously is incompatible with the absolute possibility which falls under divine omnipotence."[41] What Aquinas meant is that anything involving a contradiction does not fall within the scope of omnipotence.

Since the Judeo-Christian God is a maximally great being who is morally perfect, he must be consistent with His own nature. He will not violate His own character. He will not lie, He will not break a promise, He will not become imperfect, He will not change, He will not sin, He will not commit evil, and He will not abandon those in covenant with Him. In other words, He is totally dependable and unchanging. The apostle Paul described God's character well when he wrote: "If we endure, we will also reign with Him. If we disown Him, He will also disown us; if we are faithless, He remains faithful, for He cannot disown himself" (2 Timothy 2:12-13).

Reason 70: If God Is Real, Why Doesn't He Appear to Us?

Despite the evidence and arguments presented thus far, some may be haunted by the question: Why doesn't God appear to us? In one sense, He appeared 2000 years ago and people crucified Him! It is no wonder He does not make too many appearances.

In another sense, God is invisible and therefore cannot fully represent Himself visibly. One cannot know God's existence as one knows the existence of a rock or a plant. How can what is infinite become finite? How can the eternal become temporal? God is not a physical object that can be scientifically examined, since He transcends the very universe itself.

Having said that, it is God's prerogative to hide Himself, so we can come to Him in the right mode. God is truth, but truth by itself is not enough to convince us. It is the mode in which truth is discovered that makes it acceptable. As the Danish philosopher Søren Kierkegaard points out, "Even more important...is the mode in which the truth is accepted, and it is of slight help if one gets millions to accept the truth if by the very mode of their acceptance they are transposed into untruth."[42]

Even if God revealed Himself as a man in the sky, what would that prove? Many would still doubt His identity and ask for more proofs, as they did with Jesus. Even if He showed His supernatural power and glory, what would that achieve? Power can do almost anything but it cannot control love. God is love. We are creatures created in the likeness of His love. Yet, God will not use his power to force us to love Him. This point may explain why He sometimes refrains from using His power to convince us. Kierkegaard also wrote:

> If I am capable of grasping God objectively, I do not believe, but precisely because I cannot do this I must believe. If I wish to preserve myself in faith I must constantly be intent upon holding fast the objective uncertainty so as to remain out upon the deep, over seventy thousand fathoms of water, still preserving my faith.[43]

The very essence of love is belief in the other. Love and faith are inseparable. Faith in the other person's love allows us to participate in that love for us. Without faith, love becomes tainted because love involves uncertainty. For precisely this reason, love requires trust. Without trust, there is no workable relationship.

God wants us to relate to Him in love. He wants our trust, not pitiful attempts to prove His existence. He wants us to know Him as He is, with a faith that compels us to remain "seventy thousand fathoms" over the deep. Let us therefore be content with objective uncertainty, so God can communicate Himself to us in beauty, in truth, in goodness, and ultimately in the revelation of His only Son, in whom He offers us a qualitative kind of certainty that would not be possible if He were visible. Only in this kind of relationship can we be swept by the eternal, infinite and transcendent glory of His love.

Reason 71: Is the Bible Distorted?

The Bible is a coherent historical masterpiece. Composed of 66 books written by 40 different authors from 1400 BC to circa 100 AD, it is backed up by archaeological and extra-Biblical evidence.[44] Whilst the Bible addresses many themes, its focus is on one man, the Messiah, and it includes 333 predictive prophecies confirming him as Jesus.[45] However, considering the age of the Bible and the number of versions in circulation, it is understandable why some would question its authenticity and reliability. Although the Bible's original manuscripts are lost or non-existent, a surprising amount of evidence exists confirming their accurate preservation over many centuries.

The original Biblical manuscripts would have been written on papyri (paper like material) or animal skins. But over time, these would have naturally decayed by use or humidity. To preserve their texts, scribes such as the Masoretes copied them by hand in meticulous detail to maintain their authenticity and circulation. To give you an idea of the incredible accuracy of the Bible, between 1946 and 1956 a collection of 981 different Old Testament texts (known as the Dead Sea scrolls) and dating as far back as 250 BC, were found in Qumran caves near the Dead Sea. One of these scrolls, the book of Isaiah, has a difference of just three words that only differ in spelling, compared to a more recent Masoretic text from the same book. This finding means that over a period of 1000 years, only a few minor spelling errors exist between texts.[46]

The New Testament's transmission is vastly more reliable than any other piece of ancient literature. For example, the earliest surviving manuscript of Aristotle's biological works (held at Corpus Christi College, Oxford) is dated circa 850 AD, some 1172 years after he wrote it.[47] Yet, scholars count Aristotle's biological works as reliable. In contrast, the earliest surviving fragment of the book of John is from 150 AD, some 50 years after it was written, a mere moment compared to other ancient literature.[48] In fact, texts from the oldest Bible (the Codex Vaticanus), which is no more than 250 years older than original New Testament texts,[49] match extant Bibles today. While minor differences exist, scholars agree they are mere syntax variations or spelling errors, posing no doctrinal impact.[50]

A concern for some people is the different Bible versions that exist. Although up to 50 different English Bible versions are in circulation, they differ mainly in style and grammar, not in theology and doctrine. In reality, multiple versions help us understand the meaning of Biblical texts.

In conclusion, the Bible has been remarkably preserved over the centuries and can be regarded as trustworthy. Good reasons exist for believing that our current day Bible is faithful to what its authors originally wrote, in both Old and New Testaments.

Reason 72: Does the Bible Contradict Itself?

Atheists, skeptics, and even apologists from other religions sometimes cite contradictions in the Bible as a way of undermining its credibility. What is interesting is that they usually find these alleged contradictions in sources committed to the subject. This point shows that if people have an *a priori* commitment to find contradictions, they will find them. Conversely, if people apply themselves to a sincere and diligent study of the Bible, they will find no contradictions, but supplementations.

A contradiction happens when two facts are mutually exclusive, but a supplementation is when two facts complement one another. Aristotle, who wrote extensively on the law of contradiction argues: "It is impossible for the same thing to belong and not to belong at the same time to the same thing and in the same respect."[51] The point here is that a contradiction can only apply when a number of conditions are in play; namely, the same thing or person is in consideration in the same time period and in the same context. So for example, if one part of a text states,

"John Smith is poor," and another states, 'John Smith is rich,' these two statements would only be contradictory if they referred to the same John Smith in the same time period and in the same context. If they referred to two different John Smith's or the same John Smith in two different time periods or contexts, no contradiction would exist. The text could mean John Smith was poor, but later became rich or that he was spiritually poor but financially rich.

As simple as the John Smith example sounds, it illustrates how we must not jump to conclusions when reading texts, especially ancient texts that may lack detail and context. What seems contradictory may in fact be supplementary, resulting in a more complete understanding of the narrative being analyzed. It follows that by applying the law of contradiction, apparent conflicts in the Bible can be resolved. In fact, books and websites on the topic of Biblical contradictions refute each and every contradiction posed by critics.

In closing, if we are to arrive at a valid understanding of Bible texts, we must be careful to interpret them from the perspective of the author. We must also remember that over a period of 1500 years, 40 different authors wrote the Bible. Inconsistencies between them are therefore bound to appear, especially since each author wrote in a different way, from a different time, in a different context, and in some cases a different language. Finally, conflicts between Biblical accounts not only show us that authors wrote independently of each other, but also demonstrate they were not in collusion, a point that underscores the Bible's authenticity.

Reason 73: What About the Crusades?

Another objection posed by critics is the Crusades. These were a series of expeditions by Christian armies who fought against Muslim forces to recover the Holy land during the middle ages. The Crusades have been a topic of debate for centuries, a topic often used to bring a bloody stain on Christianity. When other objections fail, critics sometimes leap to their proverbial feet, and like courtroom barristers wield the fatal question: "What about the Crusades?" The answer here is that the Crusades were defensive wars against Muslim conquests.[52]

Whilst it is commonly accepted that the Crusades are a stain on the history of the Catholic Church, misconceptions about them are common. These misconceptions drive the belief that the Crusades were unprovoked attacks by Christian zealots against a peaceful Muslim world. These misconceptions are helped by historian Sir Steven Runciman, who published a large volume of work in the 1950s that shaped the modern view of the Crusades. However, since the 1970s the Crusades have attracted attention from hundreds of scholars. As a result, much more is known about them than when Runciman published his work. The position now is that many Crusade historians disagree with Runciman's ideas, although the fruits of their research have been slow to enter the public mind.[53]

According to various credible historians, the view that Crusades were wars of unprovoked aggression is a myth.[54] From the time of Muhammed, Muslims have sought to conquer the Christian world. After the birth of Islam in the seventh century, it only took a few hundred years for Muslim armies to take all of North Africa, the Middle East, Asia Minor, and most of Spain. In fact, by the end of the eleventh century, Islamic forces had captured two-thirds of the Christian world. These conquests included communities at the core of Christianity, such as the ancient land of Israel (the place of Christ's birth and death), Egypt (the origin of Christian monasticism), and Asia Minor (the place where the apostle Paul planted some of the first gentile churches).[55]

What is even more astonishing is that Muslim armies continued to move westward until they entered Europe itself. In terms of unprovoked aggression, history reveals it was all Muslim. At some point however, the Christian world had to defend itself, and that call came from Pope Urban II in 1095. He called the first

Crusade in response to an urgent plea from the Byzantine Emperor Alexios I Komnenos, whose empire was attacked by Muslim Turks who seized most of the formerly Byzantine Anatolia (modern day Turkey). Pope Urban called upon the knights of Christendom from across Europe to rescue their besieged eastern brethren, and to reclaim Holy places seized by Muslim invaders. According to Professor Thomas Madden, a leading Crusade historian, the entire history of the Crusades is one of response to Muslim aggression.[56]

Although Crusades were brutal and many were killed, many were also set free, and Muslims who surrendered were allowed to retain their property and to freely worship. Nevertheless, blood was shed on all sides, and a catastrophic toll of 1.7 million lives were lost.[57] As awful as this sounds, one should remember that up to eighty million people died in the six years of World War II,[58] almost fifty times more than in the entire 200 years history of the Crusades. And as for the claim that Crusaders filled the streets with blood, no serious historian accepts this claim.[59]

In closing, the Crusades were errands of mercy to liberate eastern Christians from Muslim conquests. In the same way the allies of World War II had the right to retake lands seized by Nazi invaders, the Crusaders had the right to retake lands seized by Muslim invaders. From this view, the purpose of the Crusades was entirely justified.

PART VI

Prominent People Who Found Christ

Reason 74: Legendary Author and Philosopher, C.S. Lewis

Clive Staples Lewis is without doubt one of the greatest academics and fictional writers of the twentieth century. After graduating from Oxford with triple first class honors, he became an English professor who taught at both Oxford and Cambridge. His fictional work, *The Chronicles of Narnia*, has sold over 100 million copies and has been adapted for both stage and film.[1]

Although Lewis grew up in a Christian family, he abandoned his Christian faith at the age of 15 after his mother's death from cancer in 1908. Disillusioned because God had not healed his mother, Lewis committed himself to a path of atheism and rationalism, winning the highest honors in the disciplines of Classical Literature, Philosophy, and English. After being elected a Fellow of Magdalen College at Oxford where he worked for almost thirty years, he was awarded the newly found chair of Mediaeval and Renaissance Literature at Cambridge University, where he finished his career.

Despite having been an atheist for over 16 years, Lewis returned to Christianity after being influenced by arguments from his Oxford friend J.R.R. Tolkien (author of *Lord of the Rings and the Hobbit*), and by *The Everlasting Man*, a book by G.K. Chesterton. Speaking of his conversion experience in his autobiographical book, *Surprised by Joy*, Lewis notes, "That which I greatly feared had at last come upon me. In the Trinity Term of 1929, I gave in, and admitted that God was God, and knelt and prayed: perhaps, that night, the most dejected and reluctant convert in all England."[2]

Having come to Christ like a prodigal son, "Kicking, struggling, resentful, and darting his eyes in every direction for a chance to escape,"[3] Lewis's conversion influenced millions who were perhaps tempted to think Christianity is for shallow intellectuals. On the contrary, Lewis showed us that faith and reason could blend perfectly together, a blend epitomized so eloquently in his books, *Mere Christianity, Miracles, and The Problem of Pain.* In fact, Lewis became such a great defender of the Christian faith that he challenged notorious atheists like Sir Antony Flew in open debates at Oxford.

The writings of C.S. Lewis, a literary genius, are still inspiring many today. The following is a befitting final thought from Lewis— the man who brought us many great fictional works: "Look for yourself, and you will find in the long run only hatred, loneliness, despair, rage, ruin, and decay. But look for Christ and you will find Him, and with Him everything else thrown in."[4]

Reason 75: Former LGBT Activist, Professor Rosaria Butterfield

Another English professor who found Christ is Rosaria Butterfield. At the age of 34, Butterfield was a lesbian, atheist and senior academic at Syracuse University. As an academic author and LGBT activist, she was a fervent advocate for the worldviews of Freud, Hegel, Marx, and Darwin. By her own admission, she used her tenure as a university professor to advance her leftist lesbian agenda. But in 1999 at the age of 36, her life dramatically changed when she accepted Christ, describing her experience as a "train wreck" conversion.[5]

Butterfield's conversion happened after she began a research project on the Religious Right and their politics of hatred toward "queers." To complete her research, she had to read the one book she believed had led many people astray—the Bible. While looking for a Bible scholar to aid her research, she launched her first attack against Christianity in the form of an article she wrote for a local newspaper. Whilst this article garnered a mixed response, one letter from a local pastor challenged her to defend her own presuppositions. Instead of arguing, he asked the kinds of questions she admired as an academic: How did you arrive at your interpretations? How do you know you are right?

The letter prompted Butterfield to meet with this local Syracuse pastor, and that meeting led to a close friendship with him and his wife. They exchanged views and books, had meals together and openly talked about sexuality and politics, all of which inspired her to read the Bible many times over. As she read, little did she know her heart would ultimately be overwhelmed by the truth of its pages. Hours each day, she poured herself over Bible texts, arguing at first, then eventually surrendering.

During those times of intense Bible reading, Butterfield states that three principles became insurmountable to her: God's goodness, God's holiness, and the authority of Scripture. The Bible passage that finally nailed her to the cross is Romans 1:22-26:

> Although they claimed to be wise, they became
> fools and exchanged the glory of the immortal
> God for images made to look like a mortal human
> being...Therefore God gave them over in the sinful
> desires of their hearts to sexual impurity...Even
> their women exchanged natural sexual relations
> for unnatural ones.

When Butterfield realized that homosexuality was not a fixed part of her identity but a consequence of original sin, she turned to God with a sincere remorse for her wrongdoing and accepted Christ's atoning sacrifice on the cross. Today, Butterfield lives in Durham, North Carolina with her husband and children. As a committed Christian, she believes the goal of Christianity is repentance and victory over sin through God's grace. Her full conversion story can be read in her book, *The Secret Thoughts of an Unlikely Convert.*[6]

Reason 76: Famous Astronomer, Allan Sandage

Widely regarded as one of the greatest astronomers of the twentieth century, Dr. Allan Sandage published more than 500 papers and won many esteemed accolades. Among his many achievements, he calculated the age of the universe, determined the first reasonably accurate value for the Hubble constant (expansion rate of the universe) and discovered the first quasar (a very bright celestial object powered by a massive black hole).[7]

Driven by an insatiable pursuit for the discovery of things in the world, Sandage decided to be an astronomer at the age of eleven. After receiving his PhD in physics in 1952, he began working as an assistant to Edwin Hubble at Mt. Wilson and Palomar Observatories, remaining there until he retired in 1997. However, from his early twenties Sandage was plagued by questions regarding the purpose of life and why there is something rather than nothing.[8] After thirty years of research, he came to the conclusion that science could not answer these questions, and the mystery of existence could only be explained through belief in the supernatural. It was at this point he began studying the Bible, and at the age of 57 took a leap of faith to become a born-again Christian, reasoning that he could no longer live a life of cynicism. When he decided to believe, he claims, "A peace of mind came over me."[9]

After coming to Christ, Sandage joined a faith community in California and wrote several essays on the subject of religion and science. While some critics argue that he only became a believer because of earlier socialization of Christian beliefs, Sandage maintains he did not really learn anything about Christianity until he was perhaps forty years of age.[10] His passion for truth ultimately led him to a passion for the Bible, believing it was God's inerrant word.

Sandage did not come to Christ because of what science answered, but because of what it could not answer. Science cannot answer questions on the meaning of life, human consciousness, free will, morality, and the appreciation of music and beauty. Sandage believed that science and faith complement each other, as the two answer very different questions. Science answers the what, when and how, but faith answers the why. Why are so many processes so deeply interconnected? Why is the design of the universe so truly miraculous?

For Sandage, science explains the laws of the universe and its incredible natural order, whilst the Bible explains the laws humans should live by and the spiritual reality of the universe. In Sandage's own words:

> I find it quite improbable that such order came out of chaos. There has to be some organizing principle. God to me is a mystery but is the explanation for the miracle of existence, why there is something rather than nothing.[11]

Reason 77: World Renowned Mathematician, George Ellis

George F. R. Ellis is a distinguished Professor of Applied Mathematics at the University of Cape Town in South Africa and a Templeton Prize Laureate.[12] As one of the world's leading theorists in cosmology, he has written over 500 academic articles and authored many books, one of which was co-written with Professor Stephen Hawking, entitled: *The Large Scale Structure of Space-Time*. As an active Christian, Ellis is known for his bold contributions to the dialogue between science and religion.

After Ellis completed a Bachelor of Science degree with honors in South Africa, he went to Cambridge where he received a PhD in applied math and theoretical physics in 1964. Ellis stayed at Cambridge as a lecturer before returning in 1974 to South Africa, where he worked as a professor until he retired in 2005. However, soon after returning to South Africa, Ellis joined the Religious Society of Friends (Quakers), a historical Christian group who believe in the direct inner working of Christ within the soul. He became a Quaker because he found their theology was congenial for scientists like him and deemed their commitment to philanthropy and peaceful principles especially important for apartheid South Africa.[13]

Alongside his contribution to science, over many decades Ellis has been involved in social activism, such as fund raising for the poor, protesting against apartheid in nonviolent ways, and devising a low-income housing policy that eventually guided national policy in South Africa. In other words, Ellis's contributions to science, faith and social activism make him an exemplary Christian in so many ways.[14]

Much like Alan Sandage, Ellis contends there is no conflict between science and faith. Despite those who claim the powers of science are limitless, he asserts that science has boundaries. Ellis refutes a materialist worldview by acknowledging multiple metaphysical properties of existence that physics cannot encompass; in particular, ethics, social constructions, human thoughts, emotions, and intentions.

As a moral realist, Ellis believes we do not invent ethics, we discover them, because a moral character exists in the universe that reflects the very nature of God.[15] Ellis unveils the identity of this divine nature: "God's nature is revealed most perfectly in the life and teachings of Jesus of Nazareth, as recorded in the New Testament of the Bible, who was sent by God to reveal the divine nature, summarized in 'God is Love.'"[16]

A befitting final thought about Ellis is that his faith never interfered with his science, and likewise, science never interfered with his faith. Knowing the limitations of science enabled him to maintain the belief that "God has an active presence in the world that still touches the lives of the faithful today."[17]

Reason 78: Evolutionary Biologist, Professor Richard Lumsden

After graduating from Harvard, Richard D. Lumsden became a Professor of Parasitology and Cell Biology at Tulane University in Louisiana, where he served as Dean of the Graduate School of Biological Sciences.[18] Throughout his academic career, he published many papers in peer-reviewed journals and in 1975, he received the highest award in the field of parasitology, the Henry Baldwin Ward Medal.[19] However, before Lumsden's death in 1997,[20] he made the startling choice to reject Darwinian evolution and became a Christian, a choice that cost him tenure at Tulane University.

As an evolutionist and atheist, Lumsden viewed the Genesis account of creation as mere "mythology."[21] His view however, dramatically changed after Louisiana introduced legislation in the early 1980s, requiring public schools to give equal time to the subject of creationism alongside evolution. This legislation so enraged Lumsden that he used one of his lectures to deliver a full intellectual assault on creationism, with as much mockery and cynicism he could muster. Though he received a standing ovation from his students, he had no idea of what was to follow—that his atheistic world of Darwinian evolution would come crashing down.

Following the lecture, one of his top students came and praised him for his impressive oratory. While Lumsden felt flattered by her remarks, he noticed she had prepared a writing pad with a series of questions. Consequently, Lumsden invited her to his office that same afternoon. Whilst listening to her during the meeting, he was stunned by the pertinence of her questions. She challenged him on issues that so many scientists overlook because of blind faith in Darwinian evolution. Her questions included: How could amino acids have randomly assembled themselves to form genes and proteins? When explaining the origin of life, why do textbooks propose chemical equations and reactions that defy the laws of chemistry? If mutations are genetic disasters, how can they be used by natural selection to produce new and better structures?[22]

Throughout the meeting, Lumsden found defending himself very difficult. Their meeting lasted over three hours, but it only took Lumsden half that time to acknowledge Darwinian evolution was intellectually bankrupt. His worldview had just been turned upside down. After realizing his answers were scientifically and logically inadequate, he asked himself, "If life did not originate by a naturalistic process, what was the alternative explanation?" He answered with a cry toward God, not in blasphemy, but in awe.[23] This was his eureka moment, the juncture where he discovered God exists. Soon after, Lumsden became a creationist and gave his life to Christ. For the years that followed before his death, he openly debated evolutionists, showing them that the evidence they relied upon actually supported the Genesis account of creation.

Reason 79: Outstanding Geneticist, Francis Collins

Francis S. Collins is one of the world's most outstanding scientists. After earning his PhD at Yale University in physical chemistry, Collins developed a strong interest in genetics. As a consequence, he became a Doctor of Medicine in 1977, and rose to the rank of Professor after becoming known for his gene hunting discoveries. However, his greatest discovery came in 2000 when he mapped the human genome. When invited to the White House to announce this discovery, Collins said, "It is humbling for me, and awe inspiring to realize that we have caught the first glimpse of our own instruction book, previously known only to God."[24] Describing himself as a "serious Christian,"[25] Collins wrote many books, including *The Language of God: A Scientist Presents Evidence for Belief.*

Surprisingly, Collins was raised in a non-Christian family. During his childhood, he claims, "Faith was not really on the list of things that were talked about."[26] Therefore, one cannot accuse Collins of turning to Christ because of earlier socialization. After he left home to study the physical sciences, Collins maintained he was an atheist, having convinced himself that everything in the universe could be reduced to equations. However, as a physician, his view began to change when confronted by death and dying among his patients.

Although Collins read many of the arguments for atheism, he explains, "The harder I looked at them, the flimsier they were."[27] Then after somebody gave him the book *Mere Christianity* by C.S. Lewis, Collins was in trouble. He states, "In the very first few pages of that book, all of my arguments against the plausibility of faith were rapidly dismantled. I saw them then as the arguments of a schoolboy."[28] Impacted by the Oxford scholar's arguments, Collins developed the view that each and every one of us has a moral sense of right and wrong, which cannot be explained through science. This view led Collins to the conclusion that only the existence of a moral God could explain our sense of morality. Collins claims that this moral sense is

> Something written within our hearts universally in human kind, making us different from other species, and calling us to be good and holy, pointing us...to something outside ourselves that is much more good and much more holy than we can imagine.[29]

Although Collins's logic on morality was convincing, he struggled for another two years until he became a theist. Then one beautiful fall afternoon during a hike, Collins made the decision to become a Christian. As he gazed at a frozen waterfall in the shadow of the Cascade Mountains, Collins could no longer resist. He states, "I fell on my knees and accepted the truth—that God is God, that Christ is his son and that I am giving my life to that belief."[30]

Reason 80: Award Winning Journalist and Author, Peter Hitchens

Peter Hitchens is an award winning English journalist, broadcaster and prominent author. Unlike his late brother, the notorious atheist Christopher Hitchens, Peter is a staunch defender of the Christian faith. He wrote the book *The Rage Against God*, which not only describes his journey from atheism to faith, but also provides a robust rebuttal against the anti-theist intelligentsia of our age.

Although both Peter and his brother grew up in a religiously conscious household, they both became full-bodied atheists, completely rebelling against the Christian values they were taught at home. In fact, Peter's rebellion was so intense, he set fire to his Bible whilst a teenager at his Cambridge boarding school, an act that sealed his defiance against God. For the next 20 years, Peter adopted liberal positions on marriage, abortion and homosexuality—positions that countered his conservative Christian upbringing. Referring to his brand of atheism: "We were full of our own righteousness...we knew we were right, we knew we were good, we defined our own goodness."[31] Uncannily, it was Peter's awareness of this elitist thinking of "we know better and everybody else is stupid" that finally led him to embrace Christ.

Around the age of 30, Peter began to seriously question his views on atheism and socialism. As he considered his Christian forebears, he realized they were neither crude nor ignorant, but people of great skill, men and women whose genius was not hindered by faith, but enhanced by it.[32] Although Peter admits his journey to Christ was rather slow, he points to a life changing moment when he genuinely feared God. That moment happened when he gazed at Rogier van der Weyden's painting, *The Last Judgment*, showing the terrified faces of those condemned to hell. As he gazed at this sobering work of art, Peter says, "It just came through that I might be judged, and I was scared. I still am…But then again, the fear of the Lord is the beginning of wisdom.[33]

After he came to Christ, Peter claims, "It was the first properly grown-up thing I had ever done."[34] Despite Peter finding his way back to the altar rail, his brother waxed even more virulent in his passion against God. He claims Christopher was a repressed seeker whose views epitomize a new kind of atheism—one that is self satisfied, arrogant, intolerant and resistant to any kind of counter argument, including arguments about how we decide what is unalterably good.[35] When asked in an interview about how he would define good and evil, Peter gave an astonishing answer:

> I believe in the absolute goodness of God. Evil is
> the absence of God, or the willful denial of God's
> law, or the deliberate turning away of our faces
> from God. He never turns his face from us, but we
> often turn our faces away from him. [36]

Reason 81: Distinguished Academic, Professor Alister McGrath

Former atheist Alister McGrath is an astonishing intellectual. He holds three doctorates from Oxford University in the fields of molecular biophysics, divinity, and intellectual history. Alongside his role as Professor of Science and Religion at Oxford University, he is an Anglican priest, historian and Christian apologist. He is also the author of numerous highly acclaimed books, including the international bestseller *The Dawkins Delusion?*

McGrath grew up in Northern Ireland as an aggressive atheist with a keen interest in science. Whist this interest gave him insights into the marvelous world of nature, it also led him to conclude that

God was an infantile illusion, suitable for the intellectually feeble but not for serious grownups. However, that conclusion changed after he left home in 1971 to study at Oxford. As he deeply delved into the study of the natural sciences, he expected his atheism would be further strengthened. But to his surprise, it collapsed, after he realized it rested on an unsatisfactory evidential basis. What also helped McGrath change his mind were discussions with articulate Christians who challenged his views and the realization that atheists were more concerned with rubbishing religion than seeking truth.[37]

McGrath also became aware that atheism is a faith position— meaning, it is something you believe, not something you can prove. Besides, the more he learned about the Christian faith, the more meaning, dignity and purpose it brought to his life—aspects that science cannot provide. While his journey to faith did not involve any bright lights or great emotional catharsis, McGrath simply felt Christianity was right and much more intellectually robust than atheism.[38]

Since becoming a Christian, McGrath has been a vociferous opponent of the aggressive and propagandist brand of new atheism adopted by people like Richard Dawkins, whom he has debated twice. He has also publicly debated other irreligious stalwarts, such as Daniel Dennett, Peter Atkins and the late Christopher Hitchens. McGrath claims new atheists of this sort possess a pathological hostility towards faith, and a grave misapprehension that the natural sciences force us towards atheism. He argues there is no conflict between science and faith, because interpretations of the natural sciences are driven more by biases than by evidence. In other words, depending on one's agenda, scientific evidence can be viewed as supportive of faith or inimical to faith.[39]

As an academic, McGrath now spends much of his time delivering free lectures on science, faith and God.[40] As a priest, he may be found ministering in a local parish on a Sunday morning, somewhere in the quintessential English Cotswolds.

Reason 82: Former Agnostic, Dr. Josh McDowell

Former agnostic Josh McDowell is an American Christian apologist and author of some 115 books. His best-selling book, *Evidence That Demands a Verdict*, is one of the most influential evangelical books of all time.[41] Other well known titles that he authored include *More Than a Carpenter*, *A Ready Defense*, and *Right from Wrong*.

Although McDowell went on to receive a Doctor of Law degree at the age of 43, he experienced difficulties at school because his childhood was plagued by abuse. Growing up on a farm in Michigan, McDowell claims his father was an abusive alcoholic, and between the age of six and thirteen, McDowell suffered repeated sexual abuse at the hands of a farm laborer called Wayne. As a result, McDowell struggled with low self-esteem, a speech impediment and very poor grammar at school. After finishing high school, he joined the Air Force but was discharged shortly after because of an injury. At that point he decided to pursue legal studies at college.[42]

As an agnostic, McDowell was angry. He was angry at God and people. After meeting some Christians at college, he set out on a mission to disprove Christianity by writing a paper about its lack of historical evidence. But after months of study, much to his own bewilderment he discovered a great deal of extra-Biblical evidence and consequently became a Christian. Like the apostle Paul, McDowell ended up supporting the very thing he set out to destroy.[43] Speaking about his conversion, McDowell remarked:

> I had to admit that the Old and New Testament documents were some of the most reliable writings in all of antiquity. And if they were reliable, what about this man Jesus whom I had dismissed as a mere carpenter? I had to admit that Jesus Christ

was more than a carpenter. He was all He claimed
to be.[44]

After McDowell became a Christian, he knew he had to forgive
his abusers. Though he hated his father, a powerful love consumed
him when he received Christ. He claims, "God's love took that
hatred, turned it upside down, and emptied it out."[45] Consequently,
the next time he met his father, he looked him in the eyes and said,
"Dad, I love you." Having seen the transformation in his son's life,
his father said, "Son, if God can do in my life what I've seen Him
do in yours, then I want to trust Him as my Savior and Lord." His
father also gave his life to Christ.[46]

Another abuser whom McDowell had to forgive was Wayne.
When McDowell finally came face to face with Wayne, he told
him, "What you did to me was evil, but…I believe that Jesus died
as much for you as He did for me, so I forgive you."[47] Through
the power of Christ's forgiveness, McDowell finally overcame the
scars that so deeply affected his life. Now when people ask him,
'How do you know you became a Christian?' He answers them,
"It changed my life."[48]

Reason 83: Former Atheist, Professor Holly Ordway

Holly Ordway is a professor of English with a plethora of published
works, including academic articles, book reviews, and poetry.
Growing up in a non-religious home, she was convinced that
God was little more than superstition. When she left home to
attend college, her atheism hardened as she absorbed the idea that
Christianity was a mere historical curiosity. But after becoming
a professor, little did she know her formidable fortress of atheism
was to encounter a devastating assault, leading her to lay down
her arms.[49]

Atheists claim that people who come to Christ do so because
of embedded Christian norms during childhood. This cannot be
said of Ordway. In her memoir, *Not God's Type*, she explains, "I

had never in my life said a prayer, never been to a church service. Christmas meant presents and Easter meant chocolate bunnies— nothing more."[50] By the time she was thirty, not only did she delight in thinking of herself as an atheist, but viewed Christians as people who undermined the advancement of knowledge.

Instead of examining the truth claims of Christianity, Ordway says it was "easier by far to read only books by atheists that told me what I wanted to hear: that I was smarter and more intellectually honest and morally superior than the poor, deluded Christians."[51] Oddly though, her position changed when she realized that while she wanted nothing to do with faith, she could think of no good reason to reject faith. This was the moment she realized her argument for atheism was circular.

Another factor that spurred her conversion along was reading great classic works of literature from Christian authors and poets like C.S. Lewis, J.R.R. Tolkien, George Herbert and Gerard Manley Hopkins. Their works unsettled her atheist convictions. Their faith imbued her with a different way of seeing the world, a more meaningful and richer worldview than her flat and parochial atheistic world, which failed to explain her desire for beauty and truth.

As her worldview was changing, Ordway discovered that a close friend she admired was a Christian who without imposing his faith, began answering her questions. It was at this time Ordway decided to read through and analyze the gospel narratives of the New Testament. As an expert in literature, she concluded:

> I recognized that they were fact, not story. I'd been steeped in folklore, fantasy, legend, and myth ever since I was a child, and I had studied these literary genres as an adult; I knew their cadences, their flavor, their rhythm. None of these stylistic fingerprints appeared in the New Testament books that I was reading.[52]

After she concluded the claims of the Bible were true, Ordway accepted Jesus Christ. As a committed Christian and talented academic, she currently serves as director of the M.A. in Apologetics at Houston Baptist University, speaking regularly on topics related to Tolkien and Lewis.[53]

Reason 84: Former Hindu, Rabi R. Maharaj

As a descendent of a long line of Brahmin priests, Rabi Maharaj was trained as a Yogi (practitioner of meditation), destined to follow his father as an acclaimed Hindu guru. Although he respected his father, there was no meaningful relationship with him because his father maintained a trance-like state for eight years in pursuit of union with Brahman, i.e. Moksha. Consequently, Maharaj never heard his father's voice, nor was he given the slightest bit of attention.[54]

After his father's death, Maharaj was venerated as a guru, and by the time he was eleven, many were already bowing before him and laying gifts at his feet. However, during his third year of high school, Maharaj experienced a deep inner conflict with Hinduism. He became increasingly aware of God as a distinct being who was separate from His creation, a contradiction to the Hindu concept that god was essentially everything. He also reasoned that if Hinduism were true, Brahman was both good and evil, life and death, love and hate, etc. This conclusion led Maharaj to feel his life was totally meaningless and absurd. That is, until he met Molli.

During a visit to Maharaj's house, his cousin's friend, Molli, asked him various questions that further exposed his Hindu beliefs. She also told him by knowing Jesus, she had found inner peace and joy; attributes that evaded Maharaj, despite his many hours of meditation each day. "You don't seem very happy. Are you?" Molli asked. Despite his guru heritage, Maharaj surprisingly admitted, "I'm not happy. I wish I had your joy." Molli continued,

"My joy is because my sins are forgiven. Before you go to bed tonight, Rabi, please get on your knees and ask God to show you the Truth."[55]

Pride demanded he reject everything Molli shared, but later that night, he fell to his knees and prayed for God to show him the truth. For the first time in his life, he felt his prayer had been heard, not by an impersonal force, but by the true and living God.

Soon after that night, Maharaj attended a Christian meeting. While the preacher expounded on Psalm 23 and exhorted people with words like, "Jesus wants to be your shepherd. Have you heard His voice speaking to your heart?,"[56] Maharaj's heart leapt with emotion. After the sermon, he quickly found himself on his knees and gave his life to Jesus. In that moment, he knew Jesus was not just one of several million gods, but the true creator God; the God who became a man and died for his sins. As he experienced this realization of Jesus, Maharaj claims, "a darkness seemed to lift and a brilliant light flooded my soul."[57]

When he arrived home, Maharaj quickly began sharing how he had found Jesus with his family, and the following day, he did something that sealed his transformation from a Hindu guru to a follower of Christ. He walked into his prayer room and carried out every idol and Hindu scripture into the yard outside, ridding himself of every tie with the powers of darkness that blinded him for so long. He knew there was no blending of Hinduism and true Christianity. The earlier symbolized one of many roads that led to the same destruction, while the latter was the narrow way to eternal life. Once he had finished gathering all his Hindu paraphernalia into a rubbish heap, Maharaj set it on fire then gazed into the flames that engulfed his past. He claims this was his "cremation ceremony—the end of the person I had once been… the death of a guru."[58]

Maharaj went on to lead many Hindus to Christ, speaking to thousands in auditoriums and University campuses across the world. His best selling book, *Death of a Guru*, offers a full account of his remarkable conversion, a story that has inspired many in search of truth.

Reason 85: Former Buddhist, Professor Paul Williams

After completing his doctorate in Buddhist philosophy at Oxford University, Paul Williams went on to become a Professor of Indian and Tibetan philosophy at the University of Bristol. As a leading authority in Buddhist studies, he had been a practicing Buddhist for twenty years before converting to Christianity in 2000. Details of his conversion are given in his book *The Unexpected Way*, which chronicles his journey from Buddha to Christ in a most compelling way. Central to finding Christ was his growing sense of sheer rightness and truth about Christianity and its deeply persuasive rationality.[59]

Having grown up an Anglican, Williams became disenchanted with the Anglican Church, and by the time he reached his teens, he no longer considered himself a Christian. After commencing university, Williams grew an interest in Buddhist philosophy and by the end of his studies at Oxford, he became a Buddhist in the same Tibetan tradition as the Dalai Lama.[60] In the years that followed, Williams emerged as a leading figure in Buddhism. He led Buddhist retreats, appeared in radio and television programs, and presided as president of the UK Association for Buddhist studies.,[61]

Williams's attraction to Buddhism was largely garnered by the notion that "God was unlikely because there was so much evil in world,"[62] and that Buddhism seemed a more sensible option than theism. However, looking back on his Buddhist life he admits, "No real conversion took place" and that he always knew Buddhism was "deep down a sham."[63]

Another factor that led Williams to rethink his Buddhist philosophy was his growing unease with the concept of reincarnation. He realized, "Unless I attained enlightenment, or something like it, in this life...I would have no hope. Neither would any of my friends or family."[64] He essentially concluded that reincarnation was "a hope-less doctrine." To illustrate this point, he asks people during lectures, "Hands up who wants to be reborn a cockroach?"

When he discovered that "Christianity at least offers some hope,"[65] Williams decided to delve deeper into it. While examining Christianity more closely, he realized it was more appealing and rational than other religions. He notes, "Christianity is the religion of the infinite value of the person. Each person is an individual creation of God, and as such, is infinitely loved and valued by God."[66] Williams also learned, "The evidence for the resurrection being the most likely explanation of what happened at the first Easter is very strong."[67]

After exploring the arguments for the Christian faith, Williams chose to become a Christian. He says, "I believe Jesus genuinely died, the tomb was empty and he was subsequently, after his real death, physically alive."[68] Williams claims, "I now live in gratitude and hope. And I have never, ever, for one moment regretted my decision."[69]

Reason 86: Former Chief Rabbi, Israel Zoller

Israel Zoller was a Jewish Professor of Philosophy and former Chief Rabbi of Rome, credited for saving thousands of Jews when the Nazis besieged Rome in 1943. However, when the War ended in 1945, he shocked the Jewish community after he publicly announced his conversion to Christ. Even to this day, Zoller causes controversy; devout Jews call him an apostate and heretic, while others regard him as a prophet and hero.[70]

Zoller was born in Brody, a city known for its thriving Jewish community in the former eastern part of Poland. His father was a wealthy business owner in Lodz (formerly in Russia) while his mother came from a dynasty of Rabbis. When the Czar Alexander

III nationalized all foreign-owned businesses in Russia, his family moved to Italy where he changed his surname to Zolli to sound more Italian. After earning a Doctorate in Philosophy and completing his rabbinate training, in 1918 he became Rabbi of Trieste, then Chief Rabbi of Rome at the start of the war.[71]

Unlike his counterparts, Zoller foresaw the Nazis's intention to arrest and deport Rome's 8,000 Jews. He consequently warned Jewish leaders of this threat, advising them to cease Jewish functions, close administrative offices, and encourage fellow Jews to disperse. In 1943, when the Gestapo began arresting Jews in Rome, Zoller was proved right. Fortunately, only 1,259 Jews were arrested after Zoller pleaded with the Vatican to give Jews sanctuary in churches and monasteries.[72]

In his book *Before the Dawn*, Zoller wrote about a vision he had of Jesus while praying on the holy day of Yom Kippur in 1944. In the vision, he felt unspeakable joy as he saw Jesus standing in a bright meadow clothed in a white mantle. Jesus told him, "You are here for the last time. From now on you will follow me."[73] And so it was. Zoller, along with his wife and daughter, who also had visions of Jesus, became believers and were baptized. To honor the Pope for his part in saving Roman Jews, Zoller later changed his first name from Israel to Eugenio.

Zoller's conversion caused no small stir among the Jewish community. Many claim it had more to do with his excommunication by Jews for hiding in the Vatican during Rome's siege, than a deep spiritual conviction. However, Zoller maintained his conversion was a "slow evolution, altogether internal."[74] He argued that his book *The Nazarene*, written years before, is proof of his gradual move to Christianity.

When asked why he gave up the synagogue for the church, Zoller replied, "I have not given it up. Christianity…is the crown of the synagogue. For the synagogue was a promise, and Christianity is the fulfillment of that promise."[75] Eugenio Zolli, the name he became known by after his baptism, went on to become Professor at the Pontifical Biblical Institute, inspiring many Jews to believe in Jesus as their Messiah.[76]

Reason 87: Former Muslim, Professor Mark Gabriel

Formerly known as Mustafa, Dr. Mark Gabriel was born and raised in Egypt. By the age of 12, he was a child prodigy, having memorized the entire Quran. He later graduated from Cairo's Al-Azhar University, the most prestigious Islamic University in the world, where he taught Islamic history as a professor. He also served as an Imam, preaching at a Mosque in Giza. In short, Gabriel was a distinguished figure in Islamic society. But that was about to change.[77]

Gabriel became concerned about the truth claims of Islam when he discovered a conflict. The University's politically correct version of Islam, which focused on love and peace, conflicted with many of the violent and hateful Quranic verses Gabriel had memorized as a young boy. For instance, verse 2:62 says Jews and Christians are good people who worship one God, while verses 9:29-30 commands them to convert, pay the tax (jizya) or be killed. This unsettling discovery led Gabriel to research every interpretation of the Quran in the hope of finding a version devoid of jihad and killing. Instead, he kept finding references to these practices.[78]

This finding caused a dilemma for Gabriel: either he should continue to embrace the University's version of Islam or become an Islamic fundamentalist in accordance with the Quran. He tried to rationalize the University's sanitized version of Islam by ignoring jihadi verses, but could not. Rather, because of the Quran's discrimination of non-Muslims and women, he reasoned that Islam was built on hate not love. His research also found that Islam's entire history was filled with violence and bloodshed, making him question, "What religion would condone such destruction of human life?"[79]

After much deliberation, Gabriel concluded the Quran was not a revelation from God, and began questioning Islam with students at the University, an approach that led to his expulsion. Soon after, he was kidnapped by the Egyptian secret police, who interrogated and tortured him unmercifully for days until he was released with help from his family.

After his release, Gabriel lived for a whole year absent of any faith, until one day someone handed him a Bible. He took it home, and beginning from Matthew chapter five, he read Jesus's Sermon on the Mount. He claims, "My whole body began trembling. I had studied the Quran my whole life – not once did I find words as inspiring as this. I had come face to face with the Lord Jesus Christ."[80] Gabriel continued reading the Bible until the early hours of the morning. By dawn, he had given his heart to Jesus.

Unfortunately, when Gabriel's father learned his son had converted to Christ, he tried to kill him. Consequently, Gabriel fled the country and after much travelling, now lives in the United States where he is free to share his story and preach the gospel. Gabriel is the author of numerous acclaimed books on Islamic affairs, and advises governments on anti-terrorism policy. [81]

Reason 88: Harvard Law School Professor, Simon Greenleaf

Widely considered as one of the most brilliant minds to grace the legal profession, Simon Greenleaf was a Dane Professor of Law at Harvard Law School and contributed extensively to its development. His famous work, *A Treatise on the Law of Evidence*, is considered a classic of American jurisprudence, hailed as the standard in that branch of law since its publication in 1842.[82]

Greenleaf was an agnostic who believed Christianity was a ridiculous myth. He was never shy in making this view known to his students. In the classroom, he spoke often and overtly about his belief that the resurrection of Jesus was a legend or hoax, which only ignorant fools believed. One day however, some of his students challenged him to investigate the evidential basis for the resurrection. Greenleaf took up that challenge with the aim of exposing the resurrection as a myth. As a world-renowned expert on evidence, he was perfectly placed to deliver a deathblow to Christianity, should he prove the resurrection was false.[83]

As Greenleaf focused his brilliant mind on applying his acclaimed rules of evidence to the four gospels of Matthew, Mark, Luke and John, he surprisingly changed his mind. Also, the more he examined the historical records, the more stunned he became by the evidence for Christ's resurrection. His conclusion can be summed up as follows:[84]

1. Present day copies of the original gospels were at least as authentic as other works of antiquity, the authenticity of which was acceptable in courts of law.
2. The veracity of gospel testimonies was demonstrable by internal examination (i.e., examining consistencies and resolving paradoxes between them) and external examination (i.e., comparing gospel accounts with the works of non-Christian writers like Tacitus and Josephus).
3. It was highly unlikely the apostles would have sacrificed their lives to face an executioner's death for a lie. Certainly, no man would, let alone twelve.

Greenleaf reached the opposite conclusion than he intended: that in accordance with the rules of legal evidence, the Resurrection of Jesus Christ was fact not myth. As a result, in 1874 he wrote *An Examination of the Testimony of the Four Evangelists by the Rules of Evidence Administered in the Courts of Justice*. In this book, Greenleaf declares:

> It was therefore impossible that they [the disciples] could have persisted in affirming the truths they have narrated, had not Jesus actually rose from

the dead, and had they not known this fact as certainly as they knew any other fact.[85]

Greenleaf later gave his life to Christ and became a stalwart defender of the faith. He believed any person who honestly examines the evidence as he did, would reach the same conclusion—that Jesus indeed lives!

PART VII

The Case for Heaven and Hell

Reason 89: Neurosurgeon Experiences Heaven During Coma

Dr. Eben Alexander is an accomplished American neurosurgeon who has taught at some of the most prestigious institutions, including Harvard Medical School. As a man of science trained in western medicine, he had a naturalistic view of the universe, and any notion of an afterlife was outlandish to him. That changed in 2008 after he experienced a remarkable transcendent journey during a deep coma caused by a rare form of bacterial meningitis.[1]

Alexander's story is not an afterlife account that can be easily dismissed as hallucinogenic or a projection of some inner fantasy. During his coma, the neocortex of his brain was disabled—he had no higher brain activity associated with consciousness. This condition was evidenced by CT scans and neurological examinations carried out at the time. Although medical explanations exist for out of body experiences, like hypoxia (lack of oxygen to the brain) or the overload of neurochemicals, no such explanations apply in Alexander's case. This is because the neurons of his cortex were rendered completely inactive by the bacteria.[2]

Alexander recounts how he left his body and experienced heavenly realms during his coma. His adventure began in a place of clouds set against a backdrop of deep blue sky. Whilst there, he saw flocks of shimmering celestial winged beings whose voices chanted glorious hymns and anthems like an angelic choir. These beings were simply unlike anything he had ever seen—higher, more advanced life forms that emanated joyful perfection in what they sang. He also saw a valley below with earth-like features, including beautiful flowers, butterflies, waterfalls and people dancing.

After returning to his body, Alexander was miraculously healed and wrote about his journey in his best-selling book, *Proof of Heaven*. Because his out of body experience defies any naturalistic explanation, it confirms the existence of a heavenly afterlife beyond this physical world and that humans do indeed possess an immortal soul.[3]

Alexander's experience has enabled him to see the world with fresh eyes. Describing the first time he entered a church after his coma, he wrote:

> The colors of the stained-glass windows recalled the luminous beauty of the landscapes I'd seen in the world above…and, most important, a painting of Jesus breaking bread with his disciples evoked the message that lay at the very heart of my journey: that we are loved.[4]

He says our lives on earth are a transition, a kind of test to allow our souls to mature in love and compassion.

Reason 90: Agnostic Sees Afterlife

Despite growing up in a loving Southern Baptist family, construction worker Brian Melvin disbelieved in the Christian concept of God. Nor did he believe in any afterlife. That all changed in 1980 when he contracted cholera after drinking contaminated water on a construction site.[5]

After lying in bed at home for 72 hours in severe pain, Melvin became critically dehydrated and terminally ill. His breathing was weak and his body was limp. He recalls that he left his body with a sudden "swoosh" and began hovering above his bed. Fully realizing he had just died, he notes:

> I felt myself drift through the ceiling's textured
> drywall and was engulfed in an extremely peaceful
> blackness. In this pleasant darkness I heard the
> most astounding humming/singing sounds...
> while slowly moving toward a speck of light that
> was slowly growing bigger and bigger as I neared.[6]

As Melvin drew very close to the light, which emitted hues of colors he had never seen before, he noticed its source was a person. Melvin explains:

> This marvelous person showed me my life course,
> which revealed I was without excuse. It was then
> I knew I was being judged and deserved my fate.
> You could do nothing but stand directly before
> him, whose robe's drooping hood concealed his
> face.[7]

But after looking more closely, Melvin noticed this person had terrible trauma to his hands and feet. It was then Melvin realized it was Jesus. The Lord Jesus told Melvin that He was taking him to "see another land" so he could tell others.

When Jesus pointed towards a tunnel, Melvin recounts floating toward it with a gentle force, but after entering it, he became engulfed in a violent vortex heading down to a yellowish light. After reaching the bottom of the vortex, he fell upon the ground with a great thud. "Where was I?" he asked. It did not take long for Melvin to realize he was in hell. The horrid smells and strange sounds of that place linger long in his memory, along with the sight of ghastly demons that tormented the souls of people trapped there.[8]

While in hell, he walked along a barren expanse of land. He saw countless rows of translucent cube like chambers, each one housing a person who was unable to escape. Melvin sensed they knew their fate was just, having received the full reward of their sins on earth. Because they had rejected God—a being of absolute goodness, Melvin instinctively knew they had been rightly banished to a place without God, a place of unending anguish, doom and despair. What Melvin experienced is eerily similar to the Bible's description of hell, a place of gloomy darkness, anguish and torment.[9]

Before Melvin returned to his body, he was given a glimpse of heaven, a celestial dwelling place that God created for His children. He describes it as a place of liquid love, adorned with precious jewels and streets of translucent gold, exactly as the Bible depicts. He was told that the only way one could enter this place was through the personage of Jesus Christ. After Melvin's near death experience, he committed his life to Christ and made a full recovery.[10]

Reason 9l: Atheist Dies and Comes Alive in a Morgue

From a young age, atheist Ian McCormack had a passion for sports and the ocean. After completing his college degree at the age of 24, he set off on a two year journey to visit major surfing areas around the world. Before heading back home to New Zealand in 1982, he made a final stop on the exotic island of Mauritius. Little did he know his short visit would turn into a deadly experience that would change his life.[11]

Whilst diving for lobster one night, McCormack was stung five times on his forearm by deadly box jellyfish. Just one sting from these venomous invertebrates can cause cardiovascular collapse and death within five minutes.[12] When the ambulance finally arrived, his body was already paralyzed from the poison running through his veins. On route to the hospital, pictures of his life flashed before him. McCormack knew he was going to die.[13]

As he wondered whether life after death really existed, he saw a vision of his mother praying, beckoning him to cry out to God from his heart. But he wondered which God, for there are many. At that point he remembered that his mother was a Christian, and for the first time, he prayed from his heart and gave his life to Jesus. When he finished praying, a peace came over him. Arriving at the hospital, a medical crew rushed him into an emergency room where doctors frantically tried to save his life. But it was too late. McCormack died.[13] Immediately he found himself standing in a dark room. As he stood there, he could sense evil all around him and had the eerie feeling he was being watched. He heard screams and voices telling him, "Shut up!" "You deserve to be here!" "You're in hell." Terrified by these voices, McCormack cried out to God, "I've asked you for forgiveness, why am I here?"[14]

Suddenly, an amazing beam of pure light pierced through the darkness, lifting him off his feet. The light carried him through a large circular opening above, drawing him through a long tunnel. At the far end of the tunnel, he could see the radiant source of the light, appearing as the origin of the universe. As he drew closer to that source, waves of light, which filled and overwhelmed him with pure joy, peace and love, rippled through the tunnel.[15]

When he reached the end of the tunnel, McCormack was astonished to find a man at the center of that light source. It was Jesus. As a young boy, he had seen pictures of Jesus but none of them came close to this glorious sight. Jesus wore bright shimmering garments and His face shone with an intense radiance of holiness and beauty.

As he gazed upon Jesus, McCormack heard Him say, "Ian, do you wish to return?" He thought, "Why would I want to go back?" But after further contemplation, he realized that by going back, many would hear his story and believe. The Lord said, "If you wish to return, you must see in a new light."[16] The moment he heard those words, McCormack returned to his body and came back to life in a morgue. He has since travelled the world, sharing his remarkable story.

Reason 92: Girl Falls Thirty Feet from a Tree and Gets Healed

Diagnosed with two incurable digestive disorders at the age of five, Annabel Beam was accustomed to intense pain and frequent hospital visits. Heartbreakingly, she once told her mother, "Mama, I want to die, and go to heaven with Jesus where there is no more pain."[17] At the age of nine, her wish came true after a horrifying accident in her back yard in Texas, except that she returned from heaven to tell the tale.

In December 2011 while sitting thirty feet high on the branch of a cottonwood tree, Beam plummeted headfirst into its hollow trunk. MRI scans revealed she had hit her head three times as she came hurtling down. This evidence alone demonstrates her survival was nothing short of remarkable. However Beam says that, as she lay entombed within the hollow trunk of the tree, she died and went to heaven.[18]

At first, Beam did not quite realize where she was until she met her aunt Mimi who had died two years before. Beam describes heaven as a very bright and peaceful place where everything glows, even the grass. Perhaps the best part of all is that she got to sit on the lap of Jesus, which she says was like being suspended above the universe. She said, "His eyes shine like gold glory reflected in the sun"[19] and He has a "beautiful long white robe, dark skin and a big beard."[20] Jesus told her, "When the firefighters get you out, there will be nothing wrong with you." When Beam asked Jesus if she could stay in heaven, He replied, "No Annabel, I have plans for you on earth that you cannot fulfill in heaven."[21]

After her return from heaven, Beam found herself in the hollow base of the tree, but she eventually got help when firefighters arrived with a harness to lift her out. The complicated rescue took five hours and was made easier thanks to a guardian angel who stayed with her during the whole ordeal. She claims the angel "winked" at her as if to say "everything is going to be ok."[22]

Even more remarkable than her survival is the fact she

had suffered no major physical trauma, leaving clinicians dumbfounded. The doctor treating her said, "Jesus must have been with that little girl in that tree, because we have never had anybody fall 30 feet and not suffer paralysis or broken bones."[23] What is just as bewildering is that the MRI and CT scans indicated she had no brain injury whatsoever.[24] Another great surprise was that after the accident, Beam was miraculously cured of all incurable digestive disorders. Doctors had no explanation as to why all the symptoms of her disorders had disappeared, and they subsequently released her from their care.[25]

In response to skeptics who may question Beam's story, her father says, "All I have to go on is the radiological data and the medical records from before and after. The proof is in the pudding. She wasn't well before and now she is."[26] Her mother wrote, *Miracles from Heaven*, a book on her daughter's story. The book was adapted into a major movie in 2016.

Reason 93: Man Dies in a Plane Crash and Sees Heaven

At the age of 19, Mickey Robinson was a professional skydiver. As an athletic young man, he loved adrenalin sports, especially falling from the sky. However, shortly after his plane took off for a parachute jump in August 1968, it crash landed at 100 mph, killing one person and severely injuring others. Robinson was so badly injured that doctors gave him no chance of survival. But as he lay dying on a hospital bed in Cleveland, something dramatic happened that would define the rest of his life.[27]

Apart from knowing a few Bible stories, Robinson had never met anyone who had personally told him about God, Jesus or the supernatural. Besides, he had no interest in God. He was handsome, confident and too busy living life to the full. Yet on that fateful day in Cleveland, he found himself trapped in plane wreckage, ablaze from head to toe with aircraft fuel.[28]

After a rescuer arrived on the scene, he freed Robinson from the plane then dragged his burning body to safety, before rolling him on the ground to put out the flames. When medics arrived, he was taken to the nearest hospital, but his prognosis was poor. Robinson had suffered a head trauma, massive lacerations to his body and third degree burns. Doctors told his family to expect the worst.[29]

Wracked with pain on his hospital bed, Robinson called out to a God he never knew or served, for the first time in his life. "God, please help me. I'm sorry. Give me another chance,"[30] he cried. Then something happened. Robinson claims he left his body and entered a spiritual dimension. With no control over where he was going, he found himself gliding upwards.

While travelling, he saw a portal of white light in the distance. He says, "It was whiter than the whitest snow and brighter than ten thousand suns and yet, I could look right at it."[31] As he gazed at its brightness, he noticed a horrid blackness sweeping toward him. Sensing it was evil and devoid of life, Robinson became afraid and cried out again: "No God! I'm sorry. I want to live."[32] The moment he spoke those words, he was pulled through the white portal and found himself in the presence of Almighty God.

Standing there, Robinson recounts feeling the love of God: "It's so pure, it's so perfect, it's so incredible…we're going to have to invent new words" to describe God's love.[33] But this was not the love of just any God. Robinson intuitively knew he was sensing the love of Jesus Christ. Although Robinson wanted to stay in heaven, the Lord Jesus sent him back to share this message with the world.

Robinson has written a compelling memoir about his experience, *Falling into Heaven*. Since his heavenly experience, Robinson has been travelling the world proclaiming the love of God through Jesus Christ. His message is simple: Call upon Jesus while you can. Do not to wait until you are desperate before you get saved. You may not get that second chance.[34]

Reason 94: Man Spends 23 Minutes in Hell

On the 23rd of November 1998, real estate broker Bill Wiese had a disturbing out of body experience in hell. Although he was a Christian, he knew very little about hell, as he had never studied the subject. But at three in the morning, he says his spirit was pulled out of his body and plunged into hell where he was tormented in unimaginable ways. He claims his experience was no dream; that God wanted him to witness hell to warn others of its reality. Wiese chronicled this experience in his book *23 Minutes in Hell*.[35]

When Wiese arrived in hell, he found himself in a dark, stony-looking prison cell with bars on the doors. Unlike anything he had seen before, he noticed four horrifying demon beasts towering above him at a height of about thirteen feet. Sensing they were entirely evil, Wiese was gripped with terror as these grotesque creatures gazed at him with the same unbridled hatred they had for God. Because they could not attack God, he sensed their hatred was focused on him, a person created in the image and likeness of God.[36]

Recalling what happened next, Wiese explicates in detail how these creatures threw him onto the walls of the cell and tore ribbons of flesh from his body with their giant claws. Although he did not possess a physical body in hell, Wiese claims his five senses were intact and that he felt the pain of every assault. He also claims hell was so hot that he struggled to breathe and felt extreme thirst, but he points out that no water exists in hell, not even a drop.[37]

As the torment from these demon beasts was repeated over and over, Wiese recalls how Jesus came and took him out of the cell and placed him on the edge of a great pit of fire. He says, "I could see through the flames, just enough to see bodies, people in the fire screaming...The pain I'd endured already was bad enough, but the heat from that flame I knew was worse." He claims that hell is located in the center of the earth, and once you enter it, there is "absolutely no hope of ever getting out."[38]

Eventually, Jesus took Wiese out of hell and comforted him. After regaining his composure, he asked the Lord, "Why did you send me to this place?" Jesus answered:

> Because people do not believe that this place exists....Go tell them that I hate this place, that it's not my desire for one of my creation to go to this place, not one! I never made this for man. This was made for the devil and his angels.[39]

Wiese's out of body experience sends a clear message that resonates with the Bible: hell is real. And whilst God is not willing for any to perish there, he cannot stop us if we reject the only one who can save us from it—Jesus Christ. His experience shows when people die without Christ, they are without protection, allowing demons access to drag their souls into eternal torment. Wiese's 23 minutes in hell not only confirms the reality of hell, but serves as a clarion call to "Believe in the Lord Jesus, and you will be saved" (Acts 16:31).

Reason 95: Man Dies for Two Hours and Meets Jesus

In May 2006, Dean Braxton, a born again Christian was admitted to St Francis hospital in Washington State for routine kidney stone treatment. During his stay, he unexpectedly developed multiple organ failure, leading to a prolonged cardiac arrest. Medical records show he was dead for one hour and 45 minutes. During that time he visited heaven and met Jesus, along with other Christian family members who previously died.[40]

Braxton claims he left his body on a heaven-bound journey as doctors worked furiously to revive his heart. But just before arriving there, he encountered a "thick darkness—a blackness you have never experienced here on earth."[41] As he passed through this darkness, he knew it was filled with demons and heard the screams of people in hell. He could have looked inside the darkness, but had no desire to do so. Knowing that God is not willing for anyone to perish in hell, Braxton feels sadness when reflecting on this part of his journey.

When he arrived in heaven, Braxton's first perception was how extremely bright and peaceful it was. Looking around, he observed a beautiful landscape of vibrant colors, grass and flowers. He claims that everything in heaven, including the very atmosphere, beamed with a glow of intelligence and life. He also says heaven is a place of eternal perfection where everything is right and claims he did not want to leave, especially after meeting Jesus.[42]

When Braxton saw Jesus, who appeared "brighter than the noon day sun,"[43] he fell on his knees and thanked Him repeatedly. But when he asked Jesus to let him stay, He answered, "No, it is not your time. Go back."[44] Upon hearing this, Braxton cried. But as Jesus looked into his eyes, Braxton received new understanding. He states, "The same way a computer receives information…he [Jesus] downloaded all kinds of information into me."[45] With these new insights, he realized his work on earth was not complete. His work is the same work every other Christian is called to do: tell others that God loves them and has reserved a place for them in heaven.

After he returned to his body on earth, Braxton's recovery was marked by an amazing miracle. Although Braxton had been dead for nearly two hours, his doctor, Manuel Iregui, confirmed he had no brain damage: "It's a miracle that he's alive," his doctor said. "It is a miracle that he is talking with no brain damage. But this is very exceptional, because he was really, really dead for a long time."[46] Just as amazing is that after thirteen days, Braxton walked out of the hospital healed from twenty-nine serious medical complications.

For people who find this story difficult to accept, Braxton says,

"If you do not believe me, that is ok. The most important thing is that you go to heaven. When you get there, you will see."[47]

Reason 96: Doctor Has a Heart Attack and Visits Heaven

Whilst present at home on March 24, 1979, Dr. Gerry Landry felt a crushing, nauseating pain in his chest. He was having a myocardial infarction (heart attack). This is something he had seen in others many times before as a physician at the University of Texas Health Center. He quickly alerted his wife, and as Christians, they both began praying to Jesus. When they had finished, a great peace came over them both, as if to say that everything was going to be alright.[48] Despite this peace, his symptoms grew worse. At this point, his wife called an ambulance and contacted various friends to pray. What happened next would remain forever etched in Landry's memory.[49]

"All I remember during the ride to the hospital was calling out the name of Jesus, over and over again,"[50] Landry recalls. After Landry arrived at the same emergency room where he had treated many others, the doctor in charge showed Landry his electrocardiogram. His inferior coronary artery was "knocked out." Despite feeling a cold clamminess in his hands—a warning sign that his veins were collapsing, he says, "The sweet peace of Jesus had stayed with me."[51] With his wife praying by his side, Landry's heart stopped beating.

At that moment, the peace he had previously felt now "engulfed" him, separating his spirit from his body. Suddenly, he found himself "in a place of dazzling beauty," surrounded by a multitude of radiantly beautiful people. Standing on a translucent sea of color, he noticed that each person wore a leafy crown and a pure white robe. Feeling an overwhelming sense of belonging, he thought, "This is more real than earth itself. I'm in paradise."[52]

Landry discovered that no words, only thoughts, were needed to communicate with others in heaven. People were also able to intuitively communicate their feelings, which focused on the "rapturous adoration of God and the inexpressible joy felt at welcoming yet another entrant into heaven."[53] As Landry looked around, he recognized some of his late relatives—a comforting thought for those who have lost loved ones.

Suddenly, he saw a shaft of light pierce the heavenly crowd. At the center of that light was Jesus on the cross. At first, Landry felt it strange that Christ would appear crucified when he had indeed risen. But later realized the cross is forever remembered in heaven because of its saving message. Glancing at Landry with eyes full of compassion, Jesus said, "Gerry, peace be with you." Landry thought, "Out of the billions he created, he knows me by name." Jesus continued, "Gerry, you are healed. You will have no more pain, no anxiety, no shame, and no guilt. You will be home in one week."[54]

As Jesus predicted, Landry recovered from his heart attack and was back home within a week. He later went on to obey what Christ told him in heaven: "I want you to go back and tell everyone about my love."[55] After this experience, Landry wrote, "I can tell you with certainty that death holds no terror for those who have been saved by the blood of Jesus. At the moment of death we will emerge from this body, much as a butterfly from a cocoon, to soar into the presence of our Creator."[56]

Reason 97: Man Visits Heaven after Horrific Car Crash

On 23 December 1966, Gary Wood was driving home with his younger sister, when she suddenly let out a bloodcurdling scream that pierced the night sky. She had spotted an illegally parked ten-ton truck protruding into their lane on the highway. It was too late. With no time to slow down, Wood crashed head on into the truck, suffering massive head injuries. After paramedics arrived at the scene, he was pronounced dead.[57] Recalling the fatal accident, Wood says:

> Dying is just like taking your clothes off. I stepped
> out of my body and was lifted above the top of my
> car. My whole life passed before my eyes and in
> an instant, I was caught up in a swirling massive
> funnel shaped cloud that grew wider. Angels took
> me underneath their wings.[58]

After a light engulfed him, he began walking along a pathway and heard angels sing, "Worthy is the lamb who was slain before the foundation of the world."[59] In the distance, he saw a heavenly city with twelve foundations made from different precious stones inscribed with the names of the apostles. He also noticed twelve large gates, each made from a giant pearl. As he moved closer to this heavenly city, standing in front of one of the gates was a giant angel with gold spun hair, holding a sword. Wood was told he had access to the city only because he had accepted Jesus Christ as his personal Lord and savior.[60]

Upon entering the city, he was greeted by his best friend, who a few years before, had also been killed in a car accident. After they both hugged and talked for a while, his friend took him on a tour, which included a visit to a giant library where he saw countless books. These books contained prayer requests and chronicles of those who had lived for Jesus and how they had led others to Christ. Wood claims the most exciting book of all was the *Lamb's Book of Life*, which had the names of all those who were saved. When Wood began reading this book, he noticed his name with the writing, "Paid in full by the blood of Jesus."[61]

Whilst Wood was enjoying his heavenly tour, Wood's friend told him that he had to return because his sister was frantically crying out to Jesus to revive him from the dead. Although Wood came back to life after 62 minutes, his injuries were severe. Part of his nose was torn off, his teeth were knocked out, his jaw was broken, his vocal chords were severed, and his larynx was crushed, preventing him from speaking. Despite these multiple injuries,

Wood claims that while he lay on his hospital bed, Jesus walked into his room, laid hands on him and healed him.[62]

Wood insists the Lord Jesus sent him back with the assignment of telling others that heaven is real. He also sent him to exhort the body of Christ to never accept condemnation from the devil, because Christians are redeemed and made worthy by the blood of Jesus. [63]

Reason 98: Medical Professor Sees Heaven and Hell

As a practicing Christian, Professor Richard Eby was a respected and nationally recognized gynecologist and osteopath. Among his many credits are that, in 1943 he co-founded the former Park Avenue hospital in Pomona, California, and in 1961, he became the president of the Osteopathic Physicians and Surgeons of California. In 1972, Eby had a dramatic near death experience when he landed on his head after accidentally falling three stories from an apartment building. Eby claims as soon as his head hit the sidewalk, he instantly appeared in heaven where he met Jesus.[64]

In his book, *Caught up into Paradise*, Eby gives a detailed account of heaven, describing it as a luminescent realm with ineffable music, beauty and exotic scents. He says it is a place of absolute perfection, full of light; saturated with love and peace. Recalling the occasion when he ran through a colorful valley of exquisite flowers and trees, Eby says he heard the music of heaven. It was a sound with no similarity on earth. Since he had a musical background, Eby was able to appreciate this music, claiming it had an unlimited frequency range.[65]

As a physician, Eby was also fascinated with his spiritual body. He describes it as translucent in color, similar in size and shape to his earthly body but with no bones, ligaments, tissues or organs. Because his body was weightless, he could move around wherever he wished, even without touching the ground. His mind also operated differently, since he could communicate with others by mere thoughts, not words.[66]

Eby claims he saw Jesus in all His glory, floating in a glowing cloud above him, and notes one of the longest conversations with Jesus ever recorded in a near death experience. Jesus told him, "These are the last days before I return for my body of believers. I am coming for them soon."[67] Eby felt overwhelmed by Jesus's presence and wanted to stay with Him in heaven. But while engulfed in the light of His glory, everything suddenly went dark. That was the moment he returned to his body on earth.

After Eby fully recovered from his injuries, he toured Israel in 1977 and visited Lazarus's Tomb in Bethany. While in the depths of the tomb, he states that Jesus appeared to him again, this time to reveal hell. Eby notes how he found himself in the center of the earth, and for two minutes, endured unimaginable horrors. To gain some understanding of hell, Eby contends, "If you have an imagination of what real terror is, multiply it by a billion."[68]

After Jesus took Eby out of hell, He gave Eby the following mission: "You must be able to tell them. They can choose between heaven or hell, but tell them that I died to close hell and open heaven just for them."[69] Before he finally died in 2002, Eby shared his experiences of heaven and hell, telling people far and wide that Jesus is coming soon.

Reason 99: Preacher goes to Heaven and Gets a Wake-up Call

On 3 August 1979, Howard Pittman, a Baptist minister for 35 years, died during a hospital operation from severe blood loss after a main artery ruptured. But knowing before the operation that he might not survive, he pleaded with God to extend his physical life on earth.[70]

The moment he died, Pittman recounts how angels lifted his spirit from his body and carried him to heaven. On the way there, the angels showed him a hierarchy of different demons too hideous to imagine, inhabiting and controlling the earth. In the lower hierarchy, demons resembled animals, but the higher ones resembled humans, except they were eight feet tall. He claims the chief demon in this group was greed, followed by hate, lust and strife. In the lower hierarchy, he noticed demons of fear, self-destruction and murder, as well as those skilled in the art of witchcraft.[71]

After Pittman had seen enough of these demons, he was finally brought to the gates of heaven. As he watched many people entering heaven, he noticed that angels only permitted people to enter one at a time. While pondering on this arrangement, he realized the angels were saluting each individual in honor of using his or her sovereign free will in choosing Christ.[72]

As Pittman stood at heaven's gates, one angel told him to present his case before God to extend his life on earth. When he finally mustered enough courage to speak, Pittman reminded God of all his good works on earth, stating he had lived a faithful life of love, sacrifice and worship. The moment he finished stating his case, God spoke. Pittman claims the sound of God's audible voice knocked him off his feet. Lying face down, he was confronted by a holy God. He was told that his works were unacceptable, his faith was dead, and it was an abomination to live the way he did and call it a life of worship.[73]

Pittman was stunned by God's rebuke, and quickly realized that his good works were done for himself, to soothe his own guilty conscience. Instead of serving others from a motive of love, his deeds served his own sense of religious piety. He knew he had fallen short of God's righteousness. As he reflected on God's indignation, Pittman found himself back in the hospital room. "No! God did not answer me," he cried. "He did not say yes or no to my request! Please, take me back,"[74] he asked the angels"

The angels obeyed Pittman and carried him back to heaven. This time, he pleaded God to forgive him of his sins and quoted

Hezekiah from the Bible who repented and pleaded with God to extend his life. In that moment, he felt God's awesome love engulf him, not as a distant deity, but as a heavenly Father. Instead of anger, this time God's voice expressed tenderness and mercy, the likes of which he had never experienced before. Now that the prodigal son had returned to his Father, God allowed Pittman to return to his body to share his story.[75]

Reason 100: Saved by a Mother's Prayers

The life and death story of former boxer and pastor, Curtis Kelley, is one of the most dramatic you will ever read. Even before he was born, death stalked him when his Haitian father, a practitioner of voodoo, forced his mother to attempt an abortion. Having been inducted into the occult from a young age, Kelley learned many forms of witchcraft, including how to cast spells and summon evil spirits to torment people. Despite his involvement in the dark arts, he had a praying mother who pleaded with God everyday for the salvation of his soul.[76]

Growing up, Kelley was also exposed to a plethora of drugs. At the age of six he began smoking marijuana, and by the age of ten, he was sniffing cocaine. After overdosing on drugs at the age of fifteen, Kelley claims he died and went to hell, describing it as a dark reddish pit, full of every foul imaginable thing. As he was being tormented by hellish demons, he says two hands lifted him out, after he heard a voice say, "Because of your mother's prayers and because you were chosen to do a work for us, you were saved."[77]

Soon after his experience of hell, Kelley gave his life to Jesus at a revival meeting in 1971, and from 1986 began boxing as a heavyweight professional. During his boxing career, he started a ministry to help drug addicts, and in 1991 became a pastor of a local church in California. Sadly, in 1998 while he was happily married as a pastor with three sons, tragedy struck. His son Scott was shot and instantly killed in a random carjacking. Although he was filled with grief, this tragedy did not stop Kelley from ministering to the needy, a promise he made to his son before he died.[78]

In 2004, tragedy struck again when he suffered a brain aneurysm and died. Kelley claims he was lifted out of his body and transported to a lush green garden in heaven. He says the lawn was manicured better than any golf course, with a jewel embedded in each blade of grass. As he gazed at his surroundings, he saw a large gold building glistening in the distance. From this building flowed a liquid diamond river that moved with the sound of heavenly music.[79]

To his astonishment, standing on the other side of this river was his son Scott. Overwhelmed with joy, Kelley attempted to cross the river to hug him. "Dad, remember when you made me that promise,"[80] Scott cried. Kelley remembered his promise and was told that if he stepped over to the other side, he could never return to finish his earthly ministry.

As Kelley backed away from the river, he noticed a group of children happily playing in the distance. When he asked God about them, he was told they were children who had died from wars, accidents and sickness. After observing another group of children, he asked the same question. In a tearful voice, God replied, "That group are children who were aborted and sent back to me."[81] When Kelley's heavenly experience ended, he returned to his body to continue his ministry. A full account of his story is given in his book *Bound to Lose Destined to Win*.

Reason 101: Doctor Turns to Christ After
Near Death Experience

As well as practicing medicine in Oklahoma and Texas, Dr. Donald Whitaker was a pioneer in nutritional medicine who developed his own brand of nutritional supplements.[82] Yet, he was not always conscious of natural health, as he led a wild lifestyle of drink and drugs until his early forties. As a self-confessed "hard core atheist," he never believed in God, a virgin birth or a resurrection. He was a physician who relied solely upon research science, until a near death experience on a hospital bed.[83]

Whitaker's reveling and alcohol abuse finally caught up with him in February 1975, when he was admitted to Wadley Hospital in Texarkana with acute hemorrhagic necrotic pancreatitis. His prognosis was poor. Even after a long operation, Doctors told his family he would be dead by the morning.[84]

Whilst dying on his bed, Whitaker found it very difficult to remain an atheist because of various "what if" questions that plagued his mind. He thought, "What if I was wrong?" "What if God exists?" Suddenly he began thinking of a man by the name of Ron Short, a person who had spoken to him about the love of Jesus for five years before he became ill. Although he had debated Ron many times about his faith, Whitaker respected him. He respected Ron because he was a man of integrity. He practiced what he preached; he did what he said he was going to do.[85]

Knowing he was going to die, Whitaker thought, "What if Ron is right?" "What if there is a heaven and a hell?" Immediately, the most pressing question on his mind was, "How do I get saved?" Although he did not know the answer to this question, he knew Ron did. He needed what Ron had. That same night, he telephoned Ron but discovered he was out of town. After leaving an urgent message asking Ron to come quickly to the hospital, Whitaker lay on his bed waiting for a response.[86]

Looking back on that night, Whitaker comments, "That night was the longest night that I've ever had in my entire life." Whitaker's life faded with every passing minute, and on several occasions he felt himself slipping out of his body. Each time he did, Whitaker says he travelled down into an intense darkness that was so tangible, it penetrated the fabric of his soul, gripping him with untold terror. He fought for his life, knowing that if his soul slipped all the way down into that hellish blackness, he would never return.[87]

The longer he waited for Ron, the more he felt a bone-chilling coldness spread from his lower extremities to his upper body. Death was creeping up on him like a deadly viper, ready to pounce on its prey. Somehow, by a mere thread, Whitaker managed to cling onto dear life till the morning.[88]

Finally, he felt a sense of relief when Ron arrived at about ten in the morning. Ron rushed to Whitaker's bedside and asked, "Doc, what did the doctors say your chances are?" "I have none," Whitaker answered. "Now is the time," Ron told him. "You're right" Whitaker remarked, "I may have cursed Him, spit at Him, but now is the time to accept Jesus."[89]

Ron explained to Whitaker how Jesus died for his sins and quoted scriptures from the Bible. When he finished, Ron took Whitaker by the hand and led him through a sinner's prayer. Although Whitaker had no idea what a sinner's prayer was, he trusted Ron. Recounting the moment they finished praying, Whitaker says, "A peace came over me like I had never known. I had searched for that peace in bottles, alcohol, needles, drugs, women and all types of places. But once I accepted Jesus Christ as my Lord and savior, I was no longer afraid."[90]

Ron also showed Whitaker the scripture, "And these signs shall follow them that believe…they shall lay hands on the sick, and they shall recover" (Mark 16:17-18). In simple obedience to God's word, Ron laid hands on Whitaker and he was healed.[91] Years later, Whitaker testified:

> I walk around on planet earth today, taking no insulin, taking no enzymes, eating whatsoever I desire, and God produces in my body every day the correct material for me to function without taking medication…It doesn't take a rocket scientist to figure out the Bible is true.[92]

Whitaker went on to share his faith around the world for more than thirty years and had his own successful television program entitled, *Calling Dr. Whitaker*. At the age of 75 on August 10, 2007, Whitaker's body was laid to rest and his soul finally went to be with the Lord.[93]

CONCLUSION

In this book, 101 valid reasons were given to believe in God. Not only do they warrant the existence of God, but they also form a comprehensive case for Christianity. The author cited a broad range of evidence (i.e., cosmological, biological, paleontological, historical and empirical). Yet, his approach was not to arrive at an irrefutable conclusion, but a highly probabilistic one based on confirmation theory. The overall conclusion is that faith in God is entirely reasonable, and Christianity is a valid belief.

In the first part of this book, philosophical reasons were presented for the existence of God. These reasons demonstrate that belief in God is neither irrational nor unjustifiable, but defensible. They also show that theism is a more plausible explanation than atheism for the existence of metaphysical realities like objective morals, consciousness and our desire for beauty.

What adds even more support for God's existence is the case for creation and intelligent design in part two. Cosmological, biological and paleontological findings over the last 60 years were cited, along with assessments from credible scientists, many of whom are Nobel laureates. These findings refute the notion of a strictly material and meaningless universe in which life originated by purposeless chance. Instead, the evidence points to the necessary existence of a transcendent, maximally great Being who intelligently designed the universe and all living organisms. This outcome not only supports the existence of the Judeo-Christian God, but also the Genesis account of the Bible.

In essence, the combined reasons of parts one and two provide a cogent case for God's existence. One unfortunate feature of Christian apologetics has been the tendency to treat each argument for God's existence in isolation. However, the author's approach in this book has been to present overlapping arguments to form a coherent case.

In part three, the Biblical and extra-Biblical evidence presented provides a compelling case for the existence, crucifixion and resurrection of Jesus. Arguments for His uniqueness, historical impact, virtuosity, miracles and deity, set Jesus apart from any other figure in human history. Yet, the greatest confirmation of who Jesus claimed to be is His own resurrection. On this subject, nearly all historical scholars agree on four facts; 1) Jesus died by crucifixion, 2) the disciples saw Jesus after His resurrection, 3) James, the skeptical brother of Jesus became a believer, and 4) Paul, the persecutor of the church, became a preacher of the resurrection. On this basis, one can reasonably conclude that Jesus actually rose from the dead, and by doing so validated Himself as the Son of God.

Another impressive argument for the deity of Jesus is His fulfillment of hundreds of detailed Messianic prophecies. Since it would be impossible for one man to fulfill all these prophecies by chance, the only plausible explanation is that Jesus fulfilled them by divine agency, confirming His identity as the Jewish Messiah and savior of the world.

In part four, Christianity was compared with all other major religions. One implication of this analysis is that vast theological differences exist among religions. While similarities are superficial, their differences are fundamental, enough to categorically state that all religions do not lead to the same God.

Christianity is often singled out for making exclusive truth claims. Yet, every major religion makes exclusive truth claims. Take for example Hinduism and Buddhism. These are often espoused as the most tolerant and inclusive religions. But that is not true. Hindus and Buddhists have two uncompromising doctrines— karma and reincarnation—that will never be surrendered because they are fundamental to their beliefs. If you do not believe this, try persuading a Hindu or Buddhist otherwise. Islam and Judaism are other religions that make exclusive claims about God. A Muslim or a Jew will never tell you that all religions are true, or that it does not matter what you believe. This predicament begs the question: How can we determine which religion is true? An indication of which religion is true is how it answers life's most important questions on 1) origin, 2) meaning, 3) morality, and 4) destiny.

A religion is not based on a single argument, but on a series of interrelated arguments that overlap to form a worldview. But for a worldview to be valid, its answers must fulfill two evaluative criteria. First, they must correspond with truth through empirical testing or logical reasoning. Second, its answers must create a coherent whole. Among all the major religions examined in this book, only the Christian worldview answers life's most important questions with corresponding truthfulness and the coherence of a worldview.

In part five, common questions from critics of Christianity were answered. These answers not only redress common objections toward Christianity, but also give Christians theologically sound answers to defend it. These answers may not satisfy everyone, nor do they answer every possible question. But when combined with arguments given elsewhere in this book, this information should go a long way in directing people toward Christ.

The Christian faith is not merely a destination, but a journey. The excitement of that journey involves having one's mind illuminated with each step of faith. Anselm of Canterbury's maxim describes this point well: "I believe that I may understand."[1] As we trust in Christ, our understanding of truth deepens, allowing us to enjoy a relationship with God that abounds with ever increasing freedom and confidence. As Jesus said, "If you hold to my teaching, you are really my disciples. Then you will know the truth, and the truth will set you free" (John 8:31-32).

In part six, the stories of prominent people who found Christ richly illustrate the power of the gospel to change and transform lives. The experiences of how these individuals came to faith adds veracity to the claims of Christianity, especially when one considers that some of these individuals had no earlier socialization of Christian beliefs. What adds further credibility to their testimonies is that they were all intellectual stalwarts, many of whom made an incredible impact on their chosen fields; e.g., philosophy, science, mathematics, astronomy and English literature. Their acceptance of Christ as the Son of God invokes the argument: They would only have believed if the claims of Christ were true.

In the seventh and final part of this book, empirical accounts of near death experiences were given from Christians and non-Christians alike. What they have in common are real experiences of the afterlife, which match Biblical descriptions of heaven and hell. If their stories are true, and their experiences actual, the implication is of eternal importance, meaning, each of us will one day face an eternity in heaven or hell, depending on our acceptance of Christ in this life. As C.S. Lewis noted, "Christianity is a statement which, if false, is of no importance, and if true, of infinite importance."[2]

Another point to mention is that most of these near death accounts include post-resurrection experiences of Jesus, seen as the source of a very great light. These encounters hold similarities with the experience of the apostle John, as recorded in Revelations 1:10-16: "On the Lord's Day I was in the Spirit, and I heard behind me a loud voice...I turned around to see the voice that was speaking to me...The hair on His head was white like wool, as white as snow, and His eyes were like blazing fire. His face was like the sun shining in all its brilliance."

In closing, I urge readers to weigh up all the arguments presented. The more arguments are taken as reasonable, the more plausible theism becomes. The crucial issue is whether the balance of all the arguments herein favors the truth claims of Christianity. If they do, we ought to act.

The highest duty and most essential behavior of all humanity is to worship God. This is our supreme responsibility, and relates to the greatest commandment that God gave Moses: "Love the LORD your God with all your heart and with all your soul and with all your strength" (Deuteronomy 6:5). My purpose in writing this book has been to give you good reasons to believe in the one true God, and to worship Him alone. By doing so, you not only fulfill your highest duty, but also avoid breaking the commandment: "You shall have no other gods before me" (Exodus 20:3).

Is it right for a child to call a stranger "father?" How would you feel if your own child, whom you procreated and profoundly loved, never acknowledged you as his or her parent? So it is with our heavenly Father. He loves you with an everlasting love. He longs to fill you with a peace so full and so divine, so you can live in the acknowledgment: "I am His and He is mine." As St Augustine said, "You made us for yourself O Lord, and our hearts are restless until they can find rest in you." [3]

I pray that everyone examining the reasons herein would reach the same conclusion as Harvard Professor Simon Greenleaf: that Jesus lives. And by believing in Him, you may have life in His name. If you reached this conclusion while reading this book, another step awaits you. The Bible says, "If you declare with your mouth, 'Jesus is Lord,' and believe in your heart that God raised Him from the dead, you will be saved" (Romans 10:9). To be saved, it is not good enough to merely believe. We must also confess. If you are ready to make a confession of faith in Jesus Christ, find a quiet place and declare the following prayer out loud with your mouth:

> Lord Jesus, I come to you now. I repent of all my sins and ask your forgiveness. I believe in my heart that God raised you from the dead, and I confess with my mouth you are the Son of the God and Lord of all. Wash me from my sins by your blood, and make me a new creation. I choose to serve you

for the rest of my life. Thank Jesus you for saving
me, and for giving me everlasting life. Amen.

If you confessed this prayer, I would like to welcome you
into the family of God. You will never be the same again. It is
important to tell someone that you are now a Christian, and to
find a faith community where you can grow in the grace and the
knowledge of the Lord Jesus Christ. However, if you have yet to
confess the prayer above, please take the time to revisit the 101
reasons given in this book. You could also explore the books listed
in the further reading section.

Whatever the outcome, my sincere hope is that you find the
truth, not truth that is relative to the culture of our times, but
objective and eternal truth, for it is this truth that will ultimately
lead you to Christ. As Arthur Holmes eloquently noted, "All truth
is God's truth."[4]

NOTES

Introduction

1 John Worrall, "Does Science Discredit Religion," in *Contemporary Debates in Philosophy of Religion*, ed. Michael L. Peterson and Raymond J. VanArragon (Oxford: Blackwell, 2004), 60.

2 James Hannam, *God's Philosophers: How the Medieval World Laid the Foundations of Modern Science* (London: Icon Books, 2009).

3 Ibid.

4 Melissa Cain Travis, "Three-part Harmony: The Remarkable Relationship Between Mind, Matter, and Mathematics," *Science and Faith by Houston Baptist University*, March 28, 2017, https://www.hbu.edu/news-and-events/2017/03/28/three-part-harmony-remarkable-relationship-mind-matter-mathematics/.

5 Thomas Martin, *Character of Lord Bacon: His Life and Works* (London: Maxwell, 1835), 600.

6 Richard Lewontin, "Billions and Billions of Demons," review of *The Demon-Haunted World*, by Carl Sagan, *New York Review of Books*, January 9, 1997, http://www.nybooks.com/articles/1997/01/09/billions-and-billions-of-demons/.

7 Richard Dawkins, review of *Blueprint: Solving the Mystery of Evolution*, by Maitland Edey and Donald Johanson, *New York Times*, April 9, 1989.

8 Paul R. Myrant, *The Challenge of Evolution*, (Oklahoma City: Tate Publishing, 2009), 37.

9 John Lennox, "The Battle is Not Between God and Science," *Christianity Today*, July, 25, 2013, http://www.christiantoday.com/article/john.lennox.the.battle.is.not.between.god.and.science/33364.htm.

10 C.S. Lewis, *God in the Dock* (Grand Rapids, MI: William B. Eerdmans Publishing, 1970), 187.

Part One

1 William L. Craig, "Does God Exist: William Lane Craig vs. Dr. Michael Tooley," *Reasonable Faith*, November 2004, http://www.reasonablefaith.org/does-god-exist-the-craig-tooley-debate#section_3.

2   Francis Beckwith and Gregory Koukl, *Relativism: Feet Firmly Planted in Mid-Air* (Grand Rapids, MI: Baker Books, 1998), 59.

3   J. L. Mackie, *The Miracle of Theism* (Oxford: The Clarendon Press, 1982), 115-116.

4   Charles Darwin, *The Descent of Man: Volume 1* (New York: Appleton, 1871), 34.

5   George Gaylord Simpson, *The Meaning of Evolution* (New York: Mentor, 1951), 179.

6   Richard Dawkins, *River Out of Eden: A Darwinian View of Life* (New York: Basic Books, 1995), 131-132.

7   J. P. Moreland, "Intelligent Design Psychology and Evolutionary Psychology on Consciousness," *Journal of Psychology and Theology* 30, no. 1 (2002): 51-67.

8   Anthony O'Hear, *Beyond Evolution: Human Nature and the Limits of Evolutionary Explanation* (New York: Oxford University Press, 1997).

9   Gerald M. Edelman, *Bright Air, Brilliant Fire: On the Matter of the Mind* (London: Penguin Books, 1992).

10   Phil Johnson and Joanne Duberley, *Understanding Management Research* (London: Sage Publications, 2000).

11   J. P. Moreland, *The Soul: How We Know It's Real and Why It Matters* (Chicago: Moody Publishers, 2014).

12   Renee Descartes, *Discourse on the Method of Rightly Conducting the Reason and Seeking Truth in the Sciences* (Project Gutenberg EBook, 2008), 159, accessed July 30, 2015, http://www.gutenberg.org/files/59/59-h/59-h.htm.

13   Johnson and Duberley, *Understanding Management Research*.

14   John C. Eccles and Daniel N. Robinson, *The Wonder of Being Human: Our Brain and Our Mind* (New York: The Free Press, 1984), 17.

15   Jerry A. Fodor, "The Big Idea: Can There be a Science of Mind?," *Times Literary Supplement*, July 3, 1992, 5.

16   Donald C. Johanson and Blake Edgar, *From Lucy to Language* (New York: Nevraumont, 1996), 107.

17   Steven Pinker, "Will the Mind Figure Out How the Brain Works?" *Time Magazine*, April 4, 2000, accessed August 1, 2015, http://stevenpinker.com/files/pinker/files/will_the_mind.pdf.

18   Daniel C. Dennett, *Consciousness Explained* (London: Penguin Books, 1993).

19   Oliver Burkeman, "Why Can't the Worlds Greatest Minds Solve the Mystery of Consciousness?" *The Guardian*, January 21, 2015, http://

www.theguardian.com/science/2015/jan/21/-sp-why-cant-worlds-greatest-minds-solve-mystery-consciousness.

20 Stephen J. Gould, Challenges to Neo-Darwinism and Their Meaning for a Revised View of Human Consciousness. *The Tanner Lectures on Human Values, delivered at Cambridge University*, April 30 and May 1, 1984, 64, http://tannerlectures.utah.edu/ documents/a-to-z/g/gould85.pdf.

21 Karl R. Popper and John C. Eccles, *The Self and Its Brain* (Berlin: Springer-Verlag, 1977), 129.

22 Yiannis Gabriel, *Organizations in Depth: The Psychoanalysis of Organizations* (London: Sage Publications, 1999).

23 Ibid.

24 Charles Darwin, *The Descent of Man.*

25 Sigmund Freud, *Group Psychology and the Analysis of the Ego* (New York: WW Norton & Company, 1975).

26 Michael Jacobs, *Sigmund Freud* (London: Sage Publications, 2003), 124.

27 Marjorie Rosenberg, "The Mindless Self: Freud Triumphant," *First Things*, accessed August 3, 2015, http://www.firstthings.com/article/1991/12/002-the-mindless-self-freud-triumphant.

28 Robert M. Kadar, "Evolution and Morality: The Biology and Philosophy of Human Conscience," *The Evolution Institute*, June 25, 2012, https://evolution-institute.org/article/evolution-and-morality-the-biology-and-philosophy-of-human-conscience/.

29 Fiona Macrae, "Have Scientists Found the Conscience? Region of Brain Discovered That Makes You Feel Bad About Poor Choices," *Mail Online*, January 29, 2014, http://www.dailymail.co.uk/sciencetech/article-2547942/The-brain-bad-decision-detector-Scientists-discover-region-prevents-humans-making-mistake-twice.html.

30 Alvin Plantinga, *The Nature of Necessity* (Oxford: Oxford University Press, 1974).

31 Richard Dawkins, *The God Delusion* (New York: Mariner Books, 2008), 72.

32 "Platonism in Metaphysics," *Stanford Encyclopaedia of Philosophy*, last modified March 9, 2016, http://plato.stanford.edu/entries/platonism/.

33 Craig, "Does God Exist: William Lane Craig vs. Dr. Michael Tooley."

34 Alvin Plantinga, "Two Dozen (or So) Theistic Arguments," (paper presented at the 33rd Annual Philosophy Conference, Wheaton College, Illinois, October 23-25, 1986, 4) https://www.calvin.edu/

academic/philosophy/virtual_library/articles/plantinga_alvin/two_dozen_or_so_theistic_arguments.pdf.

35 Paul M. Gould, *Beyond the Control of God?* (London: Bloomsbury Publishing, 2014).

36 Craig, "Does God Exist: William Lane Craig vs. Dr. Michael Tooley."

37 Hilary Putnam, *Philosophy Papers: Volume 1, Mathematics, Matter and Method* (Cambridge: Cambridge University Press, 1979), 323-357; Willard V. O. Quine, *From a Logical Point of View: Nine Logico-philosophical Essays* (Cambridge: Harvard University Press, 1980).

38 Gould, *Beyond The Control of God?*

39 Arthur C. Danto, "Naturalism" in *The Encyclopaedia of Philosophy*, ed. Paul Edwards, (New York: Macmillan, 1972); Alan Lacey, "Naturalism" in *The Oxford Companion to Philosophy*, ed. Ted Honderich (Oxford: Oxford University Press, 1995).

40 Feng Ye, "Naturalism and Abstract Entities," *International Studies in the Philosophy of Science* 24, no. 2 (2010):129-146.

41 John P. Burgess, "Why I Am Not α Nominalist," *Notre Dame Journal of Formal Logic* 24, no. 1 (1983): 93-105; Paul Forster, *Peirce and the Threat of Nominalism* (Cambridge: Cambridge University Press, 2011).

42 E. M. Curley, "Descartes on the Creation of the Eternal Truths," *The Philosophical Review* 93, 4 (1984): 569-597.

43 Descartes, *Discourse on the Method of Rightly Conducting the Reason and Seeking Truth in the Sciences*, 159.

44 G. K. Chesterton, *The Everlasting Man* (New York: Dover Publications, 2007), 99.

45 Johnson and Duberley, *Understanding Management Research.*

46 Arthur F. Holmes, *All Truth is God's Truth* (Cambridge: Williams B. Eerdmans Publishing, 1977).

47 Peter Kreeft and Ronald K. Tacelli, *Handbook of Christian Apologetics* (Illinois: IntraVarsity Press, 1994).

48 Bertrand Russell, *The Autobiography of Bertrand Russell* (Oxon: Routledge, 2000), 303.

49 Steve Antinoff, *Spiritual Atheism* (Berkeley: Group West, 2009), 38.

50 Blaise Pascal, *Pensees* (London: Penguin Books, 1966), 45.

51 Clive Staples Lewis, *Mere Christianity* (London: Harper Collins, 2012), 136-137.

52 Clive Staples Lewis, *The Weight of Glory* (London: William Collins, 1949), 42.

53 Alan Lacey, "Naturalism"; Clive Staples Lewis, *Miracles: A Preliminary Study* (London: Harper Collins, 1947); Mackie, *The Miracle of Theism*; Pinker, "Will the Mind Figure Out How the Brain Works?"

54 Denis Dutton, "Aesthetics and Evolutionary Psychology" in *The Oxford Handbook for Aesthetics* ed. Jerrold Levinson (New York: Oxford University Press, 2003).

55 Richard Swinburne, *The Existence of God* (Oxford: Oxford University Press, 2004).

56 O'Hear, *Beyond Evolution: Human Nature and the Limits of Evolutionary Explanation*, 214.

57 F. R. Tennant, *Philosophical Theology Vol. I* (London: Cambridge University Press, 1956), 93.

58 Lewis, *Miracles*, 1947.

59 J. B. S. Haldane, *Possible Worlds* (New Jersey: Transaction Publishers, 2002), 209.

60 Charles Darwin, "Letter to William Graham, July 3, 1881," in *The Life and Letters of Charles Darwin Including an Autobiographical Chapter*, ed. Francis Darwin (London: John Murray, 1887), 315-316.

61 Clive Staples Lewis, *The Case for Christianity* (Los Angeles: Green Light, 2000), 32.

62 David Hume, *Philosophical Essays Concerning Human Understanding* (London: A. Millar, 1748), 180.

63 Lewis, *Miracles*, 162.

64 Johnson and Duberley, *Understanding Management Research.*

65 Hume, *Philosophical Essays Concerning Human Understanding.*

66 Ali Herbert, "Interview with Alister McGrath," *Zacharias Trust*, November 20, 2013, http://www.rzim.eu/interview-with-alister-mcgrath-2.

67 Lewis, *Miracles*, 5.

68 Ali Herbert, "Interview with Alister McGrath."

69 Richard Swinburne, *The Existence of God.*

70 Sigmund Freud, *The Future of an Illusion* (London: Penguin Books, 2008).

71 Ian Sample, "Stephen Hawking: "There is No Heaven; It's a Fairy Story," *The Guardian*, May 15, 2011, https://www.theguardian.com/science/2011/may/15/stephen-hawking-interview-there-is-no-heaven.

72 Bob Seidenstciker, "John Lennox Responds to Stephen Hawking," *Patheos*, August 29, 2011, http://www.patheos.com/blogs/crossexamined/2011/08/john-lennox-responds-to-stephen-hawking/.

73 Kreeft and Tacelli, *Handbook of Christian Apologetics.*

74 Richard Swinburne, *The Christian God* (Oxford: Clarendon Press, 1994).

75 Ibid, 341.

76 Kreeft and Tacelli, *Handbook of Christian Apologetics.*

77 "Losing Our Religion? Two Thirds of People Still Claim to be Religious," *WIN Gallup International*, April 13, 2015, http://www.wingia.com/en/news/losing_our_religion_two_thirds_of_people_still_claim_to_be_religious/290/.

78 Carl C. Jung, *Modern Man in Search of a Soul* (London: Routledge, 1933), 234.

79 Bernard S. J. Boedder, *Natural Theology* (New York: Longmans Green and Co, 1902), 47.

80 "The Global Religious Landscape," *Pew research Center*, December 18, 2012, http://www.pewforum.org/2012/12/18/global-religious-landscape-exec/?utm_content=bufferf682f&utm_source=buffer&utm_medium=twitter&utm_campaign=Buffer.

81 Anthony Flew and Roy A. Varghese, *There is a God: How the World's Most Notorious Atheist Changed His Mind* (New York: Harper Collins, 2007), 185-186.

82 Blaise Pascal, *Pensees.*

83 C.S. Lewis, *God in the Dock: Essays on Theology and Ethics* (Cambridge: William B. Eerdmans Publishing, 2014), 102.

Part Two

1 Stephen A. Gregory and Michael Zelik, *Introductory Astronomy and Astrophysics* (Fort Worth: Saunders College Publishing, 1998).

2 Gregory and Zelik, *Introductory Astronomy and Astrophysics.*

3 Simon Singh, *Big Bang: The Origin of the Universe* (New York: Harper Perennial, 2005).

4 Hermann Bondi and Thomas Gold, "The Steady-State Theory of the Expanding Universe," *Monthly Notices of the Royal Astronomical Society* 108 (1948): 252.

5 Arno Penzias and Robert Wilson, "A Measurement of Excess Antenna Temperature at 4080 Mc/s," *The Astrophysical Journal* 142 no. 1 (1965): 419-421.

6 Deuteronomy 33:27.

7 1 Timothy 1:17.

8   Genesis 17:1.

9   "Cosmology: The Study of the Universe," Universe 101: Big Bang Theory, *NASA*, accessed May 15, 2015, https://web.archive.org/web/20110514230003/http://map.gsfc.nasa.gov/universe/. "The second and third sections discuss the classic tests of the Big Bang theory that make it so compelling as the likely valid description of our universe."

10 Sing, *Big Bang.*

11 Stephen Hawking, *A Brief History of Time* (New York: Bantam, 1998).

12 George Smoot and Keay Davidson, *Wrinkles in Time* (New York: Avon Books, 1993).

13 Thomas H. Maugh, "Relics of the Big Bang, Seen for the First Time," *Los Angeles Times*, April 24, 1992, A1-A30.

14 Smoot and Davidson, *Wrinkles in Time*, 17.

15 "Relativity," *Encyclopaedia Brittanica*, last modified August 25, 2016, https://www.britannica.com/science/relativity.

16 Stephen Hawking, "The Origin of the Universe," accessed May 21, 2015, http://www.hawking.org.uk/the-origin-of-the-universe.html.

17 Kenneth W. Ford, *The Quantum world: Quantum Physics for Everyone* (Cambridge, MA: Harvard University Press, 2009), 246.

18 E. Salaman, "A Talk with Einstein," *The Listener* 54 (1955): 370-371, in Einstein and Religion, ed. Max Jammer (Princeton, NJ: Princeton University Press), 123.

19 Steven Weinberg, *The First Three Minutes: A Modern View of the Origin of the Universe* (New York: Basic Books, 1988), 5.

20 Ibid.

21 John D. Barrow and Frank J. Tipler, *The Anthropic Cosmological Principle* (Oxford: Oxford University Press, 1986), 442.

22 Hawking, *A Brief History of Time*, 46.

23 John C. Lennox, *God and Stephen Hawking: Whose Design Is It Anyway?* (Oxford: Lion Hudson Books, 2011), 47.

24 Malcolm Browne, "Clues to the Universe's Origin Expected," *New York Times,* March 12, 1978, 1.

25 Jeff Miller, "God and the Laws of Science: The Law of Causality," *Apologetics Press*, accessed June 12, 2015, http://www.apologeticspress.org/apcontent.aspx?category=9&article=3716.

26 "Cosmological Argument," *Stanford Encyclopaedia of Philosophy*, last modified November 10, 2016, https://plato.stanford.edu/entries/cosmological-argument/.

27 Fred Hoyle, "The Universe-Past and Present Reflections," *Annual Review of Astronomy and Astrophysics*, 20 (1982): 1.

28 Aristotle, *The Complete Works of Aristotle,* trans. Jonathan Barnes (Princeton, NJ: Princeton University Press, 1984).

29 1 John 4:8.

30 Revelations 4:8.

31 Psalm 116:5.

32 Psalm 139:7-12.

33 1 John 3:20.

34 Job 37:23.

35 Deuteronomy 33:27.

36 1 Timothy 1:17.

37 Hawking, *A Brief History of Time*

38 Ibid.

39 Stephen Hawking and Leonard Mlodinow, *The Grand Design* (New York: Bantam Books, 2010), 180.

40 Lennox, *God and Stephen Hawking*, 22.

41 Ibid.

42 Richard Feynman, *The Character of Physical Law* (Cambridge, MA: MIT Press, 1967).

43 Lennox, *God and Stephen Hawking*, 22.

44 Ibid.

45 Paul Davies, *The Mind of God: Science and the Search for Ultimate Meaning* (London: Simon and Schuster, 1992).

46 Ibid.

47 Hawking, *A Brief History of Time*.

48 Stephen Weinberg, *Facing Up* (Cambridge: Harvard University Press, 2003), 80-81.

49 Paul Davies, "How bio-friendly is the universe," *International Journal of Astrobiology* 2 (2003): 115.

50 Fred Heeren, *Show me God: What the Message From Space Is Telling Us About God* (New York: Bantam Books, 2000), 228.

51 Hawking, *A Brief History of Time*

52 Roger Penrose, *The Emperor's New Mind: Concerning Computers, Minds, and the Laws of Physics.* (Oxford: Oxford University Press, 1999), 445-446.

53 Henry M. Morris, "Probability and Order Versus Evolution," *Institute of Creation Research*, accessed July 1, 2015, http://www.icr.org/article/probability-order-versus-evolution/.

54   Gregg Easterbrook, "Science and God: A Warning Trend?" *Scientific Community* 277, 5328 (1977): 890-893.

55   Edward Harrison, *Masks of the Universe: Changing Ideas on the Nature of the Cosmos* (Cambridge: Cambridge University Press, 2003), 286.

56   John Noble Wilford, "Sizing Up the Cosmos: An Astronomer's Quest," *New York Times*, March 12, 1991, http://www.nytimes.com/1991/03/12/science/sizing-up-the-cosmos-an-astronomer-s-quest.html?pagewanted=all.

57   Brian Nugent, *Slí na Fírinne: The Traditional Catholic Proofs of God's Existence* (Corstown: Old Castle Company, 2011), 335.

58   George F. R. Ellis, "The Anthropic Principle: Laws and Environments" in *The Anthropic Principle,* ed. F. Bertola and U. Curi (Cambridge: Cambridge University Press, 1993), 30.

59   George F. R. Ellis, "The Theology of the Anthropic Principle," in *Quantum Cosmology and the Laws of Nature,* ed. Robert John Russell et al. (Vatican: Vatican Observatory Publications, 1993), 367.

60   George F. R. Ellis, "Does the multiverse really exist?" *Scientific American* 305 no. 2 (2011): 38-43; Stephen M. Feeney et al., "First Observational Tests of Eternal Inflation," *Physical Review Letters* 107, no. 7 (2011): 1-5; Marshall Honorof, "Multiverse or Universe? 'Physicists Debate," *Space,* June 4, 2013, http://www.space.com/21421-universe-multiverse-inflation-theory.html.

61   Brian Greene, "Welcome to the Multiverse," *Newsweek*, May 21, 2012, http://www.newsweek.com/brian-greene-welcome-multiverse-64887.

62   George F. R. Ellis, "Cosmology: The Untestable Multiverse," *Nature* 469 no. 7330 (2011): 294-295.

63   Denyse O'Leary, "Multiverse Cosmology: Assuming that Evidence Still Matters. What Does it Say?" *Evolution News,* January 6, 2014, July 6, 2015, http://www.evolutionnews.org/2014/01/multiverse_cosm080801.html.

64   Dennis F. Polis, *God, Science and Mind* (Fontana, CA: Xianphil Press, 2012), 89.

65   Tim Folger, "Science's Alternative to an Intelligent Creator: The Multiverse Theory," *Discover,* November 10, 2008, http://discovermagazine.com/2008/dec/10-sciences-alternative-to-an-intelligent-creator.

66   Alexander Vilenkin, *Many Worlds in One: The Search for Other Universes* (New York: Macmillan, 2006).

67 William L. Craig, "Multiverse and the Design Argument," *Reasonable Faith*, accessed July 6, 2015, http://www.reasonablefaith.org/multiverse-and-the-design-argument.

68 Paul Davies, *God and the New Physics* (London: Penguin Books, 2006).

69 Stephen C. Meyer, *Signature in the Cell: DNA and the Evidence for Intelligent Design* (New York: Harper Collins, 2009).

70 Clifford Pickover, *Archimedes to Hawking: Laws of Science and the Great Minds Behind Them* (Oxford: Oxford University Press, 2008), 417.

71 Brian Josephson, "A Critical Point For Science," *University of Cambridge*, April 2, 2010, http://sms.cam.ac.uk/media/749894.

72 "Teleological Arguments for God's Existence," *Stanford Encyclopaedia of Philosophy*, last modified January 15, 2015, http://plato.stanford.edu/entries/teleological-arguments/.

73 Weinberg, *Facing Up*, 233.

74 S. C. Todd, "A View From Kansas on That Evolution Debate," *Nature* 401:6752 (1999): 423-423.

75 Bruce Alberts et al., *Essential Cell Biology* (Abingdon: Garland Science, 2013).

76 E. Bianconi et al., "An Estimation of the Number of Cells in the Human Body," *Annals of Human Biology* 40 no. 6 (2013): 463-471; Shyamala Iyer, "Building Blocks of Life," *ASU School of Life Sciences*, accessed July 10, 2015, http://askabiologist.asu.edu/explore/building-blocks-life.

77 Alberts et al., *Essential Cell Biology*.

78 James Watson and Francis Crick, "Molecular Structure of Nucleic Acids: A Structure for Deoxyribose Nucleic Acid," *Nature* 4356 (1953): 737-738.

79 Meyer, *Signature in the Cell*.

80 Alberts et al., *Essential Cell Biology*.

81 Ibid.

82 Meyer, *Signature in the Cell*.

83 Bill Denton, "Debunking Charle's Darwin's Theory of Evolution," *Delaware State News*, January 21, 2017, http://delawarestatenews.net/opinion/letter-editor-debunking-charles-darwins-theory-evolution/.

84 S. L. Berger, "The Complex Language of Chromatin Regulation During Transcription," *Nature* 447:7143 (2007): 407-412; T. Head, "Formal Language Theory and DNA: An Analysis of the Generative Capacity of Specific Recombinant Behaviors," *Bulletin of Mathematical Biology* 49 no. 6 (1987): 737-759; Wentian Li, "The complexity of DNA," *Complexity 3* no. 2 (1997): 33-38.

85 Francis Crick, "On Protein Synthesis," *Symposia of the Society for Experimental Biology* 12 (1958): *138*.

86 Meyer, *Signature in the Cell*.

87 Richard Dawkins, *River Out of Eden: A Darwinian View of Life* (London: Phoenix, 1996), 20.

88 Bill Gates, *The Road Ahead* (New York: Penguin Group, 1995), 228.

89 Michael Denton, *Evolution: A Theory in Crisis* (Bethesda, MA: Adler and Adler, 1986), 145; N. E. Morton, "Parameters of the Human Genome," *Proceedings of the National Academy of Sciences*, 88, 17 (1991) 7474-7476; Mario Seiglie, "DNA: The Tiny Code That's Toppling Evolution," *Beyond Today*, May 21, 2005, http://www.ucg.org/the-good-news/dna-the-tiny-code-thats-toppling-evolution.

90 Denton, *Evolution*, 334.

91 Ajit Varki and Tasha K. Altheide, "Comparing the Human and Chimpanzee Genomes: Searching for Needles in a Haystack," *Genome Research*, 15 no. 12 (2005): 1746-1758.

92 Anthony Flew and Gary Habermas, "My Pilgrimage from Atheism to Theism," *Philosophia Christi*, 6 no. 2 (2004): 197-211.

93 Werner Gitt, *In the Beginning Was Information* (Green Forest, AR: Master Books, 2004), 67, 106.

94 Meyer, *Signature in the Cell*.

95 Alberts et al., *Essential Cell Biology*.

96 Ibid.

97 Dean Kenyon, "Unlocking the Mystery of Life," *Illustra Media*, Dec 9, 2008, https://www.youtube.com/watch?v=gdBJt6sdDfI.

98 Michael J. Behe, *Darwin's Black Box: The Biochemical Challenge to Evolution* (New York: Simon and Schuster, 2006).

99 "Neo-Darwinism," *New World Encyclopaedia*, accessed July 29, 2015, http://www.newworldencyclopedia.org/entry/Neo-Darwinism.

100 Robert W. Carter, "Can Mutations Create New Information?" *Journal of Creation* 25 no. 2 (2011): 92-98; Casey Luskin, "Can Random Mutations Create New Complex Features? A response to TalkOrigins," *Evolution News and Views*, June 22, 2012, http://www.evolutionnews.org/2012/06/can_random_muta061221.html

101 Lynn Margulis, "The Phylogenetic Tree Topples," *American Scientist* 94 no. 3 (2006): 194.

102 Jan Charles Biro, "Biological Information – Definitions From a Biological Perspective," *Information* 2 no. 1 (2011): 117-139.

103 Carter, "Can Mutations Create New Information."

104 Allen Gathman, (2005). "Why Most Mutations are Recessive and Not Dominant" *Genetics, Madsci Network*, January 18, 2005, http://www.madsci.org/posts/archives/2005-01/1106062298.Ge.r.html; Harvey Lodish et al., *Molecular Cell Biology* (New York: W.H. Freeman, 2000); Vidyanand Nanjundiah, "Why are most mutations recessive?" *Journal of Genetics*, 72 no. 2-3 (1993): 85-97.

105 Lynn Margulis and Dorion Sagan, *Acquiring Genomes: A Theory of the Origins of Species* (New York: Basic Books, 2002), 11.

106 Charles Darwin, *The Origin of Species* (New York: Modern Library, 1859).

107 Charles Darwin, *The Variation of Animals and Plants Under Domestication* (New York: D. Appleton, 1896), 349.

108 Roger Lewin, (1980). "Evolutionary Theory Under Fire," *Science* 210 no. 4472 (1980): 883-887.

109 Douglas Axe, "The Limits of Complex Adaptation: An Analysis Based on a Simple Model of Structured Bacterial Populations," *BIO-Complexity* 4 (2010): 1-10.

110 Ann Gauger et al., "Reductive Evolution Can Prevent Populations from Taking Simple Adaptive Paths to High Fitness," *BIO-Complexity* 2 (2010): 1-9.

111 Michael Behe, "Experimental Evolution, Loss-of-Function Mutations, and the 'First Rule of Adaptive Evolution,'" *The Quarterly Review of Biology* 85 no. 4 (2010).

112 Behe, *Darwin's Black Box*.

113 Jonathan McLatchie, J. (2010) "The Bacterial Flagellum – Truly an Engineering Marvel," *Uncommon Descent,* December 24, 2010, http://www.uncommondescent.com/intelligent-design/the-bacterial-flagellum-truly-an-engineering-marvel/.

114 Behe, *Darwin's Black Box*; William A. Dembski, *No Free Lunch: Why Specified Complexity Cannot be Purchased Without Intelligence* (Lanham, MD: Rowman & Littlefield, 2007).

115 Renyi Liu and Howard Ochman, (April 24, 2007). "Stepwise Formation of the Bacterial Flagellar System," *Proceedings of the National Academy of Sciences of the USA* 104 no. 17 (2007): 7116-7121; David Ussery, "A Review of Darwin's Black Box," *BIOS Magazine,* last modified August 10, 2000, http://www.cbs.dtu.dk/courses/genomics_course/BeheDBB.html.

116 Dembski, *No Free Lunch*.

117 Behe, "Experimental Evolution, Loss-of-Function Mutations, and the 'First Rule of Adaptive Evolution.'"

118 Dembski, *No Free Lunch.*

119 Darwin, *The Origin of Species,* 189.

120 McLatchie, "The Bacterial Flagellum."

121 Alan Cooper and Richard Fortey, "Evolutionary Explosions and the Phylogenetic Fuse," *Trends in Ecology and Evolution,* 13 (1998) 151-156.

122 Jeffrey Levinton, "The Big Bang of Animal Evolution," *Scientific American,* November 1, 1992, https://www.scientificamerican.com/article/the-big-bang-of-animal-evolution/.

123 Nicholas J. Butterfield, (2007). "Macroevolution and Macroecology Through Deep Time," *Palaeontology* 50 no. 1 (2007): 41–55

124 Darwin, *The Origin of Species.*

125 Jaume Baguña and Jordi Garcia-Fernández, "Evo-Devo: The Long and Winding Road," *International Journal of Developmental Biology* 47 (2003); 705-713; Stephen Jay Gould, "Is a New and General Theory of Evolution Emerging?" *Paleobiology,* 6 no. 1 (1980): 119-130.

126 Jonathan B. Antcliffe,. (2012) "Patterns in Palaeontology: The Cambrian Explosion – Paradoxes and Possible Worlds. *Palaeontologyonline,* September 1, 2012, http://pdf.palaeontologyonline.com/articles-2012/PatternsInPalaeontology TheCambrianExplosionParadoxesAndPoss ibleWorlds-Antcliffe J B-Aug2012.pdf.

127 Peter Byrne P. "Early Life in Death Valley," *Quanta Magazine,* April 24, 2014, https://www.quantamagazine.org/20140424-early-life-in-death-valley/

128 R.S.K. Barnes et al., *The Invertebrates: A New Synthesis* (Malden, MA: Blackwell Science Publications, 2001), 9-10; J. W. Valentine et al., "The Biological Explosion at the Precambrian-Cambrian Boundary," *Evolutionary Biology, 25 (1991):* 279-356.

129 Douglas H. Erwin and Eric Davidson, E. "The Last Common Bilaterian Ancestor," *Development* 129 no. 13 (2002): 3021-3032.

130 Gould, "Is a New and General Theory of Evolution Emerging?"

131 Darwin, *The Origin of Species,* 292.

132 M. J. Benton, M. A. Wills and R. Hitchin, "Quality of the Fossil Record Through Time," *Nature,* 403 (2000): 534-536.

133 N. Eldredge and I. Tattersall, *The Myths of Human Evolution* (New York: Columbia University Press, 1982), 57.

134 Erin Wayman, "How to Solve Human Evolution's Greatest Hoax," smithsonian.com, December 19, 2012,

http://www.smithsonianmag.com/science-nature/
how-to-solve-human-evolutions-greatest-hoax-167921335/?no-ist
135 Scott M. Huse, *The Collapse of Evolution*. Grand Rapids: Baker Books, 1997).
136 Richard Leakey, (2009). "Richard Leakey Talks Family and Great Discoveries," *Archaeology*, August 3, 2009, http://archive.archaeology. org/online/interviews/leakey/.
137 "Ramapithecus," *Encyclopaedia Britannica*, last modified April 20, 2015, http://www.britannica.com/topic/Ramapithecus.
138 John Pickrell, "How Fake Fossils Pervert Paleontology," *Scientific American*, November 15, 2014, http://www.scientificamerican.com/ article/how-fake-fossils-pervert-paleontology-excerpt/.
139 Marvin L. Lubenow, "Paleoanthropology in Review," *CEN Technical Journal*, 10 no. 1 (1996): 14-17
140 Ibid.

Part Three

1 Robin L. Fox, *The Classical World: An Epic History from Homer to Hadrian* (New York: Basic Books, 2005), 48; Michael Grant, *Jesus* (London: Orion Publishing, 2004), 200.
2 Richard A. Burridge and Graham Gould, *Jesus Now and Then* (London: William B. Eerdmans Publishing Company, 2004), 34.
3 James H. Charlesworth, *Jesus Within Judaism* (New York: Doubleday, 1988) 168-169.
4 Michael Grant, *Jesus: An Historian's Review of the Gospels* (London: Macmillan Publishing, 1977), 200.
5 Bruce Chilton and Craig A. Evans, *Authenticating the Activities of Jesus* (Boston: Brill Academic Publishers, 2002), 3-7; William R. Herzog, *Prophet and Teacher: An Introduction to the Historical Jesus by* (Louisville, KY: Westminster John Knox Press, 2005), 1-6; Mark A. Powell, *Jesus as a Figure in History: How Modern Historians View the Man from Galilee* (Louisville, KY: Westminster John Knox Press, 1998), 117.
6 Marcus J. Borg, *Jesus, a New Vision: Spirit, Culture, and the Life of Discipleship* (San Francisco: Harper San Francisco, 1991), 61.
7 Max Lucado, *Next Door Savior* (Nashville, TN: Thomas Nelson, 2003), 5.

8   Thomas Carlyle, *On Heroes, Hero Worship and the Heroic in History* (Boston: Adams, 1840), 127.

9   "Best Selling Book of Non-Fiction," *Guinness World Records*, accessed January 25, 2017, http://www.guinnessworldrecords.com/world-records/best-selling-book-of-non-fiction.

10   Steven Skiena and Charles B. Ward, *Who's Bigger? Where Historical Figures Really Rank* (Cambridge: Cambridge University Press, 2014).

11   George Sylvester Viereck, "What Life Means to Einstein," *The Saturday Evening Post*, October 26, 1929, 17, http://www.saturdayeveningpost.com/wp-content/uploads/satevepost/what_life_means_to_einstein.pdf.

12   Ibid.

13   Isaiah 9:6; Luke 1:35.

14   Clive Staples Lewis, *Mere Christianity* (London: Harper Collins, 2012), 54.

15   Ibid, 56.

16   Bart Ehrman, *Misquoting Jesus: The story Behind Who Changed the Bible and Why* (New York: Harper Collins, 2005).

17   Clive Staples Lewis, *Essential C. S. Lewis* (New York: Touchstone Rockefeller Center, 1996), 331.

18   John 10:33; Mark 14:63.

19   Michael L. Brown, *Authentic Fire* (Lake Mary, FL: Creation House, 2015), 51.

20   Luke 14:26.

21   Matthew 10:37.

22   Isaiah 43:25; Micah 7:18; Psalm 103:3.

23   Daniel Johansson, "Who Can Forgive Sins but God Alone? Human and Angelic Agents, and Divine Forgiveness in Early Judaism," *Journal for the Study of the New Testament* 33 no. 4 (2011): 351-374; Matt Slick, Matt, "Does John 20:23 Mean That Catholic Priests Can Forgive Sins?" *CARM*, accessed January 8, 2016, https://carm.org/John2023-priests-forgive-sins; Zenon Szablowinski, "Should Christians Forgive Always; Does God Always Forgive?." *Pacifica: Australasian Theological Studies* 22 no. 1 (2009): 36-52.

24   Johansson, "Who Can Forgive Sins but God Alone?"

25   David Instone-Brewer, "Jesus of Nazareth's Trial in the Uncensored Talmud," *Tyndale House Bulletin* 62 no. 2 (2011): 269-294. Accessed http://www.tyndale.cam.ac.uk/Tyndale/staff/Instone-Brewer/prepub/07_Instone_Brewer.pdf.

26 Josephus, "The Testimonium Flavianum," *Antiquities* 18.63-64, *The Loeb Classical Library,* accessed January 9, 2016, http://www.josephus. org/testimonium.htm.

27 Louis H. Feldman, *Josephus, the Bible and History* (Detroit, MI: Wayne State University Press, 1989).

28 Mark R. Saucy, "Miracles and Jesus' Proclamation of the Kingdom of God," *Bibliotheca Sacra* 153 (1996): 281-307.

29 Plinius Secundus, *Epistle X96*, accessed January 23, 2016, http://www. vroma.org/~hwalker/Pliny/Pliny10-096-E.html.

30 Ariel Cohen, "In Face of Beheading, Iraqi Children Proclaim Love for Jesus," *The Jerusalem Post*, December 3, 2014, http://www.jpost.com/Christian-News/ In-face-of-beheading-Iraqi-children-proclaim-love-for-Jesus-383538.

31 Allen Brent, *A Political History of Early Christianity* (New York: T&T Clark International, 2009), 32.

32 Ed Hindson and Ergun Caner, *The Popular Encyclopaedia of Apologetics: Surveying the Evidence for the Truth of Christianity* (Eugene, OR: Harvest House, 2008), 126-127.

33 Ibid, 128.

34 Instone-Brewer, "Jesus of Nazareth's Trial in the Uncensored Talmud," 275.

35 Hindson and Ergun Caner, *The Popular Encyclopaedia of Apologetics,* 128.

36 "Crucifixion," *New World Encyclopaedia*, accessed January 15, 2016, http://www.newworldencyclopedia.org/entry/Crucifixion.

37 Anthony Flew and Gary Habermas, "My Pilgrimage from Atheism to Theism: A Discussion Between Antony Flew and Gary Habermas," *Philosophia Christi*, 6 no. 2 (2004): 197-211.

38 Gary Habermas and Michael R. Licona, *The Case for the Resurrection of Jesus* (Grand Rapids, MI: Kregel Publications, 2004).

39 Gerd, Theissen and Annette Merz, *The Historical Jesus: A Comprehensive Guide* (Minneapolis: Fortress Press, 1998); Charles H. Talbert, *Reading Luke-Acts in its Mediterranean Milieu* (Boston: Brill Academic Publishers, 2003).

40 Gerd Lüdemann, *What Really Happened to Jesus?* (Louisville, KY: Westminster John Knox Press, 1995), 80.

41 Josh McDowell, *The New Evidence That Demands a Verdict* (Dallas, TX: Here's Life Publishers, 1999).

42 Isaiah 7:14.

43   Micah 5:2.

44   Genesis 12:3; Jeremiah 23:5.

45   Isaiah 35:4-6.

46   Zechariah 9:9.

47   Psalm 41:9; Zechariah 11:12

48   Psalm 118:22.

49   Isaiah 53:4-5.

50   Psalm 22:16.

51   Psalm 16:10.

52   Psalm 68:18.

53   Peter W. Stoner, *Science Speaks: Scientific Proof of the Accuracy of Prophecy and the Bible* (Chicago: Moody Press, 1969).

54   Ibid.

55   John C. Villanueva, "How Many Atoms Are There in the Universe?" *Universe Today,* December 24, 2015, http://www.universetoday.com/36302/atoms-in-the-universe/.

Part Four

1   Quran 5:17, 75; 9:30-31; 19:35.

2   Quran 4:157.

3   See reasons 41 and 42 of this book.

4   John 3:16; 8:24; Romans 10:9; 1 Corinthians 1:18, 15:17; 1 John 5:12.

5   2 Corinthians 5:21; 1 Peter 2:22; 1 John 3:5.

6   Quran 40:55; 47:19; 48:2.

7   Matthew 16:15-17; John 8:58; 10:36.

8   Quran 17:93; 41:6.

9   John 3:16-17.

10   Quran 29:50; 33:40.

11   Mark 1:10-11; John 5:19; 8:38-40.

12   Quran 53:4-9; Sahih Al-Muslim 1:1.

13   Matthew 5:44-48; John 3:16.

14   Quran 3:31-32; 30:45.

15   Matthew 15:30; Luke 7:22; Acts 10:38.

16   Quran 6:37; 29:50.

17   There is no mention anywhere in the New Testament that Jesus married or had a spouse. In 1 Corinthians 9:5, when Paul was defending his right to have a wife, he refers to other apostles and brothers of the Lord

as examples. If Jesus had been married, Paul would have more than likely mentioned it here.

18 Quran 4:24; 33:50-51; 66:1-5; Sahih Al-Muslim 8:3309.

19 John 8:3-11.

20 Sahih Al-Muslim 17:4206.

21 Matthew 5:39; 26:52; John 18:36.

22 Quran 2:190-191; 5:33; 8:12; 33:60-61; Abu Dawud 33:4390.

23 Matthew 18:21-22; John 13:34-35.

24 Quran 2:194; 8:39; 9:123; 30:45; Sahih Al-Muslim 1:33.

25 John 1:29; Colossians 1:14, 20-22; Revelations 1:5.

26 Muhammad was poisoned by a Jewess called Zaynab (Sahih Bukhari, Vol. 3, Book 47:786; Tabari, Vol. 8, p.123-124). When asked why she poisoned Muhammad, she said it was because he killed her father, uncle and husband (Ibn Sa'd p.251-252). Although Muhammad lived for another three years after he was poisoned, he continued to suffer the ill effects of the poison until his demise (Sahih Bukhari Vol. 5, Book 59:713).

27 Mark 16:5-7; Luke 24:2-3; John 20:16-18; Acts 3:15.

28 Sahih Bukhari Vol. 5, Book 59:730-739.

29 See reasons 43 and 44 of this book.

30 Muhammad does not fit the profile of any Biblical prophet, nor does he fulfill any Biblical prophecy, except those concerning false teachers (Matthew 7:15-20; 2 Peter 2:1-3; 2 John 1:7-11; Revelations 22:18).

31 Quran 29:50; Sahih Bukhari, Vol. 9, Book 92:379.

32 Quran 29:51.

33 The Bible and the Quran both espouse monotheism and creationism and share narratives of common figures like Job, Noah, Abraham, Moses and Jesus.

34 The Quran disagrees with the Bible on the trinity; the deity of Jesus; the person of the Holy Spirit; the crucifixion, death and resurrection of Jesus; salvation by grace; and the identity of the devil; the sin nature of mankind;

35 Both the Bible and Quran agree there is only one God who is eternal, transcendent, omniscient and omnipotent. However, they disagree on His identity.

36 In the Old Testament, God consistently refers to Himself using the plural pronoun 'We' or 'Us.' Examples include "Let Us make man in Our Image" (Genesis 1:26), "Man has become like one of Us" (Genesis 3:22), "Come, let Us go down and there confuse their language"

(Genesis 11:7), "…who will go for Us" (Isaiah 6:8). Psalm 45:6-7 refers to God the Father anointing God the Son: "Therefore God, your God, has anointed You" (see Hebrews 1:8), In Isaiah 48:16, the writer distinguishes the "Lord God" from "His Spirit," implying they are two distinct persons, as does Genesis 1:1-2. Moreover, the two most frequently used Hebrew names of God in the Old Testament – 'Elohim' and 'Adonai,' are plural nouns. Also, a number of Old Testament passages like Exodus 33:14, Deuteronomy 4:37 and Job 13:8, refer to the 'faces,' 'persons' or 'presences' of God, implying that whilst God is one, He manifests as more than one. Finally, Old Testament verses that make triple attributions to God, such as "Holy, Holy, Holy" (Isaiah 6:3) and "The Temple of the Lord, The Temple of the Lord, The Temple of the Lord" (Jeremiah 7:4), imply the triune nature of God as three persons. In the New Testament, references to God's triune nature are much more explicit (e.g., Matthew 3:16-17, 28:19; 1 Corinthians 12:4-6; 2 Corinthians 13:14, Ephesians 4:4-6; 1 Peter 1:2; Jude 20-21; 1 John 5:7).

37   Quran 4:171; 5:73; 112:1-4.

38   Quran 2:116; 5:17, 75; 9:30; 19:35.

39   Quran 2:174; 5:72, 78; 9:30.

40   Quran 112:1-4.

41   Quran 5:18.

42   Quran 2:191, 193; 3:151; 5:33; 8:12, 39.

43   Quran 1:1, 3; 2:192; 3:31; 5:54; 49:9; 51:25.

44   See reasons 31, 38 and 41 of this book.

45   Josh McDowell, *New Evidence that Demands a Verdict* (Dallas: Here's Life Publishers, 1999).

46   Dr. Labib, "The Prophecies in the Quran, 2016." *The Spirit of Islam,* accessed January 19, 2016, http://www.thespiritofislam.com/bible-quran/25-the-prophecies-in-the-quran.html; Matt Slick, "Differences Between the Bible and the Qur'an," *Christian Apologetics & Research Ministry,* accessed January 19, 2016, https://carm.org/differences-between-bible-and-quran; R. Totten, "The Quran Vs. The Bible: Predictions of Human Actions Show Which One is Truly From God, *Testing World Views,* accessed January 21, 2016, http://worldview3.50webs.com/quranvbible.html

47   "The Global Religious Landscape," *Pew Research Center,* December 18, 2012, http://www.pewforum.org/2012/12/18/

global-religious-landscape-exec/; "Religion Census 2011," *Census 2011*, accessed January 22, 2016, http://www.census2011.co.in/religion.php.

48 Denise Carmody et al., *Ways to the Center: An Introduction to World Religions* (Belmont, CA: Wadsworth Publishers, 1984); Carmody, *Ways to the Center.*

49 Lewis M. Hopfe, *Religions of the World* (London: MacMillan, 1987) 104-105.

50 Ibid.

51 Matthew 28:19; John 14:26; 15:26; 1 John 5:7.

52 W. H. Swatos, 2016. "Hinduism," *Encyclopaedia of Religion and Society,* accessed January 24, 2016, http://hirr.hartsem.edu/ency/Hinduism.htm.

53 Srimad Bhagavatam (Bhagavata Purana) 1:3:28.

54 Wendy Doniger, "Mahabharata Hindu Literature," *Encyclopaedia Britannica*, February 19, 2015, http://www.britannica.com/topic/Mahabharata.

55 "Shiva Maha Purana," *Hindu Online*, accessed January 26, 2016, http://hinduonline.co/Scriptures/Puranas/ShivaMahaPurana.html

56 Hymns of the Atharvaveda, Book 10, Hymn 8, Verse 1.

57 V Jayaram, "The Diversity and the plurality of Hinduism," *Hindu Website*, accessed January 26, 2016, http://www.hinduwebsite.com/hinduintrod5.asp.

58 Matthew 8:16; Luke 11:14; Acts 10:38.

59 Jeffrey Brodd, *World Religions: A Voyage of Discovery* (Winona, MA: Saint Mary's Press, 2003).

60 Matthew 28:18-20; Mark 16:15-20; Acts 2:1-47

61 Swatos, *Hinduism.*

62 John 14:6; Acts 4:12; 1 John 2:23.

63 Solomon A. Nigosian, *World Religions: A Historical Approach* (Boston: Bedford/St.Martin's, 2000).

64 Matthew 11:27; John 17:3; Ephesians 1:17-18; 2 Peter 3:18.

65 Carmody, *Ways to the Center.*

66 Deuteronomy 6:4; 1 Kings 8:60; John 17:3; 1 Timothy 2:5.

67 Carmody, *Ways to the Center.*

68 Luke 6:35; John 3:16; Romans 13:10; 1 John 4:7-8;

69 Harry Gaylord, "A Quick Comparison Between Hinduism and Christianity," *Sun and Shield*, March 7, 2007, https://sunandshield.wordpress.com/2007/03/07/a-quick-comparison-between-hinduism-and-christianity/.

70   Matthew 26:28; Luke 24:47; Acts 2:38;

71   Gaylord, "A Quick Comparison Between Hinduism and Christianity."

72   Genesis 2:17; 1 Thessalonians 4:13-17; Hebrews 9:27.

73   Gaylord, "A Quick Comparison Between Hinduism and Christianity."

74   There are many verses in the Bible that imply empirical experiences are real and can be relied upon to confirm truth. Examples include Mark 16:20; John 14:11; 20:27-29; 1 John 1:1-3.

75   In Hinduism, understanding external reality depends on understanding the godhead. According to Hindu concepts of space and time, the external world is a product of the creative play of maya (illusion) - meaning, our experience of the external world is not ultimately real. The task for the Hindu is to find moksha (release) from the bonds of time and space. When one is liberated from the finitude by finding union with atman (the universal self), one finds ultimate reality - Brahman. The atman is identical to Brahman.

76   John 8:32; 14:6; 16:13; 17:17.

77   Nigosian, *World Religions: A Historical Approach.*

78   Proverbs 22:2; Acts 10:34-35; Romans 2:11; Galatians 3:28; Ephesians 5:21; 6:9; 1 Peter 1:17.

79   Ramendra Nath, "Why I am not a Hindu," *Bihar Rationalist Society*, accessed January 24, 2016, http://infidels.org/library/modern/ramendra_nath/hindu.html.

80   Judges 4:4; Acts 2:17; Galatians 3:28; 1 Corinthians 7:4; 11:12; 1 Peter 3:7.

81   V Jayaram, "Gender Bias in Hinduism," *Hindu Website*, accessed January 24, 2016, http://www.hinduwebsite.com/hinduism/essays/bias.asp.

82   See reasons 1-9 of this book.

83   "Vedic Religion: Cosmogony and Cosmology," *Encyclopaedia Britannica*, June 20, 2016, http://www.britannica.com/topic/Hinduism/The-Brahmanas-and-Aranyakas.

84   Although there are Bible passages that present seemingly contradictory verses, one must bear in mind the Bible was written by 40 different authors over a 1500 year period. Hence, differences should be expected, especially since each author had his own prose and wrote from his own cultural perspective to a different audience for a different purpose. However, a difference is not a contradiction if the verses can be reconciled through good hermeneutic interpretation. There is a plethora of literature available from Bible scholars who have

discussed and resolved differences in the Bible. It follows that since any apparent contradiction can be explained, the Bible can be relied upon as theologically consistent.

85 Jayaram, "Gender Bias in Hinduism,"

86 Romans 5:1-2; Galatians 2:16; Ephesians 1:7; 2:8-9; Titus 3:4-7.

87 V. Jayaram, "Moksha or liberation in Hinduism," Hinduwebsite, accessed January 25, 2016, http://www.hinduwebsite.com/hinduism/h_enlighten.asp.

88 John 3:16; Acts 2:21; Romans 1:16; 10: 9-10; Ephesians 2:8-9; Philippians 3:20; 2 Timothy 1:9; Hebrews 7:25; 1 Peter 1:8-9; 1 John 5:12.

89 "Attaining Moksha," *The Hindu*, last modified May 29, 2013, http://www.thehindu.com/features/friday-review/religion/attaining-moksha/article4763267.ece.

90 The Manusmriti is one of the first Sanskrit texts to be translated to English. It records the laws of Manu (the progenitor of humanity) and is considered to be the most authoritative Hindu Law book, serving as a foundation for jurisprudence in ancient Indian society.

91 "Varna (Hinduism)," Wikipedia, accessed January 25, 2016, https://en.wikipedia.org/wiki/Varna_(Hinduism).

92 The Bhagavad Gita, referred to as simply the Gita, is a 700-verse Hindu text in Sanskrit that is part of the Hindu epic Mahabharata.

93 Bhagavad Gita, 18:41-44.

94 Eesha Pandit, "The Modern Horrors of India's Ancient Injustice: How a Government Has Abandoned Millions - and They Are Fighting Back," *Salon Magazine,* October 22, 2015, http://www.salon.com/2015/10/22/the_modern_horrors_of_indias_ancient_injustice_how_a_government_has_abandoned_millions_and_they_are_fighting_back/.

95 Arundhati Roy, "India's Shame: Democracy Hasn't Eradicated the Country's Caste System. It Has Entrenched and Modernised It," *Prospect Magazine*, November 13, 2014, http://www.prospectmagazine.co.uk/features/indias-shame; Irfan Husain, "View from Abroad: Horrors of The Caste System," *Dawn*, December 15, 2014, http://www.dawn.com/news/1150818; Hillary Mayell, "India's 'Untouchables' Face Violence, Discrimination," *National Geographic News*, June 2, 2003, http://news.nationalgeographic.com/news/2003/06/0602_030602_untouchables_2.html.

96 Mayell, "India's 'Untouchables' Face Violence, Discrimination."

97 Wendy Doniger, "Suttee," *Encyclopaedia Britannica*. March 3, 2015, http://www.britannica.com/topic/suttee.

98 Ibid.

99 "Indian Women Still Commit Ritual Suicides," *RT News*, September 10, 2009, https://www.rt.com/news/india-ritual-suicide-sati/; "Sati Widow Burning Still Going On," *Hub Pages*, June 11, 2013, http://hubpages.com/politics/Sati-Still-Being-Done-in-India.

100 In Shaktism and Shaivism, Shakti is worshipped as the Supreme Being and embodies the active feminine energy of Shiva.

101 Worshipped throughout India, Kali is Major Hindu goddess whose iconography and mythology associate her with death, sexuality and violence. In some of her later historical appearances, she is paradoxically associated with motherly love.

102 Julius Lipner, *Hindus: Their Religious Beliefs and Practices* (New York: Routledge, 1994), 185, 236.

103 "Police: Indian Child Killed as Human Sacrifice," *CBS News*, January 2, 2012, http://www.cbsnews.com/news/police-indian-child-killed-as-human-sacrifice/; "Indian Witch Doctor Beheads Toddler in Human Sacrifice to Hindu Goddess," *News24*, October 1, 2015, http://www.news24.com/World/News/Indian-witch-doctor-beheads-toddler-in-human-sacrifice-to-Kali-20151001; Daniel Miller, "Indian Father Kills His Eight-Month-Old Son With Axe to Appease Hindu Goddess of Destruction and Rebirth," *Daily Mail*, October 11, 2013, http://www.dailymail.co.uk/news/article-2454853/Indian-father-kills-month-old-son-axe-appease-Hindu-goddess-destruction-rebirth.html; John Lancaster, "In India, Sase Links Mysticism, Murder," *The Boston Globe*, November 29, 2003, http://archive.boston.com/news/world/articles/2003/11/29/in_india_case_links_mysticism_murder/.

104 Dan McDougall, "Indian Cult Kills Children for Goddess," *The Guardian*, March 5, 2006, https://www.theguardian.com/world/2006/mar/05/india.theobserver.

105 Arun Janardhanan, "After Human Sacrifice Complaint, Skeletal Remains Found in Quarry, Police Call Granite Baron Today," *The Indian Express*, September 17, 2015, http://indianexpress.com/article/india/india-others/after-human-sacrifice-complaint-skeletal-remains-found-in-quarry-police-call-granite-baron-today/.

106 Yakub Masih, *Comparative Study of Religions* (Delhi: Motilal Banarsidass Publishers, 2000).

107 Buddha believed that religious ideas (especially the god idea) have their origin in fear. The Buddha said: "Gripped by fear men go to the sacred mountains, sacred groves, sacred trees and shrines" (Dhammapada,

188); V. A. Gunasekara, "The Buddhist Attitude to God," *Budass*, last modified April 1997, http://www.budsas.org/ebud/ebdha068.htm.

108 Luis Lugo et al., "U.S. Religious Landscape Survey," *The Pew Forum on Religion and Public Life*, February 2008, http://www.pewforum. org/files/2013/05/report-religious-landscape-study-full.pdf; Janaka Parera, "Buddhism Fastest Growing Religion in the West," *Asian Tribune*, April 7, 2008, http://www.asiantribune.com/?q=node/10418.

109 According to legend, a man called Malunkyaputta approached Buddha and demanded he explain the origin of the Universe. The man even threatened to cease being a follower of Buddha if he did not answer his question satisfactorily. Buddha retorted that it was of no consequence whether or not the man followed him, because the truth did not need anyone's support. Buddha felt that questions on the origin of the Universe were irrelevant to his teachings because a man's goal was to liberate himself from the present, not the past or the future.

110 See reasons 1-10 of this book.

111 Y. D. Mosig, "Wisdom and Compassion: What the Buddha Taught, A Psycho-Poetical Analysis." *Theoretical & Philosophical Psychology* 9 no. 2 (1989): 27.

112 Edward J. Thomas, *The Life of Buddha as Legend and History* (New Delhi: Routledge, 1975), 53.

113 Matthew 11:28-30; 15:32; Mark 8:2-3; Luke 7:13; John 11:34-38; 15:13; Hebrews 2:17; 4:15.

114 Paul Edwards, *Reincarnation: A Critical Examination* (New York: Prometheus Books, 1996).

115 The Buddha taught, "I had no notion of a self, or of a being, or of a soul, or of a person, nor had I any notion or non-notion" (Vajracchedika, 14).

116 Davis Taylor and Clark Offner, *The World's Religions* (GrandRapids: InterVarsity, 1975), 177.

117 Deuteronomy 6:4; 1 Kings 8:60; John 17:3; 1 Timothy 2:5.

118 Peter Kreeft, "Comparing Christianity & Buddhism," January 30, 2016, http://www.peterkreeft.com/topics-more/religions_buddhism.htm.

119 Genesis 1:1; Isaiah 66:2; Nehemiah 9:6; Revelations 4:11.

120 "Buddhism - Major Differences," *Buddhist Studies*, January 30, 2016, http://www.buddhanet.net/e-learning/snapshot01.htm.

121 John 3:16-18; 8:24; Acts 4:12; 1 John 4:14; 5:12.

122 Kreeft, "Comparing Christianity & Buddhism."

123 Job 14:14; 2 Samuel 12:23; Luke 16:19-31; Hebrews 9:27.

124 "Buddhism - Major Differences," *Buddhist Studies.*

125 Romans 3:28; Galatians 2:16; Ephesians 1:7; 2:8-9; Titus 2:11.

126 "Buddhism - Major Differences," *Buddhist Studies.*

127 Romans 8:29; Ephesians 5:1-2; 2 Corinthians 4:10; 5:17; 1 John 2:6.

128 "Buddhism - Major Differences," *Buddhist Studies*

129 Psalm 62:1; Matthew 16:26; 1 Thessalonians 5:23; Hebrews 4:12; 3 John 1:2.

130 "Buddhism - Major Differences," *Buddhist Studies.*

131 Psalm 103:12; Isaiah 43:25-26; Acts 3:19; Ephesians 1:7; Collisions 1:14; 1 John 1:9.

132 Douglas R. Groothuis, "Jesus and Buddha: Two Masters or One," *The Christian Research Journal* 25 no. 4 (2003).

133 Exodus 20:1-10; Leviticus 26:1; Psalm 31:6; 115:4-8; Daniel 3:18; Acts 17:22-31; 1Thessalonians 1:9; Revelations 9:20-21.

134 "Why do Buddhists Bow to Statues?" *Essence of Buddhism World Press*, September 22, 2013, accessed https://essenceofbuddhism.wordpress.com/2013/09/22/why-do-buddhists-bow-to-statues/.

135 Genesis 6:5; Jeremiah 17:9; Mark 7:21; John 3:19; Romans 3:23; 2 Peter 2:14.

136 Thanissaro Bhikkhu, trans., "Avijja Sutta Ignorance," *Samyutta Nikaya 45.1*, Accessed February 1, 2016, http://www.accesstoinsight.org/tipitaka/sn/sn45/sn45.001.than.html.

137 Deuteronomy 6:5; Matthew 16:24; John 8:12; 14:15-24.

138 "Buddhism Beliefs," *About Buddhism*, February 1, 2016, accessed http://www.aboutbuddhism.org/buddhism-beliefs.php/.

139 Matthew 19:29; John 3:16; 8:51; 11:25-26; 17:3; 1 Thessalonians 5:10.

140 "Basics of Buddhism," Let us Reason, February 1, 2016, accessed http://www.letusreason.org/Buddh1.htm

141 Matthew 19:9; John 3:16; 5:24; 6:51; 11:25-26; 1 Thessalonians 4:14; 1 John 5:12; Revelations 21:4.

142 Fenggang Yang and Anning Hu, "Mapping Chinese Folk Religion in Mainland China and Taiwan," *Journal for the Scientific Study of Religion* 51 no. 3 (2012): 505–521

143 Stephen F. Teiser, "Popular Religion," *The Journal of Asian Studies*. 54 no. 2 (1995): 378-395.

144 Richard Madsen, "The Upsurge of Religion in China." *Journal of Democracy* 21 no. 4 (2010): 58-71.

145 Genesis 1:1

146 Luke 4:8

147 John Breen and Mark Teeuwen, *A New History of Shinto* (Chichester: Wiley-Blackwell Publishers, 2010).

148 Joseph M. Kitagawa, *On Understanding Japanese Religion* (New Jersey: Princeton University Press, 1987).

149 "Japanese Religion and Spirituality," *Ancient Civilisations*, February 1, 2016, accessed http://www.ushistory.org/civ/10a.asp.

150 Ian Buruma, "After Hirohito: What Remains Sacred," *New York Times*, May 25, 1989, http://www.nytimes.com/1989/05/28/magazine/after-hirohito-what-remains-sacred.html?pagewanted=all

151 Pslam 14:3; Romans 3:23.

152 Ephesians 1:7; 1 Peter 1:9.

153 John 3:16; Ephesians 2:8.

154 Khushwant Singh, *The Illustrated History of the Sikhs* (Oxford: Oxford University Press, 2006).

155 William H. McLeod, "Sikhism," *Encyclopaedia Britannica*, last modified July, 22, 2016, https://www.britannica.com/topic/Sikhism

156 Ram Gidoomal and Margaret Wardell, *Lions, Princesses, Gurus: Reaching Your Sikh Neighbour* (Guildford: Highland Books, 1997).

157 Guru Granth Sahib Ji, 70.

158 John 3:16, 36, 5:24, 11:25; Romans 10:9.

159 "The Patriarchs and the Origins of Judaism," *Judaism 101*, accessed February 2, 2016, http://www.jewfaq.org/origins.htm.

160 Matthew 5:17; Romans 10:4; Galatians 2:16, 3:11; 1 Peter 2:22.

161 Romans 1:17, 3:28, 5:1, 9; Galatians 2:16.

162 John 5:37-46.

163 Ezekiel 39:27-29; Romans 11:26.

164 Romans 3:19-23; Galatians 3:23-25; Ephesians 2:15.

Part Five

1 John 3:16.

2 Eric Hobsbawm, "War and Peace," *The Guardian*, February 23, 2002, https://www.theguardian.com/education/2002/feb/23/artsandhumanities.highereducation; "Natural Disasters Since 1900: Over 8 Million Deaths, 7 Trillion US Dollars," *Science Daily*, April 18, 2016, https://www.sciencedaily.com/releases/2016/04/160418092043.htm.

3 Jonathan R. Latham, "There's Enough Food for Everyone, But the Poor Can't Afford to Buy It," *Nature* 404 no. 6775 (2002): 222-222; Gordon

Conway and Gary Toenniessen, "Feeding the World in the Twenty-First Century," *Nature 402* (1999): C55-C58.

4   Eric H. Gimenez, "We Already Grow Enough Food for 10 Billion People - and Still Can't End Hunger," *The Huffington Post*, May 2, 2012, http://www.huffingtonpost.com/eric-holt-gimenez/world-hunger b 1463429.html; "There Is Enough Food to Feed The World," *Oxfam*, February 3, 2016, accessed http://www.oxfam.ca/there-enough-food-feed-world.

5   "Goal 2: End Hunger, Achieve Food Security and Improved Nutrition and Promote Sustainable Agriculture," *United Nations*, accessed February 3, 2016, http://www.un.org/sustainabledevelopment/hunger/.

6   "Obesity and Overweight," *World Health Organization*, February 3, 2016, http://www.who.int/mediacentre/factsheets/fs311/en/.

7   Mark 6:5-6.

8   Romans 8:18.

9   Alister McGrath, *The Mystery of the Cross* (Grand Rapids: Zondervan, 1988), 159.

10   1 Corinthians 15:35-55. 1Thessalonians 4:16-17.

11   Genesis 2:16-17; Joshua 24:15; Jeremiah 29:13; John 7:17; 2 Corinthians 9:7; 2 Timothy 2:26.

12   Isaiah 40:28.

13   Isaiah 46:10.

14   Jeremiah 1:5.

15   Psalm 139:1-6.

16   Hebrews 4:13.

17   Revelations 13:8.

18   Genesis 2:17.

19   Genesis 3:21.

20   Alfred Lord Tennyson's poem In Memoriam: 27, 1850.

21   Ezekiel 28:12-15.

22   Ezekiel 28:16-17; Isaiah 14:12-17; Revelation 12:4, 7-9.

23   1 Peter 5:8; Revelations 12:9; John 10:10.

24   John 8:44.

25   Genesis 3:6.

26   Gordon W. F. Drake, "Thermodynamics," *Encyclopaedia Britannica*, last modified, February 13, 2007, https://www.britannica.com/science/thermodynamics/Isothermal-and-adiabatic-processes#ref510511.

27 "The Consequences of Climate Change," *NASA*, February 5, 2016, http://climate.nasa.gov/effects/.

28 Romans 8:28.

29 1 Timothy 2:4; 2 Peter 3:9.

30 Philippians 2:6-8.

31 Psalm 5:4-5; Proverbs 6:16-19; 8:13.

32 J. M. Violanti and J. D. Drylie, *Copicide* (Springfield, IL: Charles Thomas Publisher, 2008).

33 Genesis 6:5,13.

34 Genesis 18:20; 19:5.

35 Deuteronomy 18:9-12.

36 Deuteronomy 20:10-12.

37 2 Corinthians 5:10; Revelations 1:7-8.

38 Alvin Plantinga, *The Nature of Necessity* (Oxford: Oxford University Press, 1974).

39 David Hume, *Philosophical Essays Concerning Human Understanding* (London: A. Millar, 1748), 164.

40 "How Old is the Universe," *NASA*, February 7, 2016, https://map.gsfc.nasa.gov/universe/uni_age.html.

41 Saint Thomas Aquinas, "Summa Theologica," *Christian Classics Ethereal Library* (1265-1274): 119, accessed February 7, 2016, http://www.documentacatholicaomnia.eu/03d/.1225-1274,_Thomas_Aquinas,_Summa_Theologiae_[2],_EN.pdf.

42 Howard V. Hong and Edna H. Hong, trans., *The Essential Kierkegaard* (Princeton, NJ: Princeton University Press, 2000): 215.

43 Howard V. Hong and Edna H. Hong, trans., *Søren Kierkegaard: Concluding Unscientific Postscript to Philosophical Fragments* (Princeton, NJ: Princeton University Press, 1992): 204.

44 See reasons 31, 38 and 41 from this book.

45 Josh McDowell, *The New Evidence That Demands a Verdict.* (Dallas, TX: Here's Life Publishers: Dallas, 1999).

46 Walter C. Kaiser Jr., *The Old Testament Documents: Are They Reliable and Relevant?* (Westmont, IL: InterVarsity Press, 2001), 45-46.

47 Jerry Norman, "The Earliest Surviving Copy of Aristotle's Biological Works (circa 850)," *History of Information*, last modified December 26, 2016, http://www.historyofinformation.com/expanded.php?id=1886.

48 F.F. Bruce, *The New Testament Documents: Are They Reliable?* (Grand Rapids: William B. Eerdman's Publishing Company, 1981), 9.

49 Bruce M. Metzger and Bart D. Ehrman, *The Text of the New Testament: Its Transmission, Corruption and Restoration* (Oxford: Oxford University Press, 2005).

50 Keith E. Gephart "Are Copies Reliable?" in *God's Word in Our Hands*, ed. James B. Williams and Randolph Shaylor (Greenville, SC: Ambassador Emerald International, 2003), 164.

51 "Aristotle on Non-contradiction," *Stanford Encyclopaedia of Philosophy*, last modified February 2, 2015, http://plato.stanford.edu/entries/aristotle-noncontradiction/.

52 Thomas F. Madden, *The Concise History of the Crusades* (New York: Rowman and Littlefield, 2013).

53 Ibid.

54 Paul F. Crawford, P. F. (2011). "Four Myths About the Crusades," *The Intercollegiate Review*, Spring (2011): 13-22; Christopher Tyerman, *Fighting for Christendom: Holy War and the Crusades* (Oxford: Oxford University Press, 2005); Alfred J. Andrea and Andrew Holt, *Seven Myths of the Crusades* (Indianapolis: Hacket Publishing, 2015).

55 Madden, *The Concise History of the Crusades.*

56 Ibid.

57 Jay Michaelson, "Was Obama Right About the Crusades and Islamic Extremism?" *Washington Post*, February 6, 2015, https://www.washingtonpost.com/national/religion/was-obama-right-about-the-crusades-and-islamic-extremism-analysis/2015/02/06/3670628a-ae46-11e4-8876-460b1144cbc1_story.html?utm_term=.66660920e439.

58 "Source List and Detailed Death Tolls for the Primary Megadeaths of the Twentieth Century," *Necrometrics*, accessed February 8, 2016, http://necrometrics.com/20c5m.htm.

59 Madden, *The Concise History of the Crusades.*

Part Six

1 Tom Peterkin, "CS Lewis, Chronicles of Narnia Author, Honoured in Poets' Corner," *The Telegraph*. November 22, 2012, http://www.telegraph.co.uk/news/uknews/9694561/CS-Lewis-Chronicles-of-Narnia-author-honoured-in-Poets-corner.html.

2 Clive Staples Lewis, *Surprised By Joy: The Shape of My Early Life* (Orlando: Harcourt, 1966), 228-229.

3 Ibid, 229.

4   Clive Staples Lewis, *Mere Christianity* (New York: Harper Collins Publishers, 1980), 227.

5   Rosaria C. Butterfield, "My Train Wreck Conversion," *Christianity Today*, February 7, 2013, http://www.christianitytoday.com/ct/2013/january-february/my-train-wreck-conversion.html.

6   Rosaria C. Butterfield, *The Secret Thoughts of an Unlikely Convert: An English Professor's Journey into Christian Faith* (Pittsburgh: Crown and Covenant Publications, 2012).

7   Martin Childs, *"Allan Sandage: Astronomer Widely Acknowledged as the Most Outstanding of the 20th Century,"* *Independent*, November 22, 2010, http://www.independent.co.uk/news/obituaries/allan-sandage-astronomer-widely-acknowledged-as-among-the-most-outstanding-of-the-20th-century-2140189.html.

8   W. Mark Richardson et al., *Science and the Spiritual Quest: New Essays by Leading Scientists* (London: Routledge, 2002).

9   "Allan Sandage," *The Telegraph*, November 21, 2010, http://www.telegraph.co.uk/news/obituaries/science-obituaries/8150004/Allan-Sandage.html.

10   Richardson et al., *Science and the Spiritual Quest.*

11   John Noble Willford, "Sizing up the Cosmos: An Astronomers Quest," The *NewYork Times*, March 12, 1991, http://www.nytimes.com/1991/03/12/science/sizing-up-the-cosmos-an-astronomer-s-quest.html?pagewanted=all.

12   "George Ellis Wins 2004 Templeton Prize," *Templeton Prize*, March 17, 2004, http://www.templetonprize.org/tpgew.html.

13   Krista Tippett, "Transcript for George F. R. Ellis - Science and Hope," *On Being*, May 10, 2007, http://www.onbeing.org/program/science-and-hope/transcript/1158.

14   Ibid.

15   George F. R. Ellis, "Statement by George F. R. Ellis: Templeton Prize News Conference," *On Being,* March 17, 2004, http://www.onbeing.org/program/science-and-hope/feature/statement-george-f-r-ellis/1161.

16   Robert J. Russell, Nancy Murphy and C. J. Isham, *Quantum Cosmology and the Laws of Nature: Scientific Perspectives on Divine Action* (Notre Dame, IN: University of Notre Dame Press, 1993).

17   Henry F. Schaefer, *Science and Christianity: Conflict or Coherence* (Athens, GA: The Apollos Trust, 2003), 71.

18   David F. Coopedge, "The World's Greatest Creation Scientists," *Bible and Science Library*, accessed February 12, 2016, http://www.creationsafaris.com/wgcs_toc.htm.

19   "Past Award Recipients," *The American Society of Parasitologists*, February 15, 2016, accessed http://amsocparasit.org/node/63.

20   Mark Armitage, M. "Death of Dr Richard D. Lumsden," January 23, 1997, accessed http://www.bio.net/mm/parasite/1997-January/001947.html.

21   "PhD Turns from Atheism to Christ," *You Tube*, June 29, 2010, https://www.youtube.com/watch?v=s91-ABJ49ho.

22   Ibid.

23   "Atheist Professor Richard Lumsden Converts to Christianity," *You Tube*, December 13, 2013, https://www.youtube.com/watch?v=hBLltwJDoX4&feature=youtu.be.

24   "President Clinton, British Prime Minister Tony Blair Deliver Remarks on Human Genome Milestone," *CNN*, June 26, 2000, http://transcripts.cnn.com/TRANSCRIPTS/0006/26/bn.01.html.

25   Bob Abernethy, "Dr. Francis S. Collins Interview" *Religion & Ethics Newsweekly*, July 21, 2006, http://www.pbs.org/wnet/religionandethics/2006/07/21/july-21-2006-dr-francis-s-collins-interview/3676/.

26   "Top Atheist Scientist Converts to Christianity," *You Tube*, June 17, 2014, https://www.youtube.com/watch?v=04V5PA5h2j0.

27   Ibid.

28   Bob Abernethy, "Dr. Francis S. Collins Interview."

29   "Top Atheist Scientist Converts to Christianity," *You Tube*.

30   Steve Paulson, "The Believer: Francis Collins - Head of the Human Genome Project Discusses His Conversion to Evangelical Christianity," *Salon*, August 7, 2006, http://www.salon.com/2006/08/07/collins_6/.

31   "Atheism Aside: Peter Hitchens' Journey to Faith - CBN.com," *You Tube*, June 23, 2010, https://www.youtube.com/watch?v=H8LqfgKuXFs&feature=youtu.be.

32   Peter Hitchens, "How I Found God and Peace With My Atheist Brother," *Daily Mail*, December 16, 2011, http://www.dailymail.co.uk/news/article-1255983/How-I-God-peace-atheist-brother-PETER-HITCHENS-traces-journey-Christianity.html.

33   "Atheism Aside: Peter Hitchens' Journey to Faith - CBN.com," *You Tube*.

34 Peter Hitchens, "How I Found God and Peace With My Atheist Brother."

35 Peter Hitchens, *The Rage Against God*. (Grand Rapids: Zondervan Publishing, 2010).

36 Chris Ahrens, "The Brother of Atheist Christopher Hitchens Speaks Out About God: Peter Hitchens returns to faith," *Risen Magazine*, accessed February 15, 2016, http://www.risenmagazine.com/prominent-author-peter-hitchens/.

37 "Alister McGrath," in *Beyond Opinion: Living the Faith We Defend*, ed. Ravi Zacharias (Nashville: Thomas Nelson Publishers, 2007).

38 Ali Herbert, "Interview with Alister McGrath," *Zacharias Trust*, November 20, 2013, http://www.rzim.eu/interview-with-alister-mcgrath-2.

39 "Alister McGrath," in *Beyond Opinion: Living the Faith We Defend*.

40 "Professor Alister McGrath," *Gresham College*, accessed February 15, 2016, http://www.gresham.ac.uk/professors-and-speakers/professor-alister-mcgrath/.

41 "The Top 50 Books That Have Shaped Evangelicals," *Christianity Today*, October 6, 20006, http://www.christianitytoday.com/ct/2006/october/23.51.html.

42 Josh McDowell, J. "Evidence of a Changed Life," *Precious Testimonies*, accessed February 16, 2016, http://www.precious-testimonies.com/Hope_Encouragement/k-o/McDowellJ.htm.

43 Josh McDowell, "A Skeptic's Quest," *Josh McDowells Blog Spot*, November 30, 2007, http://joshmcdowell.blogspot.com/2007/11/skeptics-quest-my-testimony-part-1.html.

44 Josh McDowell, "My Story: Josh McDowell," *CRU*, accessed February 16, 2016, https://www.cru.org/how-to-know-god/my-story-a-life-changed/my-story-josh-mcdowell.html.

45 McDowell, "Evidence of a Changed Life."

46 Ibid.

47 Ibid.

48 McDowell, "My Story: Josh McDowell,"

49 Holly Ordway, Not God's Type: *An Atheist Academic Lays Down Her Arms* (Chicago: Moody Publishers Press, 2010).

50 Ibid, 15-16.

51 Ibid, 17-18.

52 Ibid,117.

53 Holly Ordway, *Holly Ordway.com*, accessed February 17, 2016, http://www.hollyordway.com.

54 Rabi R. Maharaj, *Death of a Guru* (Eugene, OR: Harvest House Publishers, 1984).

55 Rabi Maharaj, "Death of Guru: The Personal Testimony of Rabi Maharaj," *Christian Research Institute,* accessed December 11, 2017, http://www.equip.org/PDF/DH125.pdf.

56 Ibid.

57 Ibid

58 Rabi R. Maharaj, *Death of a Guru, 134.*

59 Paul Williams, *The Unexpected Way: On Converting From Buddhism to Catholicism* (Norfolk: Bloomsbury Publishing, 2002).

60 "Paul Williams (Philosopher)," *Wikipedia*, February 20, 2016, https://en.wikipedia.org/wiki/Paul_Williams_(philosopher)

61 "Dr. Paul Williams: Buddhist Who Became a Catholic Christian - The Journey Home Program," *You Tube*, October 29, 2014, https://www.youtube.com/watch?v=dUPC_s3i8zU.

62 "Finding a Rational Religion, *The Herald*, July 4, 2005, http://www.heraldscotland.com/news/12484272.Finding a rational religion A leading British academic has reversed the usual trend by converting from Buddhism to Catholicism Alison Chiesa hears about the reasoning behind his change of religion/.

63 Ibid.

64 Ibid.

65 Paul Williams, "On Converting from Buddhism to Catholicism," *Why I'm Catholic*, February 21, 2016, http://whyimcatholic.com/index.php/conversion-stories/buddhist-converts/65-buddhist-convert-paul-williams.

66 Paul Williams, "On Converting from Buddhism to Catholicism."

67 "Finding a Rational Religion, *The Herald.*

68 Ibid.

69 Paul Williams, "On Converting from Buddhism to Catholicism."

70 Eugenio Zolli, *Before the Dawn: Autobiographical Reflections of Eugenio Zolli Former Chief Rabbi of Rome* (San Francisco: Ignatius Press, 2008).

71 David B. Green, "This Day in Jewish History // 1944: An Italian Chief Rabbi Sees Jesus on Yom Kippur," *Haaretz*, September 17,

2013, http://www.haaretz.com/jewish/this-day-in-jewish-history/.premium-1.549212.

72 Ibid.

73 Eugenio Zolli, *Before the Dawn*, 190.

74 Ibid, 18.

75 Ibid, 9.

76 David B. Green, "This Day in Jewish History."

77 Mustafa, *Against the Tides in the Middle East: The True Story of Mustafa, Former Teacher of Islamic history* (International Academic Centre for Muslim Evangelism: International Evangelical Resource Centre, 1999).

78 Ibid.

79 Mark Gabriel, "The Story of M.A. Gabriel: The Former Professor of Islamic History at Al-Azhar University, Cairo, Egypt," *Arabic Bible*, accessed February 22, 2016, http://www.arabicbible.com/testimonials/egypt/1624-mark-gabriel-testimony.html.

80 Ibid.

81 "Dr Mark Gabriel," DrMarkGabriel.com, February 23, 2016, http://www.drmarkgabriel.com/about.html.

82 "A Treatise on the Law of Evidence," *Law Library of Queens County* accessed February 23, 2016, https://www.nycourts.gov/library/queens/Lincoln/greenleaf.shtml.

83 Robert R. Edwards, "Is Simon Greenleaf Still Relevant?" *The Lawyer's Corner, Creation Studies Institute,* accessed February 25, 2016, http://www.creationstudies.org/Education/simon_greenleaf.html.

84 Ibid.

85 Simon Greenleaf, *The Testimony of the Evangelists: The Gospels Examined by the Rules of Evidence* (Grand Rapids: Kregel Classics, 1995), 32.

Part Seven

1 Eben Alexander, *Proof of Heaven* (London: Piatkus, 2012).

2 Ibid.

3 Eben Alexander, "Proof of Heaven: A Doctor's Experience With the Afterlife," *Newsweek*, October 8, 2012, http://europe.newsweek.com/proof-heaven-doctors-experience-afterlife-65327?rm=eu.

4 Ibid.

5   Brian W. Melvin, *A Land Unknown: Hell's Dominion* (USA: Xulon Press, 2005).

6   Brian W. Melvin, "Near Death Experience of B. W. Melvin," *Bible Probe*, accessed March 1, 2016, https://www.bibleprobe.com/hells-dominion.htm.

7   Ibid.

8   Ibid.

9   Luke 16:24; 2 Peter 2:4; Revelations 14:11.

10   Melvin, *A Land Unknown*.

11   Jenny Sharkey and Ian McCormack, *Clinically Dead: I've Seen Heaven and Hell* (Louisville, KY: CreateSpace Independent Publishing, 2013).

12   Ann Salleh, "Box Jelly Venom Under the Microscope," *ABC Science*, December 13, 2012, http://www.abc.net.au/science/articles/2012/12/13/3653150.htm.

13   Sharkey and McCormack, *Clinically Dead*.

14   Ibid, 24

15   Ibid.

16   Ibid, 28

17   Lindsay Dyner and Chris Serico, "I Crossed Over: Survivors of Near Death Experiences Share Afterlife Stories," *Today*, July 15, 2016, http://www.today.com/health/i-crossed-over-survivors-near-death-experiences-share-afterlife-stories-t12841.

18   Christy W. Beam, *Miracles From Heaven: A Little Girl and Her Amazing Story of Healing* (New York: Hachette Books, 2015).

19   Kathy Schiffer Schiffer, "It's Not Our story - It's God's Story," *Aleteia*, March 9, 2016, http://aleteia.org/2016/03/09/its-not-our-story-its-gods-story-the-real-family-behind-miracles-from-heaven/.

20   Caroline Garnar, "Girl Knocked Out by 30ft Fall Inside a Hollow Tree Claims She Went to Heaven and Met Jesus," *Mail Online*, April 14, 2015, http://www.dailymail.co.uk/femail/article-3038153/Girl-knocked-30ft-fall-inside-hollow-tree-claims-went-heaven-met-Jesus-woke-cured-lifelong-illness.html.

21   Dyner and Serico, "I Crossed Over."

22   Garnar, "Girl Knocked Out by 30ft Fall Inside a Hollow Tree."

23   Rod Thomas, "Swallowed by a Tree and Fighting to Survive," *CBN*, March 15, 2016, http://www1.cbn.com/swallowed-tree-and-fighting-survive.

24   Garnar, "Girl Knocked Out by 30ft Fall Inside a Hollow Tree."

25   Thomas, "Swallowed by a Tree and Fighting to Survive."

26   Garnar, "Girl Knocked Out by 30ft Fall Inside a Hollow Tree."

27 Mickey Robinson, *Falling into Heaven* (Wisconsin: Broadstreet Publishing group, 2014).

28 Ibid.

29 Ibid.

30 Robert Hull, "Skydiver Has Visions of Afterlife Following Fiery Plane Crash, *CBN*, March 16, 2016, http://www1.cbn.com/features/skydiver-has-visions-of-afterlife-following-fiery-plane-crash.

31 "Mickey Robinson's Near Death Experience," *Eternity In Our Heart*, March 16, 2016, http://eternityinourheart.com/nde/mickey-robinson.

32 Hull, "Skydiver Has Visions of Afterlife Following Fiery Plane Crash."

33 Ibid.

34 Robinson, *Falling into Heaven*.

35 Bill Wiese, *23 Minutes in Hell* (Lake Mary, FL: Charisma House, 2006).

36 Ibid.

37 Ibid.

38 "23 Minutes in Hell," *Divine Revelations*, March 18, 2016, http://www.divinerevelations.info/documents/billwiese_23minutesinhell_text.htm.

39 "23 Minutes in Hell," *Divine Revelations*.

40 Dean A. Braxton, *In Heaven! Experiencing the Throne of God* (Maitland, FL: Xulon Press, 2009).

41 Ibid, 17.

42 Ibid, 18.

43 Ibid, 21.

44 Ibid, 18.

45 Ibid, 18.

46 Shannon Woodland, "Routine Surgery Opens Door to Heaven," *CBN*, March 20, 2016, http://www1.cbn.com/700club/routine-surgery-opens-door-heaven.

47 Braxton, *In Heaven*, .24.

48 Rita Bennett, *To Heaven and Back* (Grand Rapids: Zondervan Publishing, 1997).

49 "Dr Landry," *You Tube*, accessed March 21, 2016, https://www.youtube.com/watch?v=u70WDI0XYR0&t=199s.

50 Mark Ellis, "Medical Doctor's Heart Attack Led to Near Death Experience in Heaven, *God Reports*, August 4, 2016, http://blog.godreports.com/2016/08/medical-doctors-heart-attack-led-to-near-death-experience-in-heaven/.

51 "Gerry Landry, M.D. March 24, 1979" *Calvary Commission*, accessed March 25, 2016, http://www.calvarycommission.org/articles/doctor.asp.

52 Ibid.

53 Ibid.

54 Mark Ellis, "Medical Doctor's Heart Attack Led to Near Death Experience in Heaven."

55 "Gerry Landry, M.D. March 24, 1979" *Calvary Commission*.

56 Ibid.

57 Gary L. Wood, *A Place Called Heaven* (Kingwood, TX: RevMedia Publishing, 2014).

58 "Near Death Experience/Life After Death after Car Accident - Gary Wood/Sid Roth (Heaven Testimony)," *You Tube*, January 9, 2014, https://www.youtube.com/watch?v=nopGailnzsA&feature=youtu.be.

59 Ibid.

60 Wood, *A Place Called Heaven.*

61 "Near Death Experience/Life After Death after Car Accident," *You Tube.*

62 Wood, *A Place Called Heaven.*

63 Ibid.

64 Richard Eby, *Caught up into Paradise* (Ada, MI: Baker Publishing Group, 1990).

65 Ibid.

66 Ibid.

67 Ibid.

68 "Richard Eby Hell Vision Pt1," *You Tube*, June 3, 2001, https://www.youtube.com/watch?v=yexkcPhsJVM.

69 Eby, *Caught up into paradise.*

70 Howard Pittman, *Placebo* (Bassfield, MS: Mississippi Christian Broadcasting, 1979).

71 Ibid.

72 Ibid.

73 Ibid.

74 Ibid.

75 Ibid.

76 Earthquake Kelley, *Bound to Lose, Destined to Win* (Louisville, KY: CreateSpace Independent Publishing, 2011).

77 "Earthquake Kelley: Saved by a Mother's Prayers," *CBN*, accessed March 28, 2016, http://www1.cbn.com/700club/earthquake-kelley-saved-mothers-prayers.

78 Kelley, *Bound to Lose, Destined to Win.*

79 Ibid.

80 Ibid.

81 Ibid.

82 "Donald Whitaker Obituary," *The Oklahoman*, August 13, 2007, http://legacy.newsok.com/obituaries/oklahoman/obituary.aspx?n=donald-whitaker&pid=92546382.

83 "Amazing Testimony of an Ax-Atheist," *You Tube*, July 4, 2011, https://www.youtube.com/watch?v=CVmNf-KtVs0&list=PLIsyfNB5hmoILki_WO8G2_-a2M4NQJ57r&index=13.

84 Ibid.

85 Ibid.

86 Ibid.

87 Ibid.

88 Ibid.

89 Ibid.

90 Ibid.

91 Ibid.

92 Ibid.

93 "Donald Whitaker Obituary," *The Oklahoman.*

Conclusion

1 Ronald H. Nash, *Faith and Reason: Searching for a Rational Faith* (Grand Rapids: Zondervan Publishing, 1994), 88.

2 C.S. Lewis, *God in the Dock: Essays on Theology and Ethics* (Cambridge: William B. Eerdmans Publishing, 2014), 102.

3 Rex Warner, Augustine: Confessions (New York: Mentor, 1963).

4 Arthur F. Holmes, *All Truth is God's Truth* (Cambridge: William B. Eerdmans Publishing, 1977).

FURTHER READING

Christy W. Beam, *Miracles From Heaven: A Little Girl and Her Amazing Story of Healing* (New York: Hachette Books, 2015).

Michael J. Behe, *Darwin's Black Box: The Biochemical Challenge to Evolution* (New York: Simon and Schuster, 2006).

F.F. Bruce, *The New Testament Documents: Are They Reliable?* (Grand Rapids: William B. Eerdman's Publishing Company, 1981).

Rosaria C. Butterfield, *The Secret Thoughts of an Unlikely Convert: An English Professor's Journey into Christian Faith* (Pittsburgh: Crown and Covenant Publications, 2012).

William A. Dembski, *No Free Lunch: Why Specified Complexity Cannot be Purchased Without Intelligence* (Lanham, MD: Rowman & Littlefield, 2007).

Anthony Flew and Roy A. Varghese, *There is a God: How the World's Most Notorious Atheist Changed His Mind* (New York: Harper Collins, 2007).

Werner Gitt, *In The Beginning Was Information* (Green Forest, AR: Master Books, 2004).

Walter C. Kaiser Jr., *The Old Testament Documents: Are They Reliable and Relevant?* (Westmont, IL: InterVarsity Press, 2001).

Earthquake Kelley, *Bound to Lose, Destined to Win* (Louisville, KY: CreateSpace Independent Publishing, 2011).

Peter Kreeft and Ronald K. Tacelli, *Handbook of Christian Apologetics* (Westmont, IL: IntraVarsity Press, 1994).

John C. Lennox, *God and Stephen Hawking: Whose Design is it Anyway?* (Oxford: Lion Hudson Books, 2011).

Clive Staples Lewis, *Mere Christianity* (London: Harper Collins, 2012).

Clive Staples Lewis, *The Case for Christianity* (Los Angeles: Green Light, 2000).

Josh McDowell, *The New Evidence That Demands a Verdict* (Dallas, TX: Here's Life Publishers, 1999).

Thomas F. Madden, *The Concise History of the Crusades* (New York: Rowman and Littlefield, 2013).

Stephen C. Meyer, *Signature in the Cell: DNA and the Evidence for Intelligent Design* (New York: Harper Collins, 2009).

Alvin Plantinga, *A Warranted Christian Belief* (Oxford: Oxford University Press, 2000).

Jenny Sharkey and Ian McCormack, *Clinically Dead: I've Seen Heaven and Hell* (Louisville, KY: CreateSpace Independent Publishing, 2013).

Henry F. Schaefer, *Science and Christianity: Conflict or Coherence* (Athens, GA: The Apollos Trust, 2003).

Richard Swinburne, *The Existence of God* (Oxford: Oxford University Press, 2004).